Palgrave Macmillan's
Postcolonial Studies in Education

Studies utilizing the perspectives of postcolonial theory have become established and increasingly widespread in the last few decades. This series embraces and broadly employs the postcolonial approach. As a site of struggle, education has constituted a key vehicle for the "colonization of the mind." The "post" in postcolonialism is both temporal, in the sense of emphasizing the processes of decolonization, and analytical in the sense of probing and contesting the aftermath of colonialism and the imperialism which succeeded it, utilizing materialist and discourse analysis. Postcolonial theory is particularly apt for exploring the implications of educational colonialism, decolonization, experimentation, revisioning, contradiction and ambiguity not only for the former colonies, but also for the former colonial powers. This series views education as an important vehicle for both the inculcation and unlearning of colonial ideologies. It complements the diversity that exists in postcolonial studies of political economy, literature, sociology, and the interdisciplinary domain of cultural studies. Education is here being viewed in its broadest contexts, and is not confined to institutionalized learning. The aim of this series is to identify and help establish new areas of educational inquiry in postcolonial studies.

Series Editors:

Antonia Darder holds the Leavey Presidential Endowed Chair in Ethics and Moral Leadership at Loyola Marymount University, Los Angeles, and is professor emerita at the University of Illinois, Urbana-Champaign.

Anne Hickling-Hudson is associate professor of Education at Australia's Queensland University of Technology (QUT) where she specializes in cross-cultural and international education.

Peter Mayo is professor and head of the Department of Education Studies at the University of Malta where he teaches in the areas of Sociology of Education and Adult Continuing Education, as well as in Comparative and International Education and Sociology more generally.

Editorial Advisory Board

Carmel Borg (University of Malta)
John Baldacchino (Teachers College, Columbia University)
Jennifer Chan (University of British Columbia)
Christine Fox (University of Wollongong, Australia)
Zelia Gregoriou (University of Cyprus)
Leon Tikly (University of Bristol, UK)
Birgit Brock-Utne (Emeritus, University of Oslo, Norway)

Titles:

A New Social Contract in a Latin American Education Context
Danilo R. Streck; Foreword by Vítor Westhelle

Education and Gendered Citizenship in Pakistan
M. Ayaz Naseem

Critical Race, Feminism, and Education: A Social Justice Model
Menah A. E. Pratt-Clarke

Actionable Postcolonial Theory in Education
Vanessa Andreotti

The Capacity to Share: A Study of Cuba's International Cooperation in Educational Development
Anne Hickling-Hudson, Jorge Corona Gonzalez, and Rosemary Preston

A Critical Pedagogy of Embodied Education
Tracey Ollis

Culture, Education, and Community: Expressions of the Postcolonial Imagination
Jennifer Lavia and Sechaba Mahlomaholo

Neoliberal Transformation of Education in Turkey: Political and Ideological Analysis of Educational Reforms in the Age of the AKP
Edited by Kemal İnal and Güliz Akkaymak

Neoliberal Transformation of Education in Turkey

Political and Ideological Analysis of Educational Reforms in the Age of the AKP

Edited by

Kemal İnal and Güliz Akkaymak

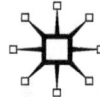

NEOLIBERAL TRANSFORMATION OF EDUCATION IN TURKEY
Copyright © Kemal İnal and Güliz Akkaymak, 2012.

All rights reserved.

First published in 2012 by
PALGRAVE MACMILLAN®
in the United States—a division of St. Martin's Press LLC,
175 Fifth Avenue, New York, NY 10010.

Where this book is distributed in the UK, Europe and the rest of the world, this is by Palgrave Macmillan, a division of Macmillan Publishers Limited, registered in England, company number 785998, of Houndmills, Basingstoke, Hampshire RG21 6XS.

Palgrave Macmillan is the global academic imprint of the above companies and has companies and representatives throughout the world.

Palgrave® and Macmillan® are registered trademarks in the United States, the United Kingdom, Europe and other countries.

ISBN: 978–0–230–34128–9

Library of Congress Cataloging-in-Publication Data

    Neoliberal transformation of education in Turkey : political and ideological analysis of educational reforms in the age of the AKP / Edited By Kemal Inal and Güliz Akkaymak.
        pages cm.—(Postcolonial studies in education)
    Includes index.
    ISBN 978–0–230–34128–9
      1. Education and state—Turkey. 2. Democracy and education—Turkey. 3. AK Parti (Turkey) I. Inal, Kemal, 1964– editor of compilation. II. Akkaymak, Güliz, editor of compilation.

LC94.T9N46 2012
379.09561—dc23   2012016019

A catalogue record of the book is available from the British Library.

Design by Newgen Imaging Systems (P) Ltd., Chennai, India.

First edition: November 2012

10 9 8 7 6 5 4 3 2 1

Transferred to Digital Printing in 2013

Contents

List of Tables	vii
Series Editors' Preface	ix
Preface	xiii
Kemal İnal and Güliz Akkaymak	

Part I   The AKP and Education in Turkey

1 The Political Economy of Education in Turkey: State, Labor, and Capital under AKP Rule   3
Gamze Yücesan-Özdemir and Ali Murat Özdemir

2 The Educational Politics of the AKP: The Collapse of Public Education in Turkey   17
Kemal İnal

Part II   Reforms, Finance, and Unions in Education in the AKP Era

3 Constructivism and the Curriculum Reform of the AKP   33
Hasan Ünder

4 The Marketization of Primary and Secondary School Curricula and Textbooks under AKP Rule   47
Ünal Özmen

5 Curriculum Change in Turkey: Some Critical Reflections   59
Hülya Koşar-Altınyelken and Güliz Akkaymak

6 Learning to FlexLabor: How Working-Class Youth Train for Flexible Labor Markets   71
Ergin Bulut

7 Turkey under AKP Rule: Neoliberal Interventions Into the Public Budget and Educational Finance   83
Nejla Kurul

8   External Education Projects in Turkey   95
    Gülay Aslan, Erdal Küçüker, and Ergül Adıgüzel

9   The New Stream of Trade Unionism: The Case of
    Eğitim-Bir-Sen in Turkey   109
    Duygun Göktürk, Gökçe Güvercin, and Onur Seçkin

Part III   The AKP and Neoliberal-Conservative Reconstruction in Education

10   The Marketization of Higher Education in Turkey
     (2002–2011)   125
     Nevzat Evrim Önal

11   Neoliberalization and Foundation Universities in Turkey   139
     Ömür Birler

12   The *Dershane* Business in Turkey   151
     Ayhan Ural

13   The Growth of Islamic Education in Turkey: The AKP's
     Policies toward *Imam-Hatip* Schools   165
     Mustafa Kemal Coşkun and Burcu Şentürk

14   Body Politics and Sexual Education under AKP Rule   179
     Serdar M. Değirmencioğlu

15   Early Childhood Education in Turkey: A Critical Overview   191
     Mehmet Toran

16   Fights over Human Rights: A Strange Story of Citizenship
     and Democracy Education   205
     Tuğba Asrak-Hasdemir

17   The System of Teacher Training during AKP Rule   219
     İ. Rıfat Okçabol

18   Transformation of the Teaching Profession in Turkey   233
     Esin Ertürk

19   Transformation of Adult Education in Turkey: From Public
     Education to Life-Long Learning   245
     Ahmet Yıldız

Contributors   259

Index   263

Tables

2.1	The budget of MoNE and the share allocated to public education (2002–2011)	22
2.2	The number of tutoring courses, teachers, and students	24
2.3	Increase in numbers of private schools and their students in years	26
9.1	Unionization rates between 2002 and 2011	112
9.2	Statistics for confederations between 2002 and 2011	113
9.3	Membership rates of public employees	113
9.4	Unions within confederations	114
10.1	Overview of Turkish higher education (2010 university quotas and entry rates)	132
12.1	The change in the *Dershane* business with figures	153
13.1	Statistics of IHSs	170
13.2	Percentages of agreement with statements about women's status	173
13.3	Religion and culture relations	174
19.1	Koran courses and number of enrolled students	253

Series Editors' Preface*

On September 12, 1980, Turkey experienced a terrible military coup that, like the 1973 coup in Chile, led to thousands of arrests and disappearances. The coup was a bid by the Turkish military, influenced by US cold-war politics, to establish conditions for bringing in neoliberal policies in this heavily populated nation covering areas in Europe and Asia. The introduction of neoliberal policies in Turkey actually occurred with decisions taken in January 1980. The main political figure behind these decisions was former World Bank employee, Turgut Özal, later to become prime minister (1983–1989) and then president (1989–1993). He was, at the time of the January 1980 decisions, undersecretary to Prime Minister Süleyman Demirel. As in Chile, after its coup of September 11, 1973 (considered by many as the first 9/11), and in other Latin American countries thereafter, forceful measures were utilized to establish and consolidate neoliberalismin Turkey.

The military coup in Turkey took place only a few years after the May 1, 1977, celebration in Istanbul's *Taksim* Square was crushed by the opening of gunfire on participants, leaving around 34 people dead. The *Taksim* May Day celebrations were, after the coup, banned for a number of years and revived after the ban was lifted in 2009 (only in 2011 and 2012 was participation allowed to all and not to just select groups). Those who witnessed the 2011 celebration, where hundreds of thousands of workers rallied anew, could readily understand why the manifestation was banned and why it required such drastic military action to usher in neoliberal policies in a country that historically has been the home of a wide variety of movements and a vibrant political left. Among the victims of the 1980 coup were activists, as well as editors of left wing publishing houses in Turkey. One of these was İlhan Erdost, editor of *Sol Yayınları*, a publisher of many Marxist classics. He was beaten to death while in custody, allegedly for publishing banned leftist books. Nevertheless, many such publishing houses and bookstores still continue to make their presence felt in and around major Turkish cities.

The army in Turkey is often regarded as the legacy of the secular policies introduced by Mustafa Kemal, known as Atatürk, the leader and military strategist who strove to modernize the country, seeking to extricate it from the grip of the Muslim Ottoman influences. The army, however, supported religious schools and included the need for obligatory religious courses in the 1982 constitution. On the other hand, it continues to play an important role in the promotion of a modernist push toward "Turkification," allowing little space for the flourishing of the various cultures, notably the Kurdish culture, that form a significant section of the Turkish mosaic. Furthermore, and here lies the connection with neoliberalism, it is largely regarded as an important US satellite force in a region of the world known for its volatility. Accordingly, in a nation where many people are schooled into its military culture from a young age and also through certain specialized university institutes, the Turkish military constitutes a formidable force as one of the world's largest armies. AKP[1] political interventions, however, have led to the army taking a backseat, and numerous high-level officers are currently in prison.

Meanwhile, the kin of those who disappeared in Turkey also continue to make their presence felt in the form of a mothers' movement that meets on Saturdays in one of Istanbul's squares, the one surrounding Galatasaray High School.[2] The parallels and influence of the *Madres* of the Plaza Cinco de Mayo in Buenos Aires are not to be missed. They provide further testimony to the fact that the process that led to transformations in different aspects of social life in Turkey, manifestations of Turkey's "growing up modern," had its birth pangs in a terrible period in the country's recent history.

The impact of neoliberalism is also highly visible within different sections of the nation's educational system. There is a noticeable,constantly increasing presence of privatization and market ideology, and instrumentalization of education as an object of consumption. While Turkey is not a member of the European Union (EU), its higher education system is not immune to the influences of the Bologna process,[3] as this gospel is being preached and taken on board by policy makers. With its large youth population, the country becomes an attractive market for European universities in their competition with the United States and Southeast Asia to recruit international fee-paying students from outside the EU as part of what is being termed the "internationalization" of higher education.

A quick glance at the faculty profiles of universities such as METU (Middle East Technical University), Boğaziçi Üniversitesi (University of the Bosphorous), Ankara Üniversitesi, and others, suggests that, traditionally, the United States has been the main postgraduate destination for promising young Turkish academics. Although many have also studied in Europe, especially Germany and the United Kingdom, exposure to the Bologna process of harmonization and credit transfer renders Turkish graduates more likely today to pursue their further education in this continent. Meanwhile, though highly selective public universities do exist in Turkey and feature among the best higher education institutions available, we also increasingly witness a plethora of private institutions where academics from nominally public institutions teach part-time at piece rate to supplement their meager salaries. This is often regarded as a win-win situation for both the private sector and the state, thus leading to the typical neoliberal blurring of the "private-public" divide, a process skewed in favor of the private sector.

Given these conditions, *Neoliberal Transformation of Education in Turkey*, through the contributions of a variety of Turkish writers in the field of education, specifically centers its analysis directly on this political–economic phenomenon. True to postcolonial concerns, a historical perspective is also well highlighted by a number of the authors. For instance, we read about the tensions that prevailed within the Ottoman Empire as a result of the nation-state's move toward modernization, while at the same time preserving and promoting Islamic values. Other important themes raised by the authors include curriculum development; the roles of IMF and World Bank; the onset of neoliberal policies in the new millennium; and the role of teachers' unions, focusing on the pro-AKP *Eğitim-Bir-Sen* whose membership increased ten times. This is not to be confused with the very visible and progressive education union, *Eğitim-Sen,* which embraces a critical pedagogy and, incidentally, produces one of Turkey's main refereed education journals. Other significant issues raised in the book include those of human rights education, the role of the "new managerialism" in Turkish education, preparation for flexi-work, adult education in the context of the recent neoliberal discourse on lifelong learning, private foundation universities, private tutoring (a phenomenon in other Mediterranean countries, as well), body politics, and sexual regulation under AKP rule, among others.

The timely view provided by this impressive group of Turkish scholars is panoramic and varied. Hence, the volume provides a much-needed comprehensive insight into educational concerns in this increasingly influential nation—a nation characterized by conditions, tensions, and struggles that result from an intermeshing of different cultures within a context of asymmetrical relations of power. In this light, Turkey serves as a perfect example of the postcolonial phenomenon of hybridity: East meets West, Europe meets Asia, secularism coexists with Islam while modernist conceptions in the form of Turkish nationalism exist side by side with postmodern ones, involving different ethnic identities seeking affirmation, greater political power or autonomy, even by armed struggle, if necessary, as has been case with the Kurds.

This thoughtful collection is a worthy contribution to the existing literature in the field. It sheds light on the pedagogical influences of a nation-state that must grapple with the inherent cultural and political conflicts and contradictions resulting from the ideological push-pull of modernizing secularization and existing religious traditions of Islam in the midst of changing economic conditions. In providing a multiplicity of scholarly perspectives across the education sector, *Neoliberal Transformation of Education in Turkey* offers a welcome, comprehensive analysis of the impact of neoliberal policies and practices on the process of Turkish education—an analysis that resonates deeply with postcolonial concerns.

Notes

* We are indebted to Professor Hasan Aksoy from Ankara University and Onur Seçkin from Boğaziçi Üniversitesi, for their important comments on earlier drafts of the Preface.

1. *Adalet ve Kalkınma Partisi,* (Justice and Development Party), which is the current ruling party in Turkey led by Prime Minister Recep Tayyip Erdoğan. It is a centre-right party that favors a conservative social agenda and a liberal market economy.
2. Incidentally this school is said to have given rise to the famous football club, Galatasaray, UEFA Cup and European Super Cup winners in 2000. The club traces its origins to the high school team.
3. This refers to the system of organization of university courses to facilitate credit transfer and overall harmonization between degree programs across the EU. By attuning people from outside the EU to this process one increases their chances of moving to universities and other higher education institutions within the union instead. The EU is bent on competing with the United States to obtain the lion's share of "international" students, that is, outside the EU. That lion's share is currently enjoyed by the United States.

Preface

Kemal İnal Güliz Akkaymak

Why did we need to write this book? Despite the many other issues related to education in Turkey, why did we prefer to write specifically on the educational politics of the Justice and Development Party (AKP)?

There are several reasons. The first reason is rooted in structural transformations of educational system in Turkey. Since the establishment of the Republic of Turkey, the education system has been restructured twice. The first structural amendment was made in the Mustafa Kemal Ataturk era (1923–1938). During the Ottoman Empire, the education system had a dual structure: traditional (religious) and modern (western) education. The republic put an end to the dual structure by closing the traditional educational institutions. Modern educational institutions, on the other hand, were considered very crucial for the construction of the "nation-state." In this respect, the Arabic alphabet was replaced with the Latin alphabet, and madrasas with universities. A coeducation system was adopted. Curricula and textbooks were written in accordance with the values of the new regime, such as democracy. A literacy campaign was launched. Religious education was trivialized. The religious discourse in education was replaced with a nationalist discourse. All these changes represent the Kemalist Reformation. Ataturk considered education as a tool with which to modernize Turkey. For him, religious educational institutions were the main reason for the country's backwardness, and modernization could only be achieved with modern educational system. For this purpose, John Dewey and many other thinkers were invited to Turkey, and their recommendations were used as a guide in the modernization of education. In short, the scholastic education system of the Ottoman Empire was reformed into a scientific-based and secular education system.

The second structural amendment started in the early 1970s and has accelerated since 2002. The economic system of Turkey was based on the planned development model and the import-substitution industrialization of the pre-1970 era. However, in line with the neoliberalization efforts in many other countries in the late 1970s, Turkey liberalized the market mechanism to converge the national economy with global capitalism. This structural change came with the January 24, 1980, measures, which were solidified with the September 12, 1980, military coup. The military officers who staged the coup implemented two policies. With the 1983 elections, they left the political power to the Özal government, which was supported by the International Monetary Fund (IMF) and the United States. Then, in order to dilute the power of the left wing, they began to implement the Turkish-Islamic Synthesis doctrine. This doctrine increased the impact of religion in political and social life, and led the pro-Islamist, anticapitalist, and antisocialist Welfare Party (RP) to come to power as part of a coalition government in 1991. The party, however, was banned by the February 28, 1997, postmodern coup for violating the principle of secularism in the constitution. After the banishment, the successors of the RP split into Radical Islamists and Moderate Islamists. Recep Tayyip Erdogan, the current prime minister, took part in the latter group and established the AKP in 2001. The party won by a landslide in the 2002 general election, winning over two-thirds of parliamentary seats[1].

The AKP considered education system, which has been based on the behaviorist education model, responsible for several problems, such as unskilled labor power and the low success of students in international exams. The party criticized the curricula for not teaching students critical thinking skills, and pointed out the necessity for a structural reform in the education system that would replace the nationalist and behaviorist education model with the liberal and constructivist model. The shift from the former model to the latter was achieved with the guidance and support (both financial and intellectual) of the World Bank (WB), the IMF, and the European Union (EU) in 2004. At the national level, the largest capitalist association, the Turkish Industry and Business Association (TUSIAD), has also been publishing reports since the early 1990s that address the necessity of reform in several fields, such as the economy, education, and law. In its reports on education, the TUSIAD states that to help Turkey play a strong role in global capitalism, the educational system needs to be reformed. The new education system, according to the TUSIAD, should aim at producing the labor force needed by the market economy. In line with the TUSIAD's report, the educational reform initiated in 2004 adopted a neoliberal discourse and changed the national stance of education into a global stance.

The AKP has made several structural changes in the educational arena since 2002. The revision of curriculum and textbooks; the introduction of Total Quality Management (TQM) and performance assessment of teachers; the abolishment of laws restricting religious education; and an increase in the number of Koran courses are among these changes. With these structural changes, the AKP, on the one hand, left the education system to the control of neoliberal ideology. On the other hand, the party integrated its conservative ideology into the system. In this book, we aim to examine and present these processes of change from a critical perspective.

The second reason is the close relation created between the economy and education. The AKP's policies have reorganized the education system to educate students/citizens in the way that the market economy requires. Almost every stage of public education has been privatized. That is, several nationwide exams have been created to determine admissions to highly ranked public schools and universities. Due to the intense competition on these exams, many students take private courses to increase their chances. Many services at schools, such as maintenance, transportation, and cafeteria work, were subcontracted to private firms. As a consequence, students are now paying more for these services, and workers in these services are now working in conditions without job security. While glorifying the relation between market and education, the educational policies of the AKP disregard social values, which should be the main part of the education system.

The third reason is an insufficient amount of the national budget spent on public education. Today, there are many public schools buildings that are not in good shape and that urgently need to be renovated. Likewise, common areas in the schools, such as restrooms and libraries, are filled with old tools and furniture. The salary of teachers in public schools is very low. The lack of enough investment in schools also dilutes the quality of public education, which leads students and parents to seek alternative educational institutions like tutoring institutions/courses. Moreover, since it came to power, the AKP has initiated a number of reforms that have led to complaint by both teachers and parents about the unstable education system.

Although the AKP considers its policies as revolutionary steps for the education system in Turkey, as the chapters in this book demonstrate, the policies have done nothing more than damage the entire system.

The fourth reason is a lack of study at the international level that critically evaluates the policies of the AKP. As opposed to international opinion, which views the party as reformist and liberal, this book highlights the necessity to present the negative aspects of the party's policies. Unlike the so-called enhancement of the Turkish economy, Turkey has a high current account deficit and, in a sense, is dependent on the flow of hot money from international financial organizations. It is not surprising, then, that under these economic conditions all public services are considered as a burden by the AKP. Erdoğan, the leader of the party, in this context, declared on several occasions that he and his supporters aim to privatize all aspects of education. However, the AKP disregards the fact that almost half of the Turkish population is under 18 and that many of them are from the lower class. Therefore, the privatization of education means both stealing the future of these young people and strengthening class differences. The privatization attempts in education also contradict the constitution, which defines Turkey as a social welfare state.

Through destroying the social composition of education, the AKP aims to restructure the education system in accordance with postmodernism. That is, the party seeks to replace the modernist role of education (i.e., the creation of a citizen) with the postmodernist role (i.e., an individual defined within a specific community). For this purpose, the emphasis on religious education has been enhanced. The party, for instance, criticizes coeducation, but it glorifies single-sex schools and classrooms, arguing that single-sex schools are more helpful for students' physiological, mental, and social well-being.

The fifth reason is the AKP's oppressive attitude toward intellectuals, professors, and all other educators. Since it came to power, the party has not allowed educators to criticize any of its policies. Its constant oppression of Eğitim-Sen, the most critical union, constitutes a significant example. Moreover, to enhance the party's power, Prime Minister Erdoğan began appointing the presidents of the main scientific institutions: the Turkish Academy of Sciences (TUBA) and the Scientific and Technological Research Council of Turkey (TUBITAK). The presidents of these institutions, however, had been selected by their members in the past. In response to this change, a great number of members of these institutions resigned. The authors of this book aim to give voice to the "suppressed academia." We believe that science and democracy cannot flourish when there is no criticism. Therefore, this book provides a well-rounded critical analysis of educational policies and reforms in the age of the AKP.

Note

1. During the period between 1997 and 2002, Turkey was ruled by unsuccessful coalition governments.

I

The AKP and Education in Turkey

1

The Political Economy of Education in Turkey: State, Labor, and Capital under AKP Rule

Gamze Yücesan-Özdemir and Ali Murat Özdemir

This chapter evaluates the political economy of education in Turkey under the rule of the Justice and Development Party (AKP). The education regime does not stand on its own and must be located within the general economic, social, and political conditions within which state, capital, and class relations are constituted. Thus, an understanding of the realities behind the education regime in Turkey requires an analysis of the Turkish economy, the transformation in the form of the Turkish state, the development of capital, and the experience of class politics. This study explores the contemporary education regime under AKP rule in the context of the historical and socioeconomic and political circumstances within which it is embedded.

In so doing, this chapter firstly aims to clarify the status of the education regime, in other words, to provide an account of how to understand the education regime. It then provides an understanding of the political economy within and beyond the education regime during the AKP years by analyzing the transformation of the state and the redefinition of labor-capital relations. Lastly, given that education is part of social policy, this chapter evaluates the social policy in Turkey under AKP rule. It discusses recent developments, describes the current scheme, and reveals the neoliberal and Islamic-conservative guises dominant in Turkish social policy and in the discoveries of policy makers.

Clarifying the Status of the Education Regime

Firstly, it is important to investigate the dynamics behind the current education policy of Turkey by way of reference to the correlation between the dynamics of accumulation and the form of the state, in which the state's realizes its function of securing the conditions necessary to reproduce the dominant ideology. The correlation between the capitalist relations of production and the surface forms, including the economy, education, politics, and the law as elements of state power, cannot be traced on the basis of linear causality. Thus, this investigation of the education regime has to take into account the imbricatedness of the relations that constitute these realms. Within this context, the process of transformation ("change") in the form of the Turkish state and the impasse related to import substitution as a chronic feature of the Turkish economy will become a point of departure for the assessment of state power, which shapes education policy and which is limited by the paradoxes of capital relations and/or the state's controversial relation to the accumulation process, which has international dimensions.

Secondly, the current education policy deals with and is characterized by significant political and institutional changes, the incentives of which cannot be understood solely by referring to the "needs" of the domestic economy. Within this context, the transitions experienced by the set of structural forms that have a certain impact on education policies and on state apparatuses that deal with education must be investigated here with reference to the ongoing crisis of capitalism after the collapse of the Fordist mode of regulation and of its corollary in peripheral countries, namely, import substitution. Neither the reason for the impasse that is related to the strategy of import substitution nor the accelerated processes of commodification of public services, including education, is related solely to the outcomes of class struggle in the domestic realm. They carry—at the same time—the footprints of the ideological and political effects of central capitalism, which provided the necessary social/structural forms in which the class struggle was shaped. The complexity of the issue makes it very difficult to establish a general theory of the politics of regime transition. It is, however, possible to view the correlation between hegemonic strategies and trends in the international division of labor. To this end, a historical evaluation must be based on an investigation of the transformation in Turkey within the world capitalist system during the last 30 years.

Thirdly, the changing balance of class forces in the realms of politics, economics, and ideology created an environment in which the democratic society is believed to have no power to challenge the choices related to the fundamental economic organization through the means of participatory democracy. For this reason, the whole neoliberal legal reform process is self-confidently conducted by the ruling AKP, which believes in a direct causal link and/or straight correlation between economic growth and the protection of private property rights, together with the enforceability of contracts, despite the growing income inequality and poverty in the society.

Fourthly, proposals for reforms—such as education, health, and social security—that have an impact on the form of the state in Turkey have been developed by commentators who judge development (a synonym for "capital accumulation" in AKP jargon) on the basis of measuring the gross domestic product (GDP). Even the "modest" goal of building the institutional framework to market products seems to be largely uncompleted. Law enforcement through a formal system has been replaced by informal methods of dispute resolution conducted by organized crime and/or clientalistic-religious networks. Possible redistributive and indirect economic goals of reforms have never come onto the agenda. Even though a detailed critique of the failures of the "old establishment" has been developing for at least the past eight years of AKP rule, nearly the same economic programs are being promoted under the auspices of the International Monetary Fund (IMF) and/or other international organizations. Under these conditions, the rule of law and the rhetoric of democracy adopted by the AKP do not represent a desire for genuine change.

Fifthly, in its attempt to depoliticize the economic decision-making process and restrict the domain of democracy as a means of fostering the smooth implementation of market-based economic reforms—including education reform—the AKP created and widely benefited from the conditions that led to the spread of generalized corruption and clientalistic/religious networks and are backed up with the generalized commodification in public services. In this respect, the changes in the form of the Turkish state that have been witnessed under the rule of the AKP have many things common with the recent changes observed in "developing" countries and with the policy recommendations of international organizations.

Last but not least, many of the so-called AKP reforms, especially those in the realm of social policy—such as education, health, and social security—correspond to a post-Washington consensus based on attempts aimed at the creation and protection of the institutions that support the market-based allocation of resources. Given the drastic consequences of income inequality, the AKP failed to mitigate the negative consequences of the market mechanism by creating new institutions. Reforms designed to secure neoliberal capitalism in Turkey provoked new problems and crises. As a result, the reforms to impose a neoliberal rationality undermined the legitimacy of democratic institutions in Turkey.

Understanding the Political Economy in and beyond Education during the AKP Years: Creating a State and Redefining Labor-Capital Relations

Throughout the 1970s, the benefits of world trade were open to peripheral countries that had higher degrees of control over their national work force. The traditional mode of the articulation of the Turkish economy with the international division of labor, namely import substitution, seemed unsuccessful in face of the growing amounts of exports from Newly Industrializing Countries (NICs), which were in no better position than Turkey before the 1970s, to the industrialized West. The 1980s were years in which Turkey's economic policies were radically reoriented under strict measures provided by the military coup of 1980 and by "elected" governments that followed under the 1982 Constitution, which was designed according to the demands deriving from international and domestic capital. The major footprints of the 1980 alterations can be found in the January 24, 1980, stabilization program, which could not be applied "properly" before the military coup was realized in September of that same year. The main objectives of the program were a reduction in government involvement in productive activities, an increased emphasis on market forces, and the replacement of an inward-looking accumulation strategy with an "export-oriented strategy of import substitution" (Kepenek and Yentürk 1996).

The process of the reconstruction of the state and the marketization of social reproduction owed its repressive measures to the military coup of 1980. The military intervened in the main codes that constitute the form of the semiperipheral Turkish state for the purpose of attaining a more market-directed system of resource allocation. In the 1980s, the global decline in unionization, the excessive use of repressive methods to dominate domestic politics, the rising marginalization of the work force in daily jobs, and the replacement of unionized workers by temporary employees all served to contribute to the deterioration of resistance based on labor solidarity.

After the military coup, in conformity with the rest of the peripheral world that was experiencing a debt crisis (especially after the Mexican crisis of 1982), the Keynesian-like economic policies of the pre-1980 governments of Turkey became instable and incoherent. Pre-1980 social entitlements and institutionalized compromises became threatened. In conformity with the international political climate of the 1980s, conservative/liberal calls for a reduction in the protective involvement of the state in labor issues were realized. Not only a change in the political regime but also a change in the structural forms constituting the state was on its way. Due to the fact that means of representation are themselves a part of the conjuncture that determines class interests, the balance of class forces, or, to put it in structuralist terms, the shared borderline between the classes, which were reflected in the state itself, was to be changed (Yalman 1997, 218–242).

Articulation of the Turkish economy with the new international division of labor aimed at transforming Turkey into an export-oriented country has been explicitly stated as a state policy. Post-1980 hegemonic projects succeeded in presenting the state as having no relation to class interests and in presenting the market and civil society as autonomous spheres, and concealed the fact that the state and the market are the sites where the hegemony of the bourgeoisie is exercised.

Turkey managed to obtain inflows of international credit in the first years of the neoliberal and conservative Özal governments, despite the lack of any policies to promote the introduction and effective implementation of sectorial policies necessary to effect a productive linkage to the existing division of labor (Yalman 1997, 191). The country's role in the wake of the events in Iran and Afghanistan and the so-called second cold war of the early 1980s may partly provide a reason for the Turkish success in having access to capital inflows and favorable borrowing conditions during the adjustment period (Öniş 1998, 128). Furthermore, despite the newly emerging impact of internationally conducted monetarism of the central world, major debt rescheduling did not result in spillover effects in other countries. Yet the situation was to change after the crises in Mexico, Brazil, and Argentina occurred in the first half of the 1980s. With the continuation of the borrowing facilities of the state after the January decisions, which resulted in a relaxation of supply constraints, the Turkish bourgeoisie found a base on which earlier practices could depend and did not radically opt to initiate the investments necessary for the implementation of export substitution (Öniş 1998, 77–128). Within this context, the "export-oriented strategy of import substitution" meant the government aimed to achieve structural adjustment by liberalizing finances without structurally changing the investment patterns of the Turkish bourgeoisie. The 1990s and the 2000s would witness the continuation of this vicious and blind pattern.

The neoliberal "revolution" in Turkey did not include the structuration of industrial organizations to charm international investment, and concern about a weak level of national productivity did not lead to a break with the old patterns of production norms. The stress created by the unproductive investments over the division of total income caused the 1994 crisis (Boratav et al. 2000, Yeldan 2003). The response to the reliance on domestic debt as a result of weak international competitiveness in industry was a vicious circle that had a detrimental impact on the overall productivity of capital (Boratav 2003, Kazgan 1999). In the absence of investment patterns that would "utilize" the labor dwelling in Turkey, and thus in the absence of change in the structure of industry, placing greater reliance on market forces in policy making became a political mantra. The overall structuration of industry ceased to respond on a material level to the changes in the reproduction of capitalism on a global scale. Mainly since the 1994 crisis, the fundamental dynamic of growth has become the ongoing deterioration of wages, and thus, the conditions of the reproduction of collective labor power due to the ongoing stress that derives from the structural deficiencies of import substitution. The neoliberal restructuring of the Turkish state resulted in an ongoing decline (except in the period between 1989 and 1993) (Dereli 1998) in terms of real wages and agricultural incomes throughout the 1980s, the 1990s, and the 2000s (Boratav 2003).

The discourse of the so-called "Washington consensus," in conformity with the New Right premises, provided the Turkish ruling classes with a new hegemonic apparatus that would be instrumental in dealing with the heritage of the mixed economy of the 1970s. New requirements for borrowing in the international arena included the opening of the economy, the reordering of public expenditure priorities, financial liberalization, privatization, the deregulation of labor markets, the providing of an encouraging environment for the private sector, and thus, the championing of the vigorous virtues of individuals capable of "emancipating" themselves from intermediary, democratic, and corporatist powers (Yalman 1997, 225–226). This situation was not in conflict with the strengthening of the authoritarian prerogatives of the state, which has been the case for Turkey up until now. On the contrary, this new approach was in line with the New Right thinking that a strong state was necessary as the political guarantor of economic individualism and private property.

Since 1994, accusations made in search of an excuse for the clear failure of neoliberal policies have concerned the rigidities of labor legislation and social policy regulations. Within this context, state expenditures on social services related to welfare and protective provisions that result in "rigidity" in the markets came to be considered as a source of impediment for the "successful" transformation of the existing accumulation strategy into an export-oriented strategy.

The above-mentioned noncompetitive configuration can be considered as the continuation of import substitution. Moreover, the subsequent crises of 1994, 1998, and 2001, which resulted in a major outflow of short-term capital, occurred as a result of a crisis of confidence related to the viability of an import substitution strategy as a dominant strategy, which included the majority of the industry.

In conformity with the traditional perception of liberalism, it was assumed, once again, that the Turkish market economy, like any other capitalist economy, faced instability because of the exogenous interventions of a rent-seeking state, rather than its inherent systemic characteristics. However, throughout the last two decades, the Turkish state was expected to contribute to the market in such a way that its "exogenous intervention" would socialize the risk of the private sector. To put it differently, state intervention in Turkey always enabled the financial sectors and industry to transfer its costs (whether they derived from weak levels of productivity or not) to the public sector, and therefore, to society. This is one of the inherent systemic characteristics of capitalism in Turkey (Yeldan 2001, 26). Other means of state intervention have been considered to be a source of uncertainty.

Between 1998 and 2008, IMF-oriented economic policies played a significant role in the "discoveries" of policy makers in search of credit. Given that financial or capital account liberalization had already been achieved, the promarket rhetoric became inadequate for the initiation of necessary reforms aiming to commodify the existing assets of Turkey. Turkey had to carry on with new international debts and problems if the import-oriented structure of the industry was to go on producing despite low levels of productivity with regard to new competitors in the world market, namely, the first, second, and third generations of NICs. Put differently, the price of reproducing capitalist relations of production in a peripheral country that had no conveniently disciplined labor force for international markets became greater than before.

The main axis of the IMF policies, especially after February 2001, aimed to achieve stabilization by way of rebuilding market confidence. According to this strategy, Turkey was to undertake the necessary reforms that were designed by the IMF and would be subjected to direct control by that institution on a regular basis. If, after each regular control visit, the controllers announced that Turkey was successful in meeting IMF requirements, then the markets would perceive the country as trustworthy and the aim of rebuilding market confidence would be deemed to be achieved (Yeldan 2003). The expected outcome of this "success" was the decrease of risk margins for international finance capital and a rise in consumption and investments together with total development. The last stand-by agreement between Turkey and the IMF ended in May 11, 2008. Mainly after the international crisis of 2008, the Turkish economy obtained international credit by borrowing freely from international markets and by charming the Middle East-based resources that "preferred" to invest in areas other than those provided and "offered" by Europe and the United States.

Throughout the 2000s, conditions of the reproduction of labor power consistently worsened for the individual worker. The process that officially started with an open-economy rhetoric exhausted the majority of the wage earners', including state officials', capacity to be members of the middle class. The process of informalizing wage relations had a negative impact on wages and covered all areas of productive activity. Import substitution as a hegemonic project disappeared, but it remained as a social reality that was decisive in the reproduction of the capitalist relations of production. A new institutionality in work, together with the refusal to deepen import substitution, led to a decline in the numbers of skilled workers among workers overall. Thus the main dynamic of growth after 1994 led to the ongoing deterioration of wages, and as a result, to the conditions of the reproduction of collective labor power rather than successful management of the economy led by domestic implementers of IMF-designed programs.

Understanding Social Policy in and beyond Education under the AKP's Rule: The Coexistence of Neoliberalism, Conservatism, and Islam

The AKP has described itself as a moderate Islamic political organization. Fittingly then, the reform plans in areas of social policy such as education, health, and social policy that the party initiated on its arrival to the government were an amalgam of Islamic conservatism and neoliberalism. Such a program might be further described as one in opposition to the basic premises of rights-based approaches to social policy. Firstly, the social policy regime of the AKP targets a process of transition from community-based ideals to those of individualism. The focus here is on individual responsibility, and it is stressed that there are no rights without duties. Put differently, rather than depending on the state for healthcare, education, and care for the elderly, the individual has to accept more responsibility for him/herself in accessing healthcare, education, and care in old age. Hence, personal consumption is presented as the key to a good life, and low taxation on income becomes essential. Specifically, the private pension system is a good example of this stress on individualism during the AKP's rule. The Turkish Private Pension Law was drafted in 1999 and approved by the parliament in October 2001. In the same vein, for the education regime, the transition from community-based ideals to those of individualism means a transition from public schools to private ones. The social effects of this "choice" have become visible in the towering numbers of private colleges and preparatory courses for the national university examination and for other purposes, including driving licenses, language examinations, and so forth.

Secondly, the social policy regime of the AKP emphasizes the market and its role in the reproduction of society. The party has led the process of market colonization or rather, the penetration of market norms into nonmarket spheres. In other words, under the AKP's rule, life itself, with its social, academic, and cultural dimensions, has become a marketplace. Both in the classical political economy and in neoliberal theory, the market is often defended as a sphere of freedom, of voluntary, uncoerced contracts between free and independent agents. Hence, it is assumed that in the marketplace, free women and men are able to simultaneously maximize the general interest and pursue their own interests by freely exchanging goods and services, without intervention from the state. Neoliberal writings display a profound distaste for the whole concept of an interventionist state and argue that any and every attempt to replace the market with a system of politically administered decision making is bound to end in tyranny and disaster.

The social security reform[1], which was started before the AKP came to power but was finalized under the party, is a good example of the subjection of the health and social security systems to the disciplines of the market. The prime motive of the AKP-initiated reform was to address the unsustainability of what had been the existing social security system (Arın 2002). Essentially, the rise in costs became a prominent source of legitimacy for the reform programs in social security. Meanwhile, the IMF announced that it would release a substantial loan to Turkey if the country enacted the necessary legislation to initiate the social security reform. With these looming financial concerns, the AKP set out to reorganize the system.

The social security reform is based on a view of the marketplace as the main mode of coordination in the production of services that are financed and provided by the social security system, such as pensions and healthcare. However, the campaign that was launched to legitimize the reform was based first on the equalitarian aspects of social security measures that operate independently of employment status, and secondly, on the expansion of the total coverage of the social security system. The market-based "egalitarianism" of the new reforms required different employment statutes to be calculated for even the worst positions.

Given that the social policy regime of the AKP emphasizes the market and its role in the reproduction of society, the market mechanisms and market-based discourses and practices are now saturating public education in Turkey. This agenda calls for expanding education markets and employing market principles across school systems.

Thirdly, the AKP's neoliberal agenda, which was in line with the so-called "structural reforms," was introduced in conjunction with the IMF and the World Bank (WB) (Koray 2005). One of the main requirements and/or reforms, which both the IMF and the WB established as stipulations for providing funds, is the restructuring of social policy in line with neoliberal ideas. One important example in this respect is the parallel between the structure and the application of social assistance in Turkey and the strategies envisaged by the World Bank to reduce poverty. The World Bank's Social Risk Mitigation Project (SRMP), which was initiated on September 11, 2001, and commenced in 2006, is a direct reflection of the bank's approach to reducing poverty. For this project, in which the Fund for the Encouragement of Social Assistance and Solidarity (SYDTF) acted as the implementer, the World Bank extended US$500 million over a five-year grace period and did so on the condition that it would be repaid in fifteen years.

Fourthly, the AKP's social policy regime is based on Islamic references. Indeed, in the pursuit of its reform program, the AKP refers to a Turkish culture in which Islam is situated and influences its social policy. Briefly, Islam is the point of reference for some of the most delicate issues that Turkish society needs to face: how to treat the poor, promote charity, and establish fair relations among communities and within families. Essential to all religions, charity is also a central organizing principle in Islam, to which the AKP refers rather often. The Islamic elements in the ideological orientation of the ruling party also appear to be very useful in motivating and mobilizing civil initiatives toward providing social assistance. An important example of the purpose of orienting Islamic elements is the rise of Islamic nongovernmental organizations (NGOs) in the realm of social assistance. In the same vein, the issue of Turkish social assistance, including those benefits allocated by municipalities and by the government, is not simply a matter of assistance to the poor. It is rather a strategy, which is used in the construction of the political and ideological bonds/links that keep the AKP in the power.

Under the strengthened aim of supporting market mechanisms and under conditions that had devastating effects on the social state, the education apparatus focused mainly on religious education in asserting its own legitimacy. Collective rights were supported only when they were not in contradiction to entrepreneurial (therefore individual) rights and freedoms. The right to religion is supported as a right to believe in Islam (but not as a right to believe in other religions or to reject Islam entirely). While the public role in the production of educational services declined enormously, the discussions on education that are held by big media groups on the right are limited to/focused on the right to wear Islamic clothing in classes at universities. In today's Turkey, one is free to choose to invest in/to consume anything s/he desires. On the other hand, no one is entitled to establish an association (or a union or a foundation, etc.) for the purpose of enhancing the right to education on the basis of social premises aimed at creating a form of citizenship that is backed up with social rights.

As a result, the "interests" of private capital that is "invited" to "invest" in education, healthcare, and the pension system come to the fore in the construction of "social" policies. The interests of capital, which are related to serious declines in "production costs," including raw materials and labor costs (the rise in the employment of unskilled and semiskilled personnel in addition to long working hours), savings in equipment, and shrinkages in the workplace, marketing activities require increases in the costs paid by contributors (contribution payments) and by the state as soon as possible. It has been argued that the dominance of profit-seeking activities in the production of health and education services would end with huge transfers of profit from the state to the private sector. However, in reality, it has been observed that state expenditure increased, yet the quality and amount of services produced decreased. The new system is designed to limit and then abolish the role of the state in the formation of social policy.

Conclusion

Throughout the chapter, certain aspects of changes in the economic, political, and ideological structures in Turkey were investigated. Currently, dominant perceptions of the reform proposals to restructure the state and redefine labor-capital relations indicate that state power is considered to be a means to support the neoliberal order. The separation of economic decision making from politics helps governments to empower markets against society. Legal reforms in Turkey have been undertaken to conform to a neoliberal economic rationality, which is attached to the goal of capital accumulation without any regard to the real lives of real people suffering from the economic, ideological, and political aspects of social inequality and insecurity. When the law is presented as a technical device, "reforms" help to create an institutional environment that undermines the legitimacy of democratic institutions. What the current process of transformations ("changes") is likely to achieve is the hardly "unintended" consequence of markets without democracy, if the term "democracy" refers to a social capacity to develop the means to challenge the fundamental economic basis of the whole political system.

During the AKP's rule, the plan to construct a social policy regime encompassing the essences of neoliberalism, conservatism, and Islam has widened the chasm between the rich and the poor by promoting the interests of the capitalist class over the interests of the public as a whole. It is certain that this combination of neoliberalism, conservatism, and Islam will not provide acceptable solutions to the many vulnerable sectors of the population. Indeed, it seems that the existing social policy regime will result in further diminishing the welfare of the majority of the population.

In sum, it is safe to say that the changes in Turkey's educational apparatus have become traceable with reference to the political economy of Turkey and the social policy regime of Turkey. Against this background, Turkish policy makers must make a vital distinction between the tools needed for market efficiency and the bases for fostering social education in Turkey. While the policies for fostering social education require both the enhancement of public contributions to the school system and the bestowing of democratic participatory rights on the recipients of educational services, the AKP consciously opted to strengthen the commodification, the marketization, and the privatization of the educational system.

Note

1. The neoliberal pension reform of 1999 was proposed after the social insurance system sustained significant losses. The Bill (No. 4447) enacted in 1999 was to be the very first stage of a larger reform to "neoliberalize" the system. The second stage was to be launched in 2006 with the introduction of the parliamentary bills enacted for the purpose of a shift from a publicly financed social security system to a "capitalization system." The legislation enabling this second stage is the result of the AKP's efforts since 2003. The 1999 attempt was to be supported when the AKP government initiated a neoliberal/conservative action plan for the improvement of the informative and operative capacities of the social security system and for the unification of the existing regulations in 2003.

References

Arın, Tülay. "The Poverty of Social Security: The Welfare Regime in Turkey." In *The Ravages of Neoliberalism: Economy, Society and Gender in Turkey*, edited by Neşecan Balkan and Sungur Savran, 73–91. New York: Nova Science Publishers, 2002.

Boratav, Korkut. *Türkiye İktisat Tarihi 1908–2002*. Ankara: İmge Yayınları, 2003.

Boratav, Korkut, Erinç Yeldan, and Ahmet Köse. "Globalisation, Distribution and Social Policy: Turkey: 1980–1998." *CEPA and New School for Social Research Working Paper series*, no. 20 (2000).

Dereli, Toker. *Labour Law and Industrial Relations in Turkey*. Hague: Kluwer Law International, 1998.

Kazgan, Gülten. *Tanzimattan XXI. Yüzyıla Türkiye Ekonomisi: 1. Küreselleşmeden 2. Küreselleşmeye.* Istanbul: Altın Kitaplar, 1999.
Kepenek, Yakup, and Nurhan Yentürk. *Türkiye Ekonomisi.* Istanbul: Remzi Kitabevi, 1996.
Koray, Meryem. *Sosyal Politika.* Ankara: İmge, 2005.
Öniş, Ziya. *State and Market: The Political Economy of Turkey in Comparative Perspective.* Istanbul: Bogaziçi University, 1998.
Yalman, Galip. *Transition to Neoliberalism: The Case of Turkey in the 1980s.* Istanbul: Istanbul Bilgi University Press, 2009.
Yeldan, Erinç. "Neoliberalizmin İdeolojik Bir Söylemi olarak Küreselleşme." In *İktisat Üzerine Yazılar I: Küresel Düzen: Birikim, Devlet ve Sınıflar*, edited by Ahmet Haşim Köse, Fikret Şenses, and Erinç Yeldan, 427–453. Istanbul: İletişim Yayınları, 2003.
———. *Küreselleşme Sürecinde Türkiye: Bölüşüm, Birikim ve Büyüme.* Istanbul: İletişim Yayınları, 2001.

2

The Educational Politics of the AKP: The Collapse of Public Education in Turkey

Kemal İnal

Recep Tayyip Erdoğan, the current prime minister of Turkey, and his politically oriented friends, who left the "National Outlook" formulated by Islamist politician Necmettin Erbakan, opened a new political track by establishing the Justice and Development Party (AKP) in 2002. The AKP won all the general and local political elections by 2011. The main reason for this success is that unlike previous Islamist parties and their cadres, the AKP has become highly popular by winning a significant proportion of votes among different social segments of the country. The weakening of the center right, various economic and political crises, a loss of confidence in former national leaders, the search for a new but popular leader, and a favorable global economic climate are among the major factors that have played a role in the success of the AKP.

Through the AKP's reformist policies that were implemented from 2002 to 2011, its governments exhibited some thoughts and practices that were unexpected for Islamic cadres. At first, the party implemented many reforms of Turkey's politics and economy; initiated a "democratic opening" regarding the Kurdish problem, broke the influence of the Turkish army over the country's politics, made achievements in the economic field, such as decreasing inflation to single digit numbers and curbing high growth rates in the economy, and established a "zero-problem policy with Turkey's neighbors." Meanwhile, education has also undergone some structural adjustments in the last ten years. For example, curricula and textbooks were revised, performance and career systems were introduced into the field of education, the teacher training system was changed and turned into a student-centered pedagogy, and philosophy of education was revised from a focus on behaviorism to one focusing on constructivism. All of these changes formulated in the name of reform have been justified in a language of economic relations. The logic for educational change is that globalization calls for a new work force. Therefore, the Turkish national education system must be reorganized accordingly.

This chapter is mainly based on this politically oriented change that is defined by the AKP as a "reform." This chapter argues that the AKP's educational politics are heavily oriented to the marketization of education. The party has developed a neoliberal educational concept that it hopes to realize in the context of a visible agenda consisting of market-oriented education, which would result in the collapse of the public education system.

Neoliberalism in Education

The last 20 years of capitalism are defined as "neoliberalism" (Duménil and Lévy 2007, 25), which is based on the market economy. As Peter McLaren and Ramin Farahmandpur state, it "functions as a type of binding arbitration, legitimizing a host of questionable practices and outcomes: deregulation, unrestricted access to consumer markets, downsizing, outsourcing, flexible arrangements of labor, intensification of competition among transnational corporations, increasing centralization of economic and political power, and finally, widening class polarization" (2001, 137). Neoliberal ideology aims to privatize and globalize education in order to train the work force that is needed for the highly globalized markets.

It is widely accepted that structural changes and reforms leading the development of neoliberalism in education began with the conservative governments of Ronald Reagan in the United States and of Margaret Thatcher in Great Britain in the early 1980s. These years were an adjustment period for many developing countries. The adjustment policies implemented under the supervision of the International Monetary Fund (IMF) and the World Bank aimed to correct the economic structures of these countries (Stewart 1995). Also, non-economic problems, such as "deteriorating facilities, instructional personnel who are poorly educated, over-stretched, under-paid and demoralized, inadequate teaching materials and, more recently, a lack of clear vision of how to navigate the educational demands of globalization and development" (Kanu 2005, 494) led developing countries to request that Western countries and institutions provide both financial assistance to education and recommendations and plans for educational development. Neoliberal education programs, which are presented as the only alternative to the failure of public education, have become a dominant ideology in the reorganization of education. Therefore, education has become a successful hegemonic project in redefining the preparation of the workforce, in teaching standardized skills and knowledge, in measuring the quality of education by exam results, and in "teaching as the technical delivery of that which is centrally mandated and tested"(Lipman 2009, 373). Regarding these neoliberal reforms of education, many scholars state that changes in the curriculum, policy, and content of education are designed to produce comfortable, self-interested, and market-oriented human beings (Akkaymak 2010a).

How to Define the AKP

This part of the chapter offers a definition of the AKP in order to understand its education politics. The AKP should be defined as a political party on two levels: politics and the economy. The AKP has formulated its ideology as "conservative democrat" (Yavuz 2010, 8; Özbudun and Hale 2010, 57; Akdoğan 2010, 59). The term "conservative democrat" expresses the desire to represent the party not as Islamist but as a contemporary movement in the Western democratic line. Conservatism has been politically implemented in many policies of the government. To illustrate, the party continued to implement compulsory religious education in the curriculum despite all criticism, removed the restrictions for admission to the *Imam-Hatip* schools (religious vocational schools), implemented widespread conservative staffing in the Ministry of National Education (MoNE) and primary and secondary schools, allowed the Islamic practice of wearing headscarves at universities and ended the age requirements for starting Koran courses, and achieved a political compromise with religious communities. These examples show that the AKP understands and implements conservatism in an Islamist content.

The government programs and implementations of the AKP show that it is also a neoliberal party (İnal 2006, Akkaymak 2010a, Akkaymak 2010b, Bedirhanoğlu 2010, Çulha-Zabcı 2010, İnal et al. 2010, Yıldırım 2010, İnal 2011). The AKP left economic management out of politics, and strayed instead into neoliberal populism rather than welfare state politics (Tuğal 2010, 16; Güzelsarı 2008, 25; Bedirhanoğlu 2010, 53; Yıldırım 2010; Ertuğrul 2010). Reflections of the neoliberalization process on education are clearly seen in the party's official documents and the educational applications of the MoNE, which will be discussed in the next part.

The Impact of Neoliberalism on Educational Policy of the AKP

In its government programs, the AKP considers education as the most important element of development, and looks at education within the framework of neoliberal ideology. The AKP has approached education as an economic investment to increase human capital and emphasized the importance of quality, competition, standards, and governance in education. To increase the country's competitiveness in the global economy, the AKP needs to have effective human capital. In this respect, the party aimed to implement several changes in education, such as improving the quality of education in public schools, training the citizens who will be able to use easily advanced information technology. In addition, the AKP has given special attention to the use of advanced technology in education, and declared that it will provide every school with technological devices such as PCs, tablet computers, and smart boards.[1]

The AKP announced that it would make arrangements with the private sector to ensure educational investments. It is possible to see the economy/market-oriented discourse in the AKP's government policies related to education programs, and in the publications of the MoNE's Department of Research and Development (MEB EARGED). However, it is important to note that regulation of education within the context of the fields of the economy and technology started before the AKP came to power. In his preface to a publication (Bal, Keleş, and Erbil 1999) by EARGED, the former Minister of National Education, Metin Bostancıoğlu, stressed the need to train a particular type of person who could produce and market products by using contemporary advanced technology. He also claimed that the quality of schooling depends on an increase in student achievement, and that this is possible only by developing the skills and practices of staff in school administration. In other publications by the MoNE from 1999 (MEB EARGED 1999), the Ministry designed a new model of schools (i.e., Curriculum Laboratory schools) and claimed that the quality of education being targeted was possible only by means of efficient educational practices and by raising the competitive strength of the country. In addition, the Ministry highlighted that education should adopt the philosophy of Total Quality Management (MEB EARGED 1999, 170). In short, the ministry's use of words such as "quality," "product," "marketing," and "customer" in the aforementioned publication indicates a market-oriented approach to education.

Since the AKP came to power, the language of economics has become dominant in educational literature and practices. To illustrate, efficiency and effectiveness in education are now based solely on the performance of teachers and students, and the role of inspectors in the schools is limited to performance evaluation. This style of school management, which is based on a performance system, is multidimensional, from the employing of staff to training and development activities, to career planning, to an incentive system based on rewards and encouragement. Performance evaluation in schools shows that market ideology has become a reality of the educational system (MEB EARGED 1002, 1–3 and 25). In addition, the AKP, basing its policy on the notion of the individual business model, has welcomed the student-centered pedagogy formulated in the West as a solution to Turkey's education problems nationally. In this context, the party has also justified its educational reforms through criticism of the previous educational system, especially in terms of the role of students. So the party accepted a student-centered pedagogy to minimize the role of the teacher. In student-centered pedagogy, the student rather than the teacher is at the center of the educational system. The AKP asserts that placing the student at the center will eliminate rote learning and lead to the ability to think abstractly, independently, and critically and lead to the ability to easily solve problems, to a love of learning, and to a feeling of self-worth. However, all of these developments that have been conceived as reforms cannot solve the problems of the public education system.

The Declining Share of Investment in the Public Education Budget

This part offers some explanations about the share of investment in education in the AKP period. The party has always claimed that the investment in education has increased since 2002. But the share of investment in education has continuously decreased, although

Table 2.1 The budget of the MoNE and the share allocated to public education (2002–2011)[3]

Years	Budget of the MoNE	Investment Budget of the MoNE	The share of Investment in the MoNE Budget (%)
2002	$4,168,151.40	$716,027.93	17.18
2003	$5,687,149.16	$826,284.92	14.53
2004	$7,181,364.25	$695,055.87	9.68
2005	$8,314,111.45	$687,321.79	8.27
2006	$9,255,947.21	$788,546.37	7.49
2007	$11,930,465.92	$832,402.23	6.98
2008	$12,846,684.36	$724,415.64	5.66
2009	$15,333,395.58	$701,781.11	4.57
2010	$15,775,090.50	$997,389.39	6.32
2011	$19,057,074.30	$1,114,874.30	5.85

Source: Eğitim-Sen (2011).

the budget allocated to education under the AKP governments has increased five times from 2002 to 2011. In each year, approximately 70 percent of expenditures in the budget allocated to education go to the salaries for around six hundred thousand personnel (mainly teachers). The remaining share covers maintenance service and repair costs for school buildings. Despite that, the schools still have many crucial problems such as poor structural design,[2] and incomplete and poor quality training materials. All of these issues indicate that the AKP governments have not made a sufficient investment in the field of education since the party came to power, as seen in Table 2.1.

In addition to insufficient investment, the government's share in educational funding has decreased gradually, while households' share has increased. Between 2002 and 2011, parents' annual spending on education for their children in primary school increased four times. Among the Organization for Economic Cooperation and Development (OECD) countries, Turkey spends the least amount per student. To illustrate, in the OECD, per capita in primary education is US$6.437 and in secondary education US$8.006, whereas in Turkey, it is US$1.130 and US$1.834, respectively (Aydoğanoğlu 2010, 24–28).

New Curriculum and the New Human Model for the Market in Textbooks

This part discusses the human model formulated in the new curriculum designed by the AKP. The AKP carried out its first deep-rooted reforms in education by changing the primary-education curriculum in 2004 and then the secondary-education curriculum. The revised curricula and textbooks were written in terms of the new educational philosophy, constructivism. The AKP considered constructivism as a solution for all of Turkey's educational problems. The MoNE has defined the previous educational philosophy as behaviorism, and criticized it as linear, monist, vulgar reductionist, and oriented toward rote learning-oriented. The new educational philosophy was affirmed as probabilistic, having multidirectional causality, and trendy. In fact, the new primary curriculum is closely related to the training of the workforce, to meet the needs of international competition that has been enhanced by global market economy, and the demand for an intellectual ability compatible with the highly globalized economy (Ertürk 2006, 67–68). Therefore, the emphasis here is on making national education responsive to the economy. Nationalism as the official ideology of Turkey has also been redefined in revised textbooks as "an outlook of more liberal, market-based nationalism" (Ertürk 2009, 51). That is, national interests will be realized in terms of the country's integration into global markets. While the idea of "using domestic goods" was dominant in the textbooks published before the reform, the idea of "brotherhood based on consumerism" has become dominant in the textbooks published since the reform (Ertürk 2009, 52).

The two motives have been decisive in the creation of the new primary-school curriculum: globalization and the possibility of joining the European Union (EU). In many publications, statements, and related studies of various ministries, it was expressed that the Turkish national education system needed to be adapted to the globalization taking place. Many official agencies emphasized the importance of advanced technology. The accession process to the EU has had an impact in the formulation of the new curriculum. Curriculum reform in fact was seen as an important step in harmonizing the Turkish educational system with EU countries (İnal 2005, İnal 2006, Altınyelken 2010, Ertürk 2006, Adıgüzel 2010).

The neoliberal model of the individual is evident within the revised primary-school textbooks. To illustrate, several key concepts of neoliberal ideology, such as entrepreneurism, marketing, investment, advertising, and competition, have been used more in the postreform textbooks than the prereform textbooks (Akkaymak 2010a, 79–102). "This result illustrates the fact that students educated with the new textbooks are exposed to the neoliberal discourse more than the students educated in the pre-2004 reform era ....So the post-2005 textbooks familiarize students with the neo-liberal concepts, and thus direct them to think within the framework of neoliberalism" (Akkaymak 2010a, 83). As emphasized by Apple, this shift indicates that in neoliberal times, not only are schools forced to be a marketplace, but the aim is also to transform students into a commodity and human capital, which will ensure that the system reproduces itself (Apple 2004, 105).

The Harmful Effects of Tutoring Institutions and Schools on Public Education

Under the rule of the AKP, one of the factors that has had negative effects on public education is the tutoring institutions. During the period of AKP dominance, the number of *dershane* (tutoring institutions), defined in the literature as an "alternative school to public education" (Eğitim-Sen 2011), a "complementary educational institution" (İnce 2008), or a "shadow educational system" (Özoğlu 2011) has increased dramatically. As shown in Table 2.2, while the number of tutoring institutions was 2,122 in 2002, the number increased to 4,099 in 2011. During the same period, the number of teachers in these institutions increased from 19,881 to 50,209, and the number of students from 606,522 to 1,234,738. The main reason for these increases is that Turkey's educational system has become an exam-oriented in the last two decades. There are many school entrance exams at different grade levels, such as the high school and university levels. In addition, there are also several exams one must take to become a public official. Tutoring institutions have a registration fee that is quite

Table 2.2 The number of tutoring courses, teachers, and students

Years	Number of Tutoring Courses	Number of Teachers	Number of Students
2002–2003	2,122	19,881	6,06,522
2003–2004	2,568	23,730	6,68,673
2004–2005	2,984	30,537	7,84,565
2005–2006	3,928	41,031	9,25,299
2006–2007	3,986	47,621	10,71,827
2007–2008	4,031	48,855	11,22,861
2008–2009	4,262	51,916	11,78,943
2009–2010	4,193	50,432	11,74,860
2010–2011	4,099	50,209	12,34,738

Source: Eğitim-Sen (2011).

expensive for the average family's budget. These institutions constitute a major sector in economy. This chapter argues that this is a clear indication of a neoliberal transformation of education.

The reasons behind the increasing demand for tutoring institutions necessitates further discussion. First, the various entrance exams for high-quality schools, of which there are a limited number, lead to competition among students and parents. High demand for the high-quality schools causes a supply-demand imbalance. Second, several drawbacks of many public schools, such as, crowded classes and an insufficient number of teachers, force parents to send their children to tutoring institutions. Third, the positive educational image created by social and cultural factors about these institutions causes parents believe that it is impossible to achieve academic success on entrance exams without attending the tutoring courses.

The chief problem concerning tutoring institutions is that they can be an economic burden for families, depending on their socio economic status. These institutions, in this respect, create an inequality of opportunity in education and weaken the quality of public education by encouraging high-quality teachers to work for them for high wages. However, the number of high-quality teachers in these institutions is not high, because they prefer to hire teachers who are low-paid and inexperienced and are new university graduates. On the other hand, an important aspect of tutoring institutions is that they are owned by Islamic religious circles or by secular circles, and these institutions have been established not only for economic reasons but also out of ideological motives.

Similarly, marketization of education is seen in private schools. The number of students in private schools in the 1930s was around 30,000, while it is around 500,000 in 2011 (Eğitim-Sen 2011, 59). Private schools are based on two assumptions. First, public schools do an insufficient job of providing quality education, and it is only the wealthier people who have a chance to receive a better education. Second, the upper and middle classes need private schools in order to perpetuate their socioeconomic status, namely their material advantages. Both assumptions can be considered as reasons for opening up a new space for education that stands against the sovereignty of public education (Kaymak 2006, 18). Private schools are considered as superior to all public schools for various reasons, such as the high quality of the school buildings, the rich educational materials they offer, their proficiency in teaching foreign languages, the number of students per class, and so forth. However, this is the case for very

Table 2.3 Increase in numbers of private schools and their students in years

Years	Number of Schools	Number of Students
1949–1950	181	25,146
1959–1960	278	41,989
1969–1970	377	55,384
1979–1980	241	63,465
1989–1990	681	1,41,873
1999–2000	1,788	2,46,514
2002–2003	967	2,08,822
2007–2008	1,698	3,20,029

Source: Okçabol (2009).

few private schools. Nevertheless, the AKP attaches great importance to private schools. For the party, getting educational services from private schools is a more rational approach than building new public schools. Another official, a bureaucrat from the MoNE argued that, as in some European countries, the entire cost of private schools, such as teachers' salaries, educational investments, the maintenance of school buildings, and the fees for electricity and water should be met by the Turkish state (Kaymak 2006, 19–21). These desires, as stated by the minister and the bureaucrat could not be implemented due to the criticism expressed in favor of public education, but this approach clearly indicates the AKP's educational concept. Nevertheless, the AKP gladly met some of the demands from private schools such as a reduction in taxes, various exemptions, and so on (Kaymak 2009, 71).

Table 2.3 shows that the number of private schools and their students increased more during the rule of the AKP than in previous periods. The number of private schools increased two times between 2002 and 2008, and meanwhile, the number of students increased by 50 percent. As noted above, the number of students attending private schools reached five hundred thousand.

Conclusion and Discussion

The aim of having Turkey take part on the world stage as an important actor by adapting itself to the process of globalization forced the AKP to reestablish education through a neoliberal discourse. Indeed, the concepts discussed in the party program for education, such as human capital, a chance to compete, quality in education, response to the demands of globalization, and adaptation to the needs of the business world embody this discourse The AKP worked to commodify public education through many approaches rather than to reinforce its quality. Also, encouragement and support for private schools has always been an interest of the AKP. For instance, large capital business groups have been allowed to establish and sponsor special workshops in public vocational and technical training schools in order to fulfill their staff needs (Bulut 2007). As another example, in his speech at the İstanbul Stock Exchange in 2003, Prime Minister Erdoğan said that the state should completely withdraw from public education and that this area should be left to the private sector (İnal 2010, 693). On the other hand, public schools have been forced to find solutions in order to offer quality education by using their own sources and finances. Although it is forbidden to obtain resources outside of schools, at the beginning of each academic year, money is collected from parents in the form of registration fees for public schools. The administrations at schools have attempted to create other alternative resources, such as using a school's grounds as parking and allocating school cafeterias to the private sector. As discussed above, under the AKP government, the number of entrance exams, which had been reduced in the public education system, was increased (Erdoğan 2009, 22).

To conclude, this chapter showed that while public schools and their teachers are unable to offer quality education, tutoring institutions, private schools, and private universities have created a strong notion that they provide quality education. However, the commodification of education loosens democratic, free, and mass education, To put it differently, this is the point at which public education collapses and the dominance of neoliberal ideology in education begins.

Notes

1. The MoNE suggests that the use of advanced technology in education will provide educational equality of opportunity for each student, and claims that this will increase student achievement in the near future. However, these means neither provide equality of opportunity, nor an increase in student achievement. Among the 41 OECD countries, Turkey is the only country where the difference between schools that have the best facilities and the ones that have the worst facilities is greatest. Moreover, these tools of advanced technology have an impact of marketization on education. This technology includes a large amount of equipment, and students may have

to use some other technological products such as printers, voice recorders, and video cards. Of course, this leads to students spending more money (see Özmen 2011, Kaymak 2011, Kurul 2011).
2. Many public buildings, including schools, were poorly constructed and thus completely demolished by the Marmara earthquake in 1999 and the Van earthquake in 2011. This suggests that the Turkish state is not attentive to or eager to deal with the quality construction, maintenance, and repair of public schools.
3. All numbers are converted to U.S. dollar (1 U.S. dollar = 1.79 Turkish Lira).

References

Adıgüzel, Ergül. "Eğitimde Yapısal Dönüşüm, Fonlanmış Eğitim Projeleri ve Bıraktığı Izler." *Eleştirel Pedagoji* 9 (2010): 37–53.
Akdoğan, Yalçın. "Muhafazakar-Demokrat Siyasal Kimliğin Önemi ve Siyasal İslamcılıktan Farkı." In *AK Parti Toplumsal Değişimin Yeni Aktörleri*, edited by Hakan Yavuz, 59–95. Istanbul: Kitap Yayınevi, 2010.
Akkaymak, Güliz. "Neo-Liberalism and Education: Analysis of Representation of Neo-liberal Ideology in the Primary School Social Studies Textbooks in Turkey." Master's Thesis, Koc University, Istanbul, Turkey, 2010a.
———. "Neoliberalleştirilen Öğrenciler." *Eleştirel Pedagoji* 10 (2010b): 29–38.
Altınyelken, Hülya K. *Changing Pedagogy A Comparative Analysis of Reform Efforts in Uganda and Turkey*. Enschede, NH: Ipskamp Drukkers, 2010.
Apple, Michael. *Neoliberalizm ve Eğitim Politikaları Üzerine Eleştirel Yazılar*. Translated by Fatma Gök et al. Ankara: Eğitim-Sen Yayınları, 2004.
Aydoğanoğlu, Erkan. "Eğitimde Kaynak Sorunu var mı?" *Eleştirel Pedagoji* 10 (2010): 24–28.
Bal, Hatice, Metehan Keleş, and Oğuz Erbil. *Eğitim Teknolojisi Kılavuzu*. Ankara: Milli Eğitim Bakanlığı Eğitimi Araştırma ve Gelişitrme Dairesi Başkanlığı, 1999.
Bedirhanoğlu, Pınar. "Türkiye'de Neoliberal Otoriter Devletin AKP'li Yüzü." In *AKP Kitabı: Bir Dönüşümün Bilançosu*, edited by İlhan Uzgel and Bülent Duru, 40–65. 2nd ed. Ankara: Phoenix, 2010.
Bulut, Ergin. "Transformation of the Turkish Vocational Training System: Creation of Lifelong Learning, Loyal Technicians." Master's Thesis, Boğaziçi University Atatürk Institute, Istanbul, Turkey, 2007.
Çulha-Zabcı, Filiz "Bağımlılığın İçselleştirilmesinde AKP ve Dünya Bankası." In *AKP Kitabı: Bir Dönüşümün Bilançosu*, edited by İlhan Uzgel and Bülent Duru, 139–150. 2nd ed. Ankara: Phoenix, 2010.
Duménil, Gerard, and Dominique Lévy. "Neoliberal (karşı) devrim." In *Neoliberalizm, Muhalif Bir Seçki*, edited by Alfredo Saad-Filho and Deborah Johnson, translated by Şeyda Başlı and Tuncel Öncel, 25–41. İstanbul: Yordam, 2007.
Eğitim-Sen. *2011–2012 Eğitim-Öğretim Yılı Başında Eğitimin Durumu*. Ankara: Eğitim-Sen Bülteni, 2011.

Erdoğan, İrfan. *Eğitime Dair* Ankara: PEGEM Akademi, 2009.
Ertuğrul, N İlter. "AKP ve Özelleştirme." In *AKP Kitabı: Bir Dönüşümün Bilançosu*, edited by İlhan Uzgel and Bülent Duru, 522–556. 2nd ed. Ankara: Phoenix, 2010.
Ertürk, Esin. "Yeni Ders Kitapları ve Milliyetçilik." *Eleştirel Pedagoji* 1 (2009): 51–55.
———. "Ders Kitaplarında Toplum, Yurttaşlık, Vatanseverlik ve Ekonomi Anlayışının Dönüşümü: 1997 ve 2004 İlköğretim Sosyal Bilgiler Ders Kitapları Üzerine Bir İçerik Analizi." Master's Thesis, Mimar Sinan Güzel Sanatlar Üniversitesi Sosyal Bilimler Enstitüsü, Istanbul, Turkey, 2006.
Güzelsarı, Selime. *Küresel Kapitalizm ve Devletin Dönüşümü: Türkiye'de Mali İdarede Yeniden Yapılanma* İstanbul: Sosyal Araştırmalar Vakfı, 2008.
İnal, Kemal. "AKP, Bildungsreform und Anpassung an den Globalen Wandel." In *Bildung und gesellschaftlicher Wandel in der Türkei-Historische und aktuelle Aspekte*, edited by Arnd-Michael Nohl and Barbara Pusch, 45–78. Würzburg: Ergon Verlag Würzburg in Kommission, 2011.
———. "AKP'nin Neoliberal ve Muhafazakâr Eğitim Anlayışı." In *AKP Kitabı Bir Dönüşümün Bilançosu*, edited by İlhan Uzgel and Bülent Duru, 689–719. 2nd ed. Ankara: Phoenix, 2010.
———. "Neoliberal Eğitim ve Yeni İlköğretim Müfredatının Eleştirisi." *Praksis* 14 (2006): 265–287.
———. "Yeni İlköğretim Müfredatının Felsefesi." *Muhafazakar Düşünce* 6 (2005): 75–92.
İnal, Kemal, Güliz Akkaymak, and Deniz Yıldırım. "The Constructivist Curriculum Reform in 2004 in Turkey: In Fact What Is the Constructed?" Paper presented at the XIV World Congress of Comparative Education Societies, Boğaziçi University, Istanbul, Turkey, June 14–18, 2010.
Kanu, Yatta. "Tensions and Dilemmas of Cross-Cultural Transfer of Knowledge: Post-Structural/Postcolonial Reflections on an Innovative Teacher Education in Pakistan." *International Journal of Educational Development* 25, no. 5 (2005): 493–513.
Kaymak, Murat. "Eğitimi ileri teknolojiye bağlamak!" *Eleştirel Pedagoji*, no. 13 (2011): 23–27.
———. "Küresel Ekonomik Krizin Eğitime Olası Etkileri Üzerine." *Eleştirel Pedagoji* 4–5 (2009): 65–72.
———. "Yeni Özel Öğretim Kurumları Yasa Tasarısı ve Özel Okullar." *Eğitim, Zil ve Teneffüs* 3 (2006): 18–22.
Lipman, Pauline "Beyond Accountability: Toward Schools That Create New People for a New Way of Life." In *The Critical Pedagogy Reader*, edited by Antonia Darder, Marta P. Baltodano, and Rodolfo D. Torres, 364–383. 2nd ed. New York and London: Routledge, 2009.
McLaren, Peter, and Ramin Farahmandpur. "Teaching against Globalization and the New Imperialism: Toward a Revolutionary Pedagogy." *Journal of Teacher Education* 52, no. 2 (2011): 136–150.
MEB EARGED (Department of Research and Development) . *Öğrenci Merkezli Eğitim Uygulama Modeli* Ankara: Milli Eğitim Basımevi, 2003.

———. *Okulda Performans Yönetimi Modeli (Taslak)*. Ankara: Milli Eğitim Bakanlığı, 2002.

———. *Müfredat Laboratuar Okulları: MLO Modeli*. Ankara: Milli Eğitim Basımevi, 1999.

Okçabol, İ Rıfat. "Eğitimden Sapma II: Eğitimin Seçkincileşmesi." *Eleştirel Pedagoji* 3 (2009): 24–31.

Özbudun, Ergun, and William Hale. *Türkiye'de İslamcılık, Demokrasi ve Liberalizm: AKP Olayı*. İstanbul: Doğan Kitap, 2010.

Özmen, Ünal. "'Elektronik Kitap Projesi' Üzerine Eleştiri ve Öneri." *Eleştirel Pedagoji* 17 (2011): 3–6.

Özoğlu, Murat. *Özel Dershaneler: Gölge Eğitim Sistemiyle Yüzleşmek*. Ankara: SETA, 2011.

Stewart, Frances. "Eğitim ve Uyum: 1980'lerin Deneyimi ve 1990'lar İçin Bazı Dersler." In *Piyasa Güçleri ve Küresel Kalkınma*, edited by Renee Prendergast and Frances Stewart, translated by İdil Eser, 169–203. İstanbul: YKY, 1995.

Tuğal, Cihan. *Pasif Devrim: İslami Muhalefetin Düzenle Bütünleşmesi*. Translated by Ferit Burak Aydar. İstanbul: Koç Üniversitesi Yayınları, 2010.

Yavuz, Hakan. "Giriş; Türkiye'de İslami Hareketin Dönüşümünde Yeni Burjuvazinin Rolü." In *AK Parti: Toplumsal Değişimin Yeni Aktörleri*, edited by Hakan Yavuz, 7–28. İstanbul: Kitap Yayınevi, 2010.

Yıldırım, Deniz. "AKP ve Neoliberal Popülizm." In *AKP Kitabı: Bir Dönüşümün Bilançosu*, edited by İlhan Uzgel and Bülent Duru, 66–107. 2nd ed. Ankara: Phoenix, 2010.

II

Reforms, Finance, and Unions in Education in the AKP Era

3

Constructivism and the Curriculum Reform of the AKP

Hasan Ünder

The Westernization policy of the Ottoman Empire that began at the start of the eighteenth century gave rise to a cultural duality with different and incompatible worldviews: the traditional Islamic culture on the one hand, and the new, modern or secular Western culture on the other. Turkey's politics in the last two centuries can be seen as an open or disguised clash between traditionalists and modernists. While traditionalists limit modernization to the military, the scientific, and the technological spheres and strongly oppose a morality and lifestyle related to the modern West, modernists defend the modernization of all aspects of life, including the philosophical, political, cultural, legal, familial, and so forth. Since the early nineteenth century, modernists have increasingly gained hegemony over traditionalists, and with Mustafa Kemal Atatürk, the founder of the republic, the modernists took complete control of politics, and modernity became one of the primary defining characteristics of the Turkish republic.

After the Young Turk Revolution in 1908, the Islamist movement emerged as a radical response to modernization's challenges to a traditional religious worldview, and has become one of the most important political ideologies in Turkey since then. The movement was suppressed during the single-party decades (1925–1945) and reemerged in the multiparty period that began in 1946. The Islamist movement was represented first within center-right parties and then by openly Islamist parties under the leadership of Necmeddin Erbakan after 1970. The Justice and Development Party (AKP), as an

Islamist-rooted political party, was founded by a group that separated from Erbakan's Welfare Party after its banishment in 1998, and rose to power in 2002.

In order to weaken the modernist discourse, Islamists have used postmodern or postpositivist arguments, directed against modernism or an enlightenment worldview, partly because of the risk of being openly Islamist in a secular Turkey and partly because of the attraction and sophistication of these ideas. Constructivism, postmodernism, and the postpositivist philosophy of science have in common a relativist, antiobjectivist, and antipositivist epistemological view of scientific knowledge. In the curriculum reform, which began in a period when the AKP did not have the ability to control the state apparatus, constructivism was used as an "approach" considered in educational literature as a learning theory in psychology, as a pedagogical method, or as a relativist and antiobjectivist epistemological view of scientific knowledge. In this chapter, I will explain why constructivism as an epistemological view has been adopted in the curriculum reform initiated by the AKP government in its early years in power.

Constructivism as a Basic Approach in Education

Constructivism has become the most influential approach in science teaching since the 1980s (Matthews 1994, 137). While its critics see it as a "secular religion" (Phillips 1995, 5), its supporters present it as a panacea that will solve all educational problems. It has become a guiding approach or official philosophy of educational practices in such countries as Canada, many states of the United States, Thailand, Greece, New Zealand, India, and Taiwan. It was also adopted as a basic approach in the curriculum reform in Turkey in 2004. It was declared in the introductions to many curricula that constructivism, along with multiple intelligence theory, the cognitive approach in psychology, and the theory of the multiplicity of learning styles had been their guiding theories and that textbooks, learning and teaching environments, teacher and student relationships, and evaluation had been restructured in accordance with the demands of those theories or approaches.

Constructivism in education is distinct from constructivism in art and international relations. It refers to a learning theory associated with Jean Piaget and Lev Vygotsky that says that when learner tries to make sense of new experiences, either the learner's new experiences are assimilated into his/her present mental schemes or, if that is not possible, then the learner's present mental schemes change or generate new schemes and accommodate the experience. What is meant by constructivism in the Ministry of National Education's (MoNE's) documents (e.g., MoNE 2005) is constructivism in this sense. The term sometimes refers to pedagogical methods that emphasize the importance of the awareness of the learner's previous experiences and schemes, of the realization of how the information taught and the learner's present schemes interact, of meaningful learning rather than a lot of rote learning, and of the student's inquiry, discovery, and active participation in the learning process, all of which were derived from constructivist learning theory and the propositions characterizing Ernest von Glasersfeld's (1990) radical constructivism. And lastly, the term "constructivism" refers to an epistemological view that emphasizes the active role that the knowing subject plays in the production of knowledge or beliefs rather than the known object.

What is new in educational, but not philosophical, circles is epistemological constructivism, because educationists have been familiar with Piaget's learning theory for a long time, and those aspects that distinguish pedagogical constructivism have been the usual practices since Jean-Jacques Rousseau and progressive education. I think the main theses of epistemological constructivism as educationists understand it have been stated succinctly and clearly by Glasersfeld (1990), who formulates the two principles of his radical constructivism as follows:

- Principle I: (a) Knowledge is not passively received either through the senses or by way of communication; (b) knowledge is actively built up by the cognizing subject (Glasersfeld 1990, 22).
- Principle II: (a) The function of cognition is adaptive, in the biological sense of the term, tending towards fit or viability; (b) cognition serves the subject's organization of the experiential world, not the discovery of an objective ontological reality (Glasersfeld 1990, 23).

The first principle of radical constructivism requires the active participation of the learner in the learning process. Principle I (a) is related to learning and rejects the traditional teaching practice in which the teacher presents the subject and the students passively listen. Principle II (b) confirms the progressive conception of knowledge, understood as a "personal acquisition and obtained from experience" (Darling and Nordenbo 2003, 298), and advanced by leading progressivists like Rousseau, John Dewey, William H. Kilpatrick, and Piaget. Principle II substantiates the epistemological position of radical constructivism. Principle II (a) shows radical constructivism's close connection with functionalism, instrumentalism, and the pragmatic theory of truth, and rejects the spectator theory of knowledge. While, on the one hand, Principle II (b) denies realism, objective knowledge, and by implication, the correspondence theory of truth, on the other hand, it endorses the instrumentalist concept of knowledge and cognition and the coherence theory of truth.

Epistemological theses of radical constructivism draw on a number of philosophical and psychological theories. Among the most important of them are Immanuel Kant's phenomenalism, George Berkeley's subjective idealism, Thomas Kuhn's and Paul Feyerabend's antiobjectivist accounts of scientific knowledge, and William James's instrumental conception of knowledge and pragmatic theory of truth. The fundamental view of radical constructivism, that is, that knowledge is not the reflection of the object in the subject but rather is constructed by the active subject, comes from Kant. The views that the knowing subject cannot have access to reality beyond itself, that there is no external reality or that, even if there is one, it cannot be known, and that knowledge and its objects are constructed by the knowing subject, come from Berkeley and Kant. The view that the mental schemes of the learner evolve in interaction with the environment come from Piaget. The uninhibited instrumentalism of radical constructivism (Glasersfeld 1995, 21–22) comes from James. The views that perception is theory laden, that scientific knowledge and theories are not about objective reality and that scientific knowledge is not cumulative come from Kuhn and Feyerabend.

The above views that characterize epistemological constructivism have not been explicitly stated in curricula of the MoNE; however, we can find some hints of it in the documents of the ministry. In one of the documents, it is stated that while truth in the former social studies curriculum was understood as something independent of the knowing subject and as based on objective reality, in the new curriculum it was conceived as being constructed individually and socially and grounded in subjective reality. Moreover, the basic philosophy of the new science curriculum takes a constructivist approach (MoNE n.d., 38–41).

Why Constructivism?

The reasons that lead decision makers to constructivism can be various. It is possible that its modishness might be attractive to some of them. But more serious reasons are pedagogical and ideological. To start with the pedagogical reasons, it is the failure of the Turkish student in international assessments, such as the Trends in International Mathematics and Science Study (TIMMS) and the Program for International Student Assessment (PISA). The results of such assessment systematically show that Turkish students are weak in such areas as interpretation of graphs, spatial reasoning, and reading comprehension. It is believed that this worrisome situation is a consequence of teaching methods that assign a passive role to students and promote rote learning. Pedagogical constructivism's emphasis on active student participation, the importance of the learner's past experience and schemes, and the student's understanding of the subjects, which are appreciated by such opponents of constructivism as D. C. Phillips (1995) and Michael R. Matthews (1994), make it an appealing approach for decision makers.

Another reason, which concerns us more, is ideological. I will explain in the following section why epistemological constructivism was ideologically attractive for the AKP.

The Problem with Positivism and Modernism

There are some indications of ideological motives in speeches of the Minister of Education (Kınalı 2004) and the undersecretary of the MoNE (Birinci 2006). For them, curriculum change is not a simple event but a "revolution in mentality," or a "paradigm shift," in Kuhnian terms. What reform overthrows is positivism and its associated way of thought and theory, such as the Newtonian, deterministic, linear, and analytical ways of thinking in natural science and behaviorism in psychology. What reformers aim to promote in place of it are chaos or complexity theory that emphasize, against mainstream scientific thinking, such concepts as nonlinearity, mutual causality, uncertainty, multiple causes and multiple effects, unpredictability, and cognitive psychology rather than behaviorism. What make constructivism attractive are its epistemological claims that undermine positivism and the related theories.

Islamists have strongly opposed positivism for philosophical and political reasons. The ontological and epistemological assumptions of positivistic and of religious worldviews are diametrically opposed. It is clear that the tenets of positivism or scientism are incompatible with the outlook of monotheistic religions for the following reasons. To illustrate, positivism points at science rather than holy scriptures as authority for solutions and explanations. Its identification of knowledge with scientific knowledge devaluates the claims of religion. Its restriction of the knowable world to natural phenomena relegates the supernatural realm to the unknowable, and its rejection of the existence of anything beyond this world reduces the claim of revelation to the level of hallucinations that have no objective appeal at best or to the status of untruth at worst. The disenchanted and deterministic world of positivism, to the development of which Isaac Newton, who was a good Christian, significantly contributed, leaves no room for a god hypothesis and divine intervention, or for miracles, and allows at most a first mover and designer as posited by deism. Its naturalistic account of human beings without free will as not qualitatively different from other animals implies that man can be studied like other natural entities, which is why behaviorism, which "recognizes no dividing line between man and brute" (Watson 1913), was rejected for the new curricula. Auguste Comte's theory of three stages makes theological thinking into a relic that belongs to the childhood period of mankind and places Muslim societies, which consider themselves as believers of the last and most advanced revelation, behind Western societies. All of these theories address secularization, that is, the increasing banishment of religion from political, social, and intellectual realms.

The second reason for the aversion of Islamists to positivism is its ideological function for the Westernized camp in Turkey. When the Ottoman Empire decided to modernize its military power with Western modern technology and its *sine qua non* modern science, then positivism, biological materialism, political ideas, Western etiquette, and the Western lifestyle also began to be useful. Westernization also means change in the elite structure of society, that is, the receding of the traditional religious-educated *ulama* (body of mullahs) and other officials and the advance of new intellectuals and officials educated in Western countries or Westernized schools within the empire. The new power elite used modernist discourse to legitimize its status and to delegitimize that of the older elite. In 1923, Mustafa Kemal Atatürk, a Westernizer with strong positivist leanings, founded modern Turkey along modernist lines and carried Westernization to its utmost reaches. He changed the political regime from constitutional monarchy to a secular republic, modernized education, abolished religious schools, banned religious orders, changed traditional dress and headwear, and revised the calendar to follow Western models.

Atatürk and his followers often legitimatized their policies with a modernist and scientist discourse. The following words of Atatürk reflect his radical scientific belief: "The best guide in the world for civilization, for life and for success is science. Searching other guides out of science means heedlessness, ignorance and heresy" (Atatürk 1989, 202). Modernists have often appealed to such metanarratives of the Enlightenment as progress and as a unilinear conception of history. Atatürk said that "the truest and the most genuine path is the sect of civilization [meaning modern Western civilization]. To do what the civilization ordered and demanded is enough to be human" (Atatürk 1989, 225). In labeling (some) Islamic beliefs, modernists have used such words as "ignorance," "prejudice," and "perversion," and those who hold such beliefs as "bigots," "old-fashioned," and "relics of the Dark Ages," terms that Enlightenment thinkers used for Christianity. Adülhak Adnan-Adıvar (1951) likens, with some exaggeration, the early republican era to a "positivistic mausoleum." For him, positivism as it is understood in Turkey has become "the official dogma of irreligion" (Adnan-Adıvar 1951, 129). According to him, in that period, positivism has taken the place that Islam occupied in the past. Therefore, in order to legitimate their claims to power and to desecularize the public realm, Islamists have to overcome positivism as a philosophy or ideology.

Why Epistemological Constructivism Served a Useful Function for the AKP

Epistemological constructivism serves a purpose for three aims of Islamists. One of them can be termed as "the enemy of my enemy is my friend." They are allies against a common enemy, positivism. Islamists always have had sympathy for any idea, even for Marxism, which criticizes this and that aspect of the modern West. But they have more sympathy for ideas and persons that undermine modern science, which is the basis for positivist and modernist discourse. For example, they support quantum physics, chaos theory, and complexity theory against Newtonian physics, which justifies determinism, predictability, and the orderliness of nature and thus leaves no room for the intervention of God in natural events. They do so because they believe that the former justifies indeterminism, uncertainty, long-term unpredictability, and chaos, and thus makes room for divine intervention (miracles) in nature. They have an affinity with hermeneutics, which rejects the application of natural scientific methods to the study of human beings and social events; with critical theory, which rejects the fact-value distinction of positivism; and with postmodernism, which shakes the persuasiveness of the legitimating metanarratives of modernity and suggests a tolerance for non-Western cultures. They have more sympathy for Kuhn and Feyerabend, because their views more than any other have shaken the claims of objectivity, truth, and the universality of scientific knowledge, which more than anything else give positivism and modernism their strength. Therefore, as İbrahim Kalın has observed,

> Today we can hardly come across a book or article written in English, Arabic, Turkish or Bahasa Malaysia that does not have recourse to Foucault, Kuhn, Feyerabend or Lyotard to denounce the philosophical underpinnings of modern science. From the academic papers of Muslim graduate students to the writings of the so called "ijmalis" led by Ziauddin Sardar, the names of numerous philosophers of science sweep through the literature with indigenous additions from the Islamic point of view. (Kalın 2002, n.d.)

Kuhn (1996) provides the link between constructivism and the postpositivist philosophies of science, sometimes called antiscience. According to Kuhn, scientists see the world through paradigms, and their observation is not objective but theory laden, since observation is a paradigm dependent upon scientific theories that cannot be tested by comparing them with reality and they are also incommensurable with one another; since paradigm changes are not progress toward the discovery of an objective reality; and since the choice of theory is not a rational activity made on the basis of objective evidence. In short, Kuhn (and also Feyerabend) claims that the scientific enterprise is not as positivists have described it, and that scientific knowledge is not superior to other forms of knowledge (including religion) with respect to truth and objectivity and does not deserves any privileged status among them.

Kuhn, who has become the foremost proponent of constructivism since the 1960s, profoundly influenced science educators as well as the general intellectual sphere. He supplies, as Ziauddin Sardar (2000) and Hugh G. Gauch (2003, chapter 3) pointed out, the main ideas of the relativist-constructivist front in the science wars. Matthews (2004) suggests that many science educators have become constructivists in view of Kuhn's ideas and develop their arguments by using his thought. Cathleen C. Loving and William W. Cobern (2000, 199), who researched the citations from Kuhn in two science education journals between 1982/1985 and 1998, find that Kuhn has been cited as an authority with almost no critical comment. Glasersfeld (1998) embraces Kuhn's views about the relations between scientific theories and reality and seems to regret that his views have not been utilized in science education. Like Kuhn, he maintains that scientific knowledge is not accumulative and not a discovery of an objective reality, just as the mental constructs of individual subjects are not representations of an outside objective reality (Glasersfeld 2001, 32–33).

Secondly, constructivism serves a purpose for Islamists because it leaves room for religion. The denial of the views that scientific knowledge is identical with knowledge and not objective implies that there are no significant differences with respect to objective truth between science and other forms of thinking such as religion, and that other knowledge claims are as legitimate as the knowledge claims of science. Feyerabend (1991, 91–151; 1999, 188–192) pushes the argument forward and draws some radical practical implications for the relations between science and state, and for the place of science and other forms of thinking in science. He forcefully defends the notion that the relation between science and state in a free society must be like religion and state relations in secularism, that governments must be at an equal distance in relation to all forms of thinking and practices, and that all belief systems and theories—religion, witchcraft, astrology, astronomy, creationism, evolution—must be taught in state schools impartially and in detail.

One of the main missions of the Islamic-rooted AKP has been to raise a religious generation since its rise to power in 2002. This objective was not declared openly in the years it has held power because the AKP could not control all the state apparatuses, especially the military, the Supreme Court, and civil media. When the party gained control, Recep Tayyip Erdoğan, the prime minister, openly declared that they wanted to raise a religious generation. The realization of this aim requires the desecularization of the public sphere, including schools and the larger society. Desecularization necessitates that religious beliefs, symbols, and practices be made visible and that the symbols and intellectual bases of secularism disappear. The AKP government has especially become more undisguised in its aims since 2011. It canceled some national ceremonies that would remind people of and revitalize critical events and their main actor, Atatürk, which, in a way, culminated in the secular republic. So, we can say that constructivism works to undermine positivism or scientism, which serve as the philosophical or ideological underpinning of secularism. As the AKP's former minister of education, Erkan Mumcu (2006), states, in a teacher union with Islamic leanings, it is impossible to teach religion and to defend *Imam-Hatip* schools (school to train government-employed imams) as a good model and to raise high-quality theologians unless positivism has been completely abandoned.

Thirdly, constructivist epistemology has the function related to a possible long-term aim of Islamists. Kuhn's famous book, *The Structure of Scientific Revolutions*, was published in 1962, Feyerabend's *Against Method* in 1975, Jean-François Lyotard's *Postmodern Condition* in 1979. The sociology of scientific knowledge that has taken its inspiration from Kuhn's work has was developed between late the 1970s and the 1980s. While these intellectual events occurred in the Western intellectual world, some other important developments were taking place in the Islamic world. As Sardar (1997) noted, an Islamic revolution occurred in Iran in 1979, and Organization of the Petroleum Exporting Countries (OPEC) became a more efficient organization in the region. Also, the search for Islamic identity gained momentum. Since the early 1980s, the scientific and cultural legacies of Islamic civilization, the possibility of, and the search for, an Islamic science have become subjects of interest among Muslim intellectuals.

A postpositivist or constructivist philosophy of science sheds new light on an old controversy that took place among Ottoman intellectuals at the beginning of the twentieth century, partly mentioned above, concerning the influence of culture on scientific practices. It poses for Islamists both a problem or a dilemma and a promise. The dilemma was formulated by Ottoman-Turkish Westernizers. They claimed that Western civilization is an integrated whole with its roses and thorns and cannot be taken partially, so either one must accept both the roses and their thorns or one must reject both the roses and the thorns. Westernizers affirmed the first horn of this dilemma. Islamists had tried to escape between the horns of the dilemma by means of Ziya Gökalp's (1959: 104–109) civilization-culture theory, which rejected the dilemma and made it possible for Islamists to accept the roses (science and technology) and reject the thorns (a spiritual culture somehow mingled with Christianity). But the postpositivist philosophy of science in a sense confirmed the Westernizers' thesis that science is not independent of the culture within which it developed.

It is not surprising that an Islamist would be reluctant to accept a culture colored with Christianity. Thus, it is better for them to relinquish the roses. But this is an extremely difficult choice, because Western science and technology are vital for survival and are the primary sources of Western hegemony in the world. At this point, postpositivist philosophy makes a nice but, I think, almost impossible promise. The promise is, stated by Feyerabend in the preface to the Turkish translation of his *Against Method*: "Each culture, each nation can build a science that fits its own particular needs" (Feyerabend 1989, 12). The promise is nice because it gives Islamists the hope that Islamic culture can be a self-sufficient and pure culture that does not need the Western influence. However, the promise is almost impossible because it is too difficult to create a science without the knowledge produced by the high technology that is needed immensely by Muslim societies. Nevertheless, this perspective still gives hope to Islamists.

Conclusion

Based on the constructivist understanding of scientific knowledge, which rejects objectivity and the universality of scientific knowledge, a pedagogical principle can be deduced that every student can create his/her own knowledge or science. Yet, it is almost impossible for students to construct knowledge, or rather a viable idea that can compete with established scientific knowledge. How can a student construct such concepts as photosynthesis, atom and molecular theory, and the theory of genetics, which were conceived by successive generations of passionate scientists. If what a student constructs in his/her own mind is based on the already known science outside him/her, then he/she does not need a constructive or antiobjective epistemology. Therefore, we can say that the adoption of a constructivist epistemology as a foundation for curriculum reform is due to its attractiveness from an ideological point of view, because its antirealist and relativist theses are useful in undermining the hegemony and the privileged position of science and positivism, which have buttressed modernist discourse and policies opposed by Islamism from the beginning. Islamists can employ constructivism as a way to open up some space for religion and religious education and to suggest a respect for religion. In fact, the AKP changed the public education law in March 2012 so that "Koran education" and the study of "the Prophet Mohammad's Life" became elective courses, in addition to the course "Culture of Religions" and "Knowledge about Morality," which was made compulsory by 1982 constitution. In virtue of the law a lot of *Imam-Hatip* schools was opened or many existing schools were transformed into *Imam-Hatip* schools.

Constructivism can have an instrumental value for Islamists because an Islamist epistemology and belief system is the opposite of positivism. It is obvious that a constructivist critique of science and positivism applies to the claims with respect to universality, objectivity, and certainty. It is therefore expected that Islamists will take side with constructivism and with similar views as they gain control and can speak openly. Today, in the tenth year of the AKP administration, we can unhesitatingly say that the party has begun to do this. Its most obvious and recent example is the Prime Minister Recep Tayyip Erdoğan's declaration that they want to raise religious generations in schools.

References

Adnan-Adıvar, Abdülhak. "Interaction of Islamic and Western Thought in Turkey." In *Near Eastern Culture and Society*, edited by T. Cuyler Young, 119–129. Princeton: Princeton University Press, 1951.

Atatürk, Mustafa Kemal. *Atatürk'ün Söylev Demeçleri*. 3 vols. Ankara: Atatürk Araştırma Merkezi Yayınları, 1989.

Birinci, Necat. "Protokol Konuşmaları." In *Türk Eğitim Sisteminde Yeni Paradigma Arayışları: Bildiriler Kitabı*, edited by Halil Etmeyez et al., 9–13. Ankara: Eğitim-Bir-Sen, 2006. http://www.egitimbirsen.org.tr/dokuman/sempozyum_kitabi.pdf (accessed March 2004).

Darling, John, and Sven E. Nordenbo. "Progressivism." In *The Blackwell Guide to the Philosophy of Education*, edited by Nigel Blake et al., 288–308. Oxford: Blackwell, 2003.

Feyerabend, Paul K. *Knowledge, Science and Relativism*. Cambridge: Cambridge University Press, 1999.

———. *Özgür Bir Toplumda Bilim*. Translated by Ahmet Kardam. Istanbul: Ayrıntı Yayınları, 1991.

———. *Yönteme Hayır: Bir Anarşist Bilgi Kuramının Ana Hatları*. Translated by Ahmet İnam. Istanbul: Ara Yayıncılık, 1989.

Gauch, Hugh G. *Scientific Method in Practice*. Cambridge: Cambridge University Press, 2003.

Glasersfeld, Ernest von. "An Exposition of Constructivism: Why Some Like It Radical." In *Constructivist Views on the Teaching and Learning of Mathematics*, edited by Robert B. Davis, Carolyn A. Maher, and Nel Noddings, 19–29. Washington, DC: National Council of Teachers of Mathematics, 1990.

———. *Radical Constructivism: A Way of Knowing and Learning*. London: Routledge, 1995.

———. "The Radical Constructivist View of Science." *Foundations of Science* 6 (2001): 31–43.

———. "Why Constructivism Must Be Radical." In *Constructivism and Education*, edited by Marie Larochelle, Nadine Bednarz, and James Garrison, 23–29. Cambridge: Cambridge University Press, 1998.

Gökalp, Ziya. *Turkish Nationalism and Western Civilization: Selected Essays of Ziya Gökalp*. Translated and edited by with an Introduction by Niyazi Berkes. New York: Columbia University Press, 1959.

Kalın, İbrahim. "Three Views of Science in the Islamic World." In *God, Life and the Cosmos: Christian and Islamic Perspectives*, edited by Ted Peters, Muzaffar Iqbal, and Syed Nomanul Haq, 43–75. Aldershot: Ashgate, 2002. http://www.muslimphilosophy.com/kalin/index.html (accessed December 2011).

Kınalı, Mustafa. "Hedef İyi 'Eğitim'." *Hürriyet*. August 12, 2004. http://arama.hurriyet.com.tr/arsivnews.aspx?id=248657 (accessed March 2010).

Kuhn, Thomas S. *The Structure of Scientific Revolutions*. 3rd ed. Chicago: University of Chicago Press, 1996.

Loving, Cathleen C., and William W. Cobern. "Invoking Thomas Kuhn: What Citation Analysis Reveals about Science Education." *Science and Education* 9 (2000): 187–206.

Matthews, Michael R. *Science Teaching: The Role of History and Philosophy of Science*. London: Routledge, 1994.

Matthews, Michael R. "Thomas Kuhn's Impact on Science Education: What Lessons Can Be Learned?" *Science Education* 88, no. 3 (2004): 190–118.

MoNE. *İlköğretim 1–5. Sınıf Programları Tanıtım El Kitabı*. Ankara: MONE, 2005.

MoNE. "Talim ve Terbiye Kurulu Program Geliştirme Çalışmaları." N.d. http://ttkb.meb.gov.tr/programlar/prog_giris/prg_giris.pdf (accessed February 2010).

Mumcu, Erkan. "Protokol Konuşmaları." In *Türk Eğitim Sisteminde Yeni Paradigma Arayışları: Bildiriler Kitabı*, edited by Halil Etmeyez et al., 35–40. Ankara: Eğitim-Bir-Sen, 2006 http://www.egitimbirsen.org.tr/dokuman/sempozyum_kitabi.pdf (accessed March 2004).

Phillips, D. C. "The Good, the Bad, and the Ugly: The Many Faces of Constructivism." *Educational Researcher*, 24, no. 7 (1995): 5–12.

Sardar, Ziauddin. "Islamic Science: Contemporary Debate." In *Encyclopaedia of the History of Science, Technology, and Medicine in Non-Western Cultures*, edited by Helaine Selin, 2nd ed., 455–458. Dordrecht, NH, Netherlands: Kluwer Academic Publishers, 1997.

Sardar, Ziauddin. *Thomas Kuhn and the Science Wars*. Cambridge: Icon Books, 2000.

Watson, John B. "Psychology as the Behaviorist Views It." *Psychological Review* 20 (1913): 158–177. http://psychclassics.yorku.ca/Watson/views.htm (accessed February 2011).

4

The Marketization of Primary and Secondary School Curricula and Textbooks under AKP Rule

Ünal Özmen

Turkey was introduced to liberalist policies in the economy on January 24, 1980. The military coup of 1980, by suppressing social opposition, made it easier for prospective governments to put liberal policies into effect. However, the liberalization of the educational system was to come in the 2000s. Different than previous governments, the Justice and Development Party's (AKP) governments focused more on social policies, especially on education. The first areas to be affected by neoliberal policies were the curricula and correspondingly the textbooks and auxiliary materials used by sixteen million students in the formal educational system.

For a prime minister with a religious background like Recep Tayyip Erdoğan, and a party that based its ideology on Islam, education is meant to be a tool for the promotion of religion. However, while promoting religion, the party has also tried to keep education in accordance with neoliberal ideology. Even though this seems like a dilemma, the AKP succeeded in managing the dilemma in its favor through a program called "Moderate Islam." That is, the AKP applied both religious and liberal discourses to the educational system. In this respect, the AKP proved that it had transformed its ideology from a political Islamic ideology with the ultimate goal of shariah into a domestic Islamic movement that fit with the idea of "Market Islam" (Haenni 2011).

This chapter focuses on the marketization of the educational system, focusing on the textbooks during the AKP era (i.e., 2002–2011). The purpose of this chapter, in this respect, is to examine the curricula and textbooks put into use by the AKP governments and to show the impact of neoliberal policies in education. The next part will provide a detailed analysis of the implementation processes of curricula and textbooks.

Implementation Processes of Curricula and Textbooks in Turkey

The curricula are prepared by commissions constituted within the Board of Education and Discipline (TTKB) or the relevant general directorates of the Ministry of National Education (MoNE), in accordance with the Constitution, the Fundamental Law of National Education, and relevant bylaws. After the TTKB approves the prepared curricula, they are approved by the MoNE, and then published in the *Journal of Communiqués* and come into force.

The curricula, which were written according to a behavioral education model and remained in effect between 1968 and 2004, could not be updated along with the changes and improvements in the economic and social life. This led to criticism among intellectuals and people involved in the education field. This chapter argues that the AKP governments made use of the demand for change as an opportunity to shape the basic elements of education, which has the direct power to penetrate into the subconscious of the society. The curricula in elementary and secondary education were gradually changed as of 2004.

The New Curricula

Ziya Selçuk, TTKB President in 2004, suggested that the curricula would be based on socioeconomic (globalization), political (European Union), philosophical (social constructivism) and educational (student-centered education, SCE) grounds, when explaining the reasons for developing new curricula (Sevimay 2004). In a similar vein, Hüseyin Çelik, the minister of education (2003–2009), declared on several occasions that they would adopt whichever curricula could be successfully applied worldwide. These statements show that Turkey's individual needs and conditions were not taken into account. To give further examples, the administrative court canceled the Turkish Language and Social Studies curricula in a lawsuit filed by a student's parent on grounds of the curricula, because they were against the basic principles of science and pedagogy and the facts about Turkey. The suit contended that the language used in the curricula and the facts included in the objectives lacked complementary features and did not match the social facts and realities of life because the content of these curricula were against the basic principles of science teaching and laique educational thought in schools. That is, activities used in Western countries were put into practice, the materials used in pilot schools were prepared by specialists from the European Union (EU), and assessments were performed based on the criteria and translated questionnaires from Western curricula. Moreover, even after his resignation, Selçuk, the architect of the reform (İnal 2005, İnal 2006), admitted that the curricula were not prepared in accordance with the social and cultural features of Turkey (Özmen 2007).

The change in the curricula pointed up the necessity to revise textbooks. The textbooks would by implication be one of the most important areas in the new educational approach, the theoretical framework of which was devised based on the curricula.

Textbooks in Turkey

Textbooks are the most important source of information for students in Turkey, a country that has difficulties in using scientific sources for acquiring information such as research and reading. Textbooks therefore constitute the main intellectual resource by which a person can perceive and interpret life after completing his/her schooling. It can also be said that new information is built on the information acquired from textbooks. It is important as well to underline that the knowledge offered by textbooks is taken for granted by many students, which can result in their avoiding questioning the knowledge they acquire from textbooks or their teachers. From this point of view, textbooks, specifically in Turkey, should not be seen as merely an instrument of education, and should be considered as a whole, including the language, illustrations, physical appearance, and design. It should be designed like an architectural structure, as pedagogues say.

Procedure for Preparation of Textbooks

The preparation of textbooks in Turkey is entirely under the responsibility of the state, in particular, the relevant committees (primarily the

TTKB) of the MoNE. This procedure, to the utmost, is official, unilateral, hierarchical, and authoritarian. The state, as can seen below, has established the textbook policy in the form of a detailed hierarchy of rules. Textbooks are the main material for education that is supposed to be prepared in accordance with the curricula. Textbooks are prepared by authors/publishers (as a textbook, workbook, or teacher's guidebook) and sent to the TTKB, which functions as the advisory committee for the MoNE. The Board hands the draft textbook to the Commission for Preliminary Review for review in terms of compatibility with the format. The approved textbooks are then sent to branch commissions for the main substantive reviewing in terms of content. The branch commission examines the textbook according to the relevant curriculum, the Textbooks Regulation, the Board's decision (which has jurisprudential value), and evaluation criteria of the relevant branch, and gives an assessment score. Textbooks with a score of 75 and higher (over 100) are then sent to the Evaluation Commission, which checks the propriety of the results of the main review. Textbooks with a score of 90 and higher in the main review and that are approved by this commission are presented for the approval of the Board; the Board assesses the report about the textbook, and approves or rejects it. The textbooks approved by the Board are signed by the minister, published in the *Tebliğler Dergisi* (Journal of Communiqués), and are finally given the title of textbooks. The duration of validation of a textbook approved by the TTKB is five years. Textbooks with scores between 75 and 90 are sent with the errors index card to their publishers to be corrected together with the Evaluation Commission.

The TTKB charges a fee to the author or the publisher for the revision process in advance. The fee for the revision of a ten-forme (one forme is 16 pages) textbook is 5,000TL (US$2,800) on average. The MoNE also prepares textbooks as do private publishing houses.

Textbooks and Private Publishing Houses

Textbooks have sometimes been, with the permission of official authorities, prepared by private publishing houses as well as the State. However, twenty years of experience shows that private publishing houses have not contributed to increasing the quality of textbooks (Özmen 2003). The main reason for this is that textbooks are being prepared merely based on commercial concerns. Thus, it is not possible to enrich the content and format. However, as is well known, a textbook that is well put together can present to the student the necessary information systematically and do this in correct and competent language. A high-quality textbook helps the student develop methods for creating knowledge and skills, as well as presents ways for the student to produce his/her self-interpretation in totally new circumstances and situations. A textbook that cannot achieve these goals only serves to increase individuals' dependence on others' intelligence. The following statement by the MoNE, which guides both the ministry's publishing house and private publishing houses, is thought provoking: "What is important about a textbook is the first impression. Focus on size, weight, cover, and page layout. Few people look at the content" (MoNE 2004, 39).

Although it is known that the revision of textbooks serves to redirect the profits of the book market, and for ideological purposes, the Turkish state used powerful means of publicity to convince the society about the changes in curricula and textbooks that were created for social purposes. Through deliberately spreading the belief among the private sector that a public service should always and inevitably be a bad service, the government has achieved a common public acceptance of the need to apply free market rules in the design and production of textbooks. This has led to the promotion of many companies, such as, *Selt, Harf*, and *Kelebek*. It is very significant that these companies have never published textbooks or not have ever engaged in the field of education. However, the Ministry does not regard their lack of experience in the educational field as a concern in its contracting with those companies to produce textbooks.

The review and evaluation process of the privately published companies is another important aspect of this issue. First of all, the textbooks prepared by private companies are reviewed and evaluated by the Ministry's commissions, yet not in an objective way. That is, whether the result of evaluation is positive or negative is determined by the close political relationship of the publisher with the decision-making mechanism, as well as relationships based on money (Özmen 2011). Private publishers can choose the members of the commissions via their relationships with administrative authorities, change members if they are not satisfied with the results, or even can rereview the textbook if it was rejected (Özmen 2011). What is striking is that the MoNE accepts all of these activities as normal.

Free and Nonrecyclable Distribution of Textbooks

Textbooks have been distributed to students free of charge by the AKP governments since 2003. The Constitution establishes education as a duty of the state, the vast majority of the society needs this public service, and of course the government handles this practice with a populist approach. All these facts make it more difficult to discuss and question the problems that occur with the process of the free distribution of textbooks. However, the free distribution of textbooks, contrary to popular belief, does not provide benefits to students and their parents. On the contrary, it results in the misuse of public funds. The process of the free distribution of textbooks works as follows:

- Publishing houses prepare the textbook.
- The TTKB approves the textbook.
- The MoNE initiates a public auction.
- All publishers send their textbooks to a consortium that they establish together, and join the public auction as single corporate body.
- The MoNE purchases the textbooks from the consortium, which is the single provider in three ways: auction, direct supply, or negotiated auction.
- The packaging cost of the textbooks is the MoNE's responsibility.
- The publisher sends the textbooks to warehouses in every province that are recommended by the MoNE.[1]
- The MoNE initiates a separate "public auction for distribution" of the textbooks to schools in every province.
- Students keep the textbooks they have received until the end of the academic year, and in most cases they are thrown away at the end of the academic year.

This process repeats itself every year. It is not surprising that the process creates a significant amount of profit for the private sector. In other words, transferring the responsibility for publishing textbooks to private companies also transfers public funds to private hands. This chapter, however, argues that scientific pedagogy is ignored because the textbooks are repurchased every year, and the selection of the textbooks is left to the seller-buyer relations. Privatization of the publishing and the delivery of textbooks also mean that federal funds are wasted. To illustrate, each year the MoNE buys textbooks from private publishers and pays an average of 300–400 million TL (US$225 million) to publishers and distributors. Moreover, the annual cost of distribution of textbooks is 35 million TL (US$20 million) (*Habertürk* 2012).[2] This is an unacceptable waste of public money. Moreover, although the MoNE promises to supply textbooks that will last for five years, as many textbooks as the number of students are still being bought every year. The purchase and distribution cost of the textbooks in the 2003–2004 and 2004–2005 academic years (i.e., about 350 trillion TL [US$196 trillion]) was paid from the Fund for Encouraging Social Help and Solidarity by verbal order of Prime Minister Erdoğan. According to its statute, this institution must spend its resources for the vital needs of the poorest people in the society. Resources that should be spared for people suffering from health and nutrition problems, however, have been transferred to other areas. Purchasing textbooks each year instead of collecting them back from students in order to reuse them means nothing more than that the party creates its own wealth. One of the publishing houses (i.e., *Harf* Publishing) that subsequently started a textbook publishing business and that has had a significant share in the public auction, for instance, belongs to the brother of the former minister of public works and settlement, Zeki Ergezen. If, on the other hand, the textbooks were used for five-year periods, on average 135 million TL (US$75 million) would be saved; 1, 275,000 pine trees would be saved from being cut down; and 307 million Kwh of electric power and 29 million tons of water would be saved (Öztürk 2008).

Another important factor in facilitating the privatization of publishing is that teachers have been removed from process of selecting textbooks. Until 2003, textbooks were evaluated and selected by teachers, which encouraged the publishers to obtain the approval of teachers in addition to the approval of the Ministry. The procedure, in this respect, was similar to "consumer supervision" over people who prepare and publish textbooks, which forces them to work more efficiently. Including the teachers in the determination process was thus more democratic. The purchase of textbooks by auction, however, cut out the teacher. This is because the AKP gives priority to price instead of quality.

Electronic Books (Tablet PCs)

Apart from hardcopy textbooks, the distribution of electronic books is important in understanding the AKP's approach to education. Prime Minister Erdoğan initiated an Electronic Book Project during the 2011 national elections with the slogan "A tablet PC for every student, a Smart Board for every classroom." Similar to the textbook publication process, electronic books and Smart Boards were awarded through a public auction. The initial bidding on the project took place on November 2011. The government purchased 84,921 Smart Boards for 339 million TL (US$190 million) from Vestel Company

(*Habertürk* 2012). However, a lawsuit was filed against the auction based on an accusation concerning the technical requirements listed in the patent that Vestel had registered on September 2011, which was two months before the auction. Furthermore, it was discovered that one of the designers of the patent was also a senior official at the public institution that initiated the auction (*Milli Gazete* 2012). The ministry made an announcement upon the revealing of the scandal and said, "All patent rights of the Smart Board in terms of intellectual property belong to the MoNE" (*SınavBilgisi* 2011). However, when the document was later made public, it was seen that the patent right was transferred to the MoNE after the auction date. Obviously, the products of information technologies, as well as printed materials, are subject to the self-interest, bribery, and populism of those involved in this process.

The idea of replacing printed textbooks with electronic textbooks and reinforcing classrooms with Smart Boards, as this chapter contends, did not arise from a need. The electronic book has a different meaning, beyond ordinary training material, in terms of being an economic and political project. The most significant result of this project is that the producer of the electronic book will be a constant client of a huge market. Users will become dependent on tablet PCs, and will have to buy and use (along with this device, which has a monitor size of only ten inches) constantly updated/added software and other subsidiary products, most of which are indispensable. Schools will begin to go round in circles, like armies that become obliged to constantly renew defense and assault weapons. In this respect, the electronic textbook means opening the training materials market to global capital (Kaymak 2011). Considering the financial ramifications of this device, and the global power of the actors in the industry, it could already be said that tablet PCs will soon become a new subject in the field of education.

The MoNE carries out its policy of the utilization of technology in education via loans from international financial institutions, such as the World Bank and EU funds, which it obtains on the condition that it purchases the products recommended by those institutions. The loans provided by the international institutions are quite advantageous for governments in several respects: On the one hand, the governments that adopt policies that chase development can "keep up with the times," and on the other hand, they assure that a group of capitalists is created who will permanently serve the government by sharing external sources with their supporters!

Uploading textbooks to tablet PCs will certainly meet a political expectation as well. Prime Minister Erdoğan, during the release of the Project to the public, said that, "We will give each one of our children an electronic book. Then all the curricula will be in it. They will go to school only with the electronic book, and will need nothing else" (*Radikal* 2012). The prime minister is saying in very plain language that the government will impose a single curriculum and a single book for all students. This means that students will come under the rule of a closed-minded power free from intervention in terms of content and software. The fact that tablet PCs will be remotely contolled (via the Internet) indicates another potential danger, which is the censoring of websites, or the etatization of information.

The AKP governments have a faulty perception that a person who uses technology products will inevitably be successful. However, technology products are merely tools that must be operated by people. A person's success, as well as failure, depends on her/his relationship with and use of technology, and for what purposes s/he uses technology. The more important thing is to bring the products of information technologies into use only after making them compatible with the purposes and other elements of education, that is, after the necessary infrastructure has been prepared. Moreover, they should be considered as simple objects, not the objective itself.

Conclusion

It is imperative for the State to have a fundamental approach based on the public weal in preparing, printing, and distributing textbooks. A public institution organized in good faith would able to fulfill all these services perfectly and on time, providing the quality required, and at lower costs than they are currently.

The distribution of textbooks free of charge should be continued, even without a constitutional provision for this practice. However, it is also an urgent necessity to stop the ongoing squandering of money and resources that is discussed in this chapter. It is possible to produce textbooks that can be used for at least 3 to 5 years by improving the present technical specifications and inspecting the textbooks properly. Hundreds of millions of TLs could be saved annually if there is no need to buy textbooks every year. The money saved in this way can be used in repairing and renovating schools, and in obtaining training equipment and materials to provide a higher-quality education for students. Without doubt, the teacher should regain the right to freely select the textbook that s/he will use in the classroom. Regranting this right to the teacher will lead to "user supervision" along with the inspection of the TTKB, and this will force authors and publishers to be more attentive and to produce textbooks of higher quality in all aspects, as well as reduce the burden on the state. Therefore, the opening of textbooks based on curricula designed by the State to a marketization process should be given up in order to produce an official textbook policy that is primarily based on the needs of students rather than the profit-oriented interests of the private sector, because education for the majority of people in Turkey is still perceived as a public duty of the State.

Notes

1. The MoNE has its own printing houses, which have a total capacity that is sufficient to supply all the textbooks that are required and which have a distribution network in every province. In addition to its own printing houses in Ankara and Istanbul, the MoNE also hired a printing house in Ankara that belongs to the Turkish Historical Society. The MoNE, however, does not use its own printing houses, and prefers to have even its own textbooks printed in private printing houses. The MoNE does not use the resources of provincial/district directorates to deliver textbooks to schools, as the transportation and distribution is carried out by contractors, that is, private companies.
2. Some local education directors have seen this practise as squandering and reported to higher authorities in the Ministry that they could distribute the textbooks cheaper and by using their own resources; however, despite their insistence, the procedure has not been changed (*Habertürk* 2012).

References

Habertürk. "Akıllı Tahtalar, Önümüzdeki Aydan Itibaren Sınıflarda." January 13, 2012. http://ekonomi.haberturk.com/teknoloji/haber/705667-akilli-tahtalar-on umuzdeki-aydan-itibaren-siniflarda (accessed March 2012).
Haenni, Patrick. *Piyasa İslamı. İslam Suretinde Neoliberalizm*. Translated by Levent Ünsaldı. Ankara: Özgür Üniversite Kitaplığı, 2011.
İnal, Kemal. "Neoliberal Eğitim ve Yeni İlköğretim Müfredatının Eleştirisi." *Praksis* 14 (2006): 265–287.
———. "Yeni İlköğretim Müfredatının Felsefesi." *Muhafazakar Düşünce* 6 (2005): 75–92.
Kaymak, Murat. "Eğitimi İleri Teknolojiye Bağlamak." *Eleştirel Pedagoji* 13 (2011): 22–27.

MilliGazete. "MilliEğitimBakanlığı'ndanmilyondolarlıkskandal!" December 12, 2011. http://www.milligazete.com.tr/haber/adrese-teslim-ihale-224901.htm (accessed March 2012).
MoNE (Ministry of National Education). *Temel Eğitim Ders Kitabı, Bilim ve Teknoloji 4*. Ankara: MoNE, 2004.
Özmen, Ünal. "Milli Eğitim Bakanı Bunu İzah Etsin." *BirGün*, May 5, 2011.
———. *Eğitimin AKP'si*. Ankara: SOBİL, 2007.
———. "Ders Kitapları Üzerine." *Öğretmen Dünyası* 279 (2003): 41–46.
Öztürk, Mustafa. "Basın Açıklaması." 2009. http://www.mozturk.net/?Type=1&Id=160 (accessed June 2008).
Radikal. "Başbakan'dan Çocuklara 'Elektronik Kitap' Projesi." May 7, 2011. http://www.radikal.com.tr/Radikal.aspx?aType=RadikalDetayV3&ArticleID=1048598&CategoryID=77 (accessed March 2012).
Sevimay, Devrim. "Kemalizm Eğitimin Yapı Taşı Olamaz (1)." *Vatan*, August 27, 2004.
SınavBilgisi. "Fatih Projesi ile Alakalı İddialara MEB Yanıt Verdi." December 28, 2011. http://www.sinavsiz.com/fatih-projesi-ile-alakali-iddialara-meb-yanit-verdi/ (accessed March 2012).

5

Curriculum Change in Turkey: Some Critical Reflections

Hülya Koşar-Altınyelken and Güliz Akkaymak

The revision of the primary school curriculum is one of the most significant changes the Justice and Development Party (AKP), has introduced in recent years within the Turkish education system. The need for change within the curriculum that is in line with contemporary national and international developments was highlighted in the party program before the AKP came to power in 2002 (AKP 2002, AKP 2001). The curriculum review process was initiated as early as 2004, during which the educational programs for five subjects were revised and new curricular documents were developed. The 2004 curriculum introduced substantial changes in the curriculum content, pedagogical approach, and assessment system (MoNE 2005). The content load was reduced, and a thematic approach was considered in the organization of content. It adopted a "competence-based" approach as opposed to the traditional knowledge-based (or subject-based) curriculum approach, and emphasized the development of select competencies and skills. In terms of pedagogical approach, it adopted student-centered pedagogy and encouraged student participation, classroom activities, the use of learning aids, hands-on learning, and cooperative learning. Student assessment was also revised in an attempt to move beyond testing. The new assessment system was framed as authentic assessment and aimed at evaluating students' learning processes. The newly developed educational programs were piloted in 120 public schools across the country in the 2004–2005 academic year. The nationwide implementation was launched in the following academic year in the first five grades at the same time, while it was gradually introduced to the upper three grades, one grade each year (Educational Reform Initiative [ERG] 2005).

The official account of why the primary school curriculum was changed refers to a dissatisfaction with student learning achievements, the inefficiency of the education system, and the urge to restructure the education system in line with the imperatives of the knowledge-based economy in which "we now live in, or are moving toward" (Robertson 2007, 2). The discourse on the rationale for change often reflects the primacy of economic considerations (Altınyelken 2010a), particularly the importance of preparing an adequate workforce and maintaining competitive economic power, and is part of a worldwide trend observed in the past three decades in education reforms (Levin 1998). Major lines of change within the curriculum also mirror curriculum reforms in several other countries in Asia, sub-Saharan Africa, and Latin America, in terms of shifting to a competency-based curriculum, embracing pedagogical approaches based on constructivism, and introducing continuous assessment (see Altınyelken 2011, Altınyelken 2010b, Chisholm and Leyendecker 2008).

This chapter seeks to analyze the new curriculum from a critical and empirical perspective by focusing on the educational program in Social Studies for grades four and five. The chapter locates the curriculum change within the broader framework of neoliberal reforms within the Turkish education system, and illustrates to what extent and how the recent curricular changes reflect a neoliberal agenda. The chapter draws on two studies conducted by the authors: a content analysis of social studies textbooks in grades four and five, and interviews with classroom teachers teaching grade five (a total of 19 teachers teaching at seven public schools in Ankara).

The chapter is structured in five sections: After this introductory part, the next section will inform about the Curriculum 2004 in terms of its rationale and the changes introduced. Two sections that present the findings of the empirical studies follow this. The section that draws on the content analysis attempts to uncover how the neoliberal values and discourses are promoted in the textbooks, while the following section aims at examining teachers' views on the social studies textbook and discusses broader implications of the changes introduced in the curriculum content. The final section will recapture the main findings and end with some concluding remarks.

Curriculum 2004

The Ministry of National Education (MoNE) has made several amendments to educational programs for primary education in recent decades. However, until 2004, none of the attempts have turned into a comprehensive amendment that influences all structures of education (see Akpınar and Aydın 2007, Güven and İşcan 2006). The primary school curriculum, which was last modified in 1968, was revised in 2004 under the name of 2004 Primary School Education Reform. Similar to educational reforms of many other countries, the 2004 reform reorganized primary school education according to the constructivist and student-centered educational models, and adapted a competency-based curriculum approach. The Curriculum 2004 emphasizes the development of eight competencies, namely critical thinking, creativity, communication, inquiry, problem solving, use of information technologies, entrepreneurship, and language competencies in Turkish (MoNE 2004). In the context of the reform, the MONE revised the educational programs for Turkish (grades 1–5), Life Knowledge (1–3), Science and Technology (4–5), and Social Studies (4–5).

In-depth interviews conducted with five of the architects of the reform illustrated that globalization, the economic structure of Turkey, the global shift to the constructivist model, and the insufficiency of the behaviorist model constitute the main reasons for the reform. The interviewees stated that the Curriculum 1968 was not compatible with the changes occurring in the twenty-first century, such as changes in science and technology, professional relations, and labor force quality. The new educational system had to be responsive to global, economic, and technological developments. The system had to prepare students for a competitive economy. Interviewees also noted that the low academic performance of Turkish students on international tests (such as the Program for International Student Assessment [PISA], Progress in International Reading Literacy Study [PIRLS], and Trends in International Mathematics and Science Study [TIMSS]) illustrated the inadequacy of the behaviorist educational model in terms of teaching critical thinking and questioning skills. Within the process of reforming the educational programs, the MoNE studied similar educational reforms and trends in other countries, particularly in the United States, Ireland, Israel, and Canada.

Although, neither the European Union (EU) nor the Turkish Industrialists' and Businessmen's Association (TUSIAD) had a leading role in the reform process, their reports laid the groundwork for the reform process. The accession process to the EU, which requires the implementation of several reforms in different spheres, including education, is among the reasons for the reform. In Turkey's progress reports (2001, 2002, and 2004 Progress Reports of Turkey), the EU highlights the importance of adapting the educational system to the knowledge-and competition-based economy. To illustrate, the EU states that in order to improve the efficiency of the system, curriculum and teaching techniques need to be revised, and a connection between education and the job market has to be solidified. Similar to the EU, the business world in Turkey has been emphasizing the necessity of reforms in the education system since the early 1990s. For instance, the TUSIAD report (1990) entitled *Education in Turkey: Problems and Structural Adjustment Recommendations for Change*, states that as a consequence of the shift from an industrial society to an information society, and improvements in science and technology, the structure of societies changed, signaling the necessity to restructure the education system. The report argues that the 1968 curriculum was not sufficient to respond to those changes. The new educational system has to be responsive to contemporary changes and aim at producing competitive individuals. Reports of the EU and TUSIAD underlined the necessity of improving the relevance of education for the labor market and for the economy in general. The MoNE appeared to respond to these demands during the curriculum review process as attempts were made to align the Curriculum 2004 with the needs of the market economy.

Textbook analysis

The fourth- and fifth-grade social studies textbooks that have been published by the MoNE since 1980 were analyzed utilizing qualitative content analysis. Even though the Ministry publishes textbooks each year, the content of the textbooks does not change each year. The selection of textbooks is therefore based on the changes made in the textbooks. The years that correspond with the time that the content of the textbooks was changed are 1980, 1990, 1998 and 2005. However, due to the lack of 1998 and 2005 textbooks in the MoNE's archive library, the content analysis covers the years 1980, 1990, 1999, and 2006.

The pre- and post-2005 fourth and fifth grade social studies textbooks are compared in terms of their representation of neoliberal discourse. The manifest and latent qualitative content analyses are conducted through several keys words that were selected in reference to the literature on neoliberalism, and neoliberalism and education. The literature argues that consumption has become more important since the beginning of the 1980s (Hartley 2009). Also, there has been a strong emphasis on production (Gökçe 2000). Therefore, government policies have been amended in a way that is consistent with the contemporary culture of consumption and production (Hartley 2009). Another focus in neoliberalism is on competition and entrepreneurship (Read 2009, Harris 2007). The competitive nature of neoliberalism forces individuals to invest in their skills and abilities in order to be preferred in the marketplace (Read 2009). Individuals are encouraged to see themselves as entrepreneurial and competitive (Harris 2007). Based on these arguments, the key words included consumer, consumption, shopping, purchasing, producing, production, advertisement, marketing, entrepreneurship, individual success, competition, and investment. Also, to find out whether the privatization-oriented nature of neoliberalism is present in the textbooks, privatization is also considered as a key word.

Analysis of the contextual use of the key words illustrated that the post-2005 textbooks have more emphasis on individualism, welcome participation of the private sector in public services, and represent citizens as consumers, salespersons, and entrepreneurs. In line with the argument that the educational system serves neoliberalism through leading students to skills and competencies necessary to be part of the marketplace (Apple 2001, Harris 2007, Hursh 2005, İnal 2009, Read 2009), there are several passages and exercises in the post-2005 textbooks that imply the neoliberal language, such as "individualism." The pre-2005 textbooks define the individual as a member of family and society. There is a strong emphasis on the significance of living in and for the society and the country. To illustrate, the pre-2005 textbooks have sections like *Ailenin önemi* (Importance of family) and *Toplum içinde yaşamanın önemi* (Importance of living in a society). With the 2004 reform, the focus shifts from a society-based description to an individual-based description of the individual. The post-2005 textbooks, for instance, have less emphasis on working for the society; instead, they claim that the society appreciates successful individuals. Unlike the previous books, the idea of people supporting the society is not present in the new textbooks, but rather, emphasis on the self-interested individual has become prominent.

The idea of the privatization of education is seen implicitly in the textbooks as well. Unlike the pre-2005 textbooks, participation of the business world in public services was integrated into the post-2005 textbooks. A section entitled *Onlar birer hayırsever* (They are all philanthropists) exemplifies the participation of the business sector in public services, stating that "well-known businessmen and companies of our country carry out social projects through their charitable foundations. They work for the public through being active in different social spheres, such as education, health, art and sport (Karagöz et al. 2006, 150)." Emphasis on social cooperation from this perspective represents the impact of neoliberal ideology in education. Active participation of business associations and foundations in service sectors is legitimized under the name of charity. This supports the dilution of welfare state regulations. The focus on these actors' participation in public services indicates that such services are considered as a sphere in which interest groups can play a role. In this respect, the new textbooks support privatization in education and health through highlighting the importance of business foundations' contributions.

Another difference between the pre- and post-2005 textbooks is their approach toward the concept of citizen. The post-2005 textbooks represent a citizen as a producer, consumer, and entrepreneur and consist of several passages and exercises leading students toward fields of production, marketing, advertising, consumption, and entrepreneurship. Although there are sections in the pre-2005 textbooks about production and consumption, they are different from the post-2005 books. Unlike the former, the latter contain examples directing students to become an active producer, a consumer, and even a salesperson. Passages, examples, and exercises in the new textbooks show that the focus is not only on being a producer but also that production is done with the purpose of selling, profiting, and competing.

The findings of the analysis of the textbooks demonstrate that the 2004 Primary School Education Reform introduced neoliberal discourse into the educational system of Turkey. Acknowledging that education is not a mechanical process, and thus that the educational system centered on neoliberal discourse does not mean that students will inevitably be a part of the market, this study argues that the 2004 reform facilitates the process of directing students to think within the framework of neoliberalism. In this respect, the new educational system seeks to promote neoliberal ideology and contains the possibility of creating individuals with a neoliberal orientation.

Similar concerns were raised in some other studies as well. For instance, the new curriculum was criticized for its emphasis on economic activities and individualism (Adıgüzel 2010, İnal 2009, Yıldız 2008). Rather than providing students the opportunity to develop themselves in the ways that they really want, the new curriculum appears to educate students to be economic inputs for a neoliberal economy and labor market (Yıldız 2008, 25). The Curriculum 2004 has also integrated a market-specific language into education, as in the case of performance homework and performance evaluations. Hence, the curriculum and textbooks were based on economic concepts, increasing the likelihood of transforming students intellectually toward a market-oriented outlook (Adıgüzel 2010, İnal 2009).

Teachers' Views on the Revised Social Studies Textbook

The textbook was central to the discussions on the content of the revised social studies educational program. Teachers who were interviewed for this study unanimously believed that the previous social studies textbooks were overloaded with too much information, leading to rote learning, memorization, and stress on teachers to complete the curriculum within a prescribed period. However, although teachers widely acknowledged the need for change, few welcomed the new social studies textbook for grade five.

Teachers voiced a number of criticisms with the regard to the quality of the textbook. Except for a few, the majority of them believed that the content load was reduced too much in the new textbook, as it superficially introduced themes and did not provide adequate information on the specified subjects. This confirms the findings of another study on the implementation of the social studies program in grade four, which found out that 70 percent of teachers believed that the textbook was inadequate to inform students on the subjects (Yapıcı and Demirdelen 2007). Teachers argued that the new book was filled with stories, questions, and a variety of classroom activities as well as research assignments.

Similar to other newly developed educational programs, one of the aims of the new social studies educational program is to develop students' research skills. The curriculum documents state that in the contemporary world, the future of individuals and societies is dependent on the competencies to access, use, and produce knowledge

(MoNE 2009, MoNE 2005). Research assignments were designed as an important tool to improve students' competencies to access and retrieve relevant information, and to encourage self-directed learning. However, in reality this approach did not work according to the expectations, as students delegated their responsibility to others, primarily to parents. Moreover, research assignments assume that children have access to the Internet at home or in their neighborhoods, or have access to written educational resources. These assumptions are in contradiction with the realities of many households that do not have computers, an adequate number of reference books, or the financial resources for frequent visits to Internet cafés. What is more, research assignments require parental involvement, yet parents do not always have the time or the educational background and commitment to help their children.

Because of the "emptiness" of the textbooks and too much reliance on classroom activities and research assignments, social studies emerged as the least-liked course among students and teachers alike. With a few exceptions, the teachers believed that the students did not enjoy the course since it was dull, superficial, and uninteresting. They suggested that students are more interested in courses in which they have ample opportunities to learn. Nevertheless, in social studies they often conversed about familiar issues that were not stimulating. The lack of sufficient information in the textbook was viewed as a serious concern since knowledge acquisition was considered as an important goal of education. Moreover, knowledge was essential in providing background information to students in order to enable them to do further research and support their learning.

Another significant concern was related to the perceived contradictions between the new educational program and the nationwide examination system that governs admission to secondary schools. These exams have traditionally evaluated students on the basis of their knowledge acquisition. However, there were concerns that mainstream schools fail to prepare students for the exams, because the emphasis has shifted in the curriculum from knowledge acquisition to the development of competencies and skills. Hence, demand for private tutoring has increased. Furthermore, teachers believed that previously, highly motivated, intelligent, and driven students could succeed in the nationwide exams by mastering the books, even if they did not attend any private tutoring centers, because the textbooks contained substantive information. As the new books lacked such rich content, teachers believed that in the absence of private tutoring, students from underprivileged backgrounds could hardly succeed on the exams. The quality of secondary school education has a direct impact on access to universities and employment opportunities in the labor market. Therefore, there was a strong conviction among teachers that the educational gap among income groups, and between urban and rural areas would be further accentuated, leading to an increasingly stratified society. Similar concerns were also reported in other contexts. For instance, the authorities have attempted to introduce a competency-based curriculum in China. However, these reforms have raised serious equity issues there, as examination-oriented education has long been deeply embedded in Chinese culture and society (Dello-Iacovo 2009).

Such concerns have motivated the majority of teachers to supplement the social studies textbook by searching for additional sources of information from the Internet and bookstores. Some teachers have used previous textbooks as a reference as well. Since teachers and students are not permitted to use books other than the new textbooks in the classroom, teachers have photocopied these materials to share with students or fellow teachers. Thus, some critics called the revised curriculum "photocopy-centered learning."

Conclusion

This chapter has attempted to provide an empirical and critical analysis of the Curriculum 2004 by focusing on the social studies educational program. Based on a content analysis of social studies textbooks and interviews with teachers involved in teaching social studies in primary schools, the chapter raised some critical questions about the new curriculum.

The content analysis revealed that the textbooks published after 2005 reflect a neoliberal language and agenda. The books focus on individualism and some other qualities that are highly valued in a market economy, such as consumption, competition, and entrepreneurship. This implies that the educators and curriculum designers who were involved in developing the new educational programs and textbooks aim at educating individuals according to the demands of the market. The discussions with teachers have reflected some broader societal concerns and disclosed a general dissatisfaction with the textbooks for social studies. Indeed, the majority of teachers did not approve of the substantial reductions in the content load due to concerns about students' academic success (also identified in Korkmaz 2008), the nationwide examinations, the increasing demand for private tutoring, and the deepening educational inequalities. Therefore, these teachers tended to supplement the curriculum with additional information gathered from other educational resources, and they continued to impart knowledge at a level that they believed was adequate.

The case of research assignments or the revision of textbooks illustrates the importance of considering context adequately in education reforms. When learning is increasingly directed toward student research (with the assumed benefits in terms of rendering students autonomous learners and preparing them for lifelong learning), in a country where access to information resources is uneven, or very limited in some regions or for certain segments of society, then such a policy threatens children's right to education and undermines their learning opportunities. Likewise, when textbooks are scrapped, so too is essential information on topics that are studied in a country where these books are the primary and often "the only" reference book for millions of students. Such a policy then may also further exacerbate educational inequalities and marginalize students from lower socioeconomic backgrounds. Furthermore, the chapter suggests that the revised curriculum might aggravate social inequalities, since children who have better access to cultural, economic, and social resources are placed in an advantageous position. Therefore, the new curriculum appears to have the consequence of reproducing or even aggravating existing social and economic inequalities rather than helping to ameliorate them.

References

Adıgüzel, Ergül. "Eğitimde Yapısal Dönüşüm, Fonlanmış Eğitim Projeleri ve Bıraktığı İzler." *Eleştirel Pedagoji* 9 (2010): 37–53.
AKP (Justice and Development Party). "Emergency Action Plan." 2002. http://www.akparti.org.tr/acil eylem.asp (accessed August 2009).
———. "Party Program." 2001. http://www.belgenet.com/parti/program/ak_1.html (accessed March 2010).
Akpınar, Burhan, and Kamil Aydın. "Türkiye ve Bazı Ülkelerin Eğitim Reformlarının Karşılaştırılması." *Doğu Anadolu Bölgesi Araştırmaları* 6 (2007): 82–88.
Altınyelken, Hülya K. *Changing Pedagogy: A Comparative Analysis of Reform Efforts in Uganda and Turkey*. Enschede, Netherlands: Ipskamp Drukkers, 2010a.
———. "Pedagogical Renewal in Sub-Saharan Africa: The Case of Uganda." *Comparative Education* 46, no. 2 (2010b): 151–171.

———. "Student-Centred Pedagogy in Turkey: Conceptualisations, Interpretations and Practice." *Journal of Education Policy* 26, no. 2 (2011): 137–160.
Apple, Michael W. "Comparing Neo-Liberal Projects and Inequality in Education." *Comparative Education* 37, no. 4 (2001): 409–423.
Chisholm, Linda, and Ramon Leyendecker. "Curriculum Reform in the Post-1990s Sub-Saharan Africa." *International Journal of Educational Development* 28, no. 2 (2008): 195–205.
Dello-Iacovo, Belinda. "Curriculum Reform and 'Quality Education' in China: An Overview." *International Journal of Educational Development* 29, no. 3 (2009): 241–249.
ERG (Educational Reform Initiative). "Yeni Öğretim Programlarını İnceleme ve Değerlendirme Raporu." 2005. http://www.erg.sabanciuniv.edu.tr/ (accessed August 2009).
EU (European Union). "2001 Progress Report of Turkey." 2001. http://projeler.meb.gov.tr/pkm1/index.php?option=com_content&view=article&id=142:ab-lerleme-raporlar&Itemid=78 (accessed April 2010).
———. "2002 Progress Report of Turkey." 2002. http://projeler.meb.gov.tr/pkm1/index.php?option=com_content&view=article&id=142:ab-lerleme-raporlar&Itemid=78 (accessed April 2010).
———. "2004 Progress Report of Turkey." 2004. http://projeler.meb.gov.tr/pkm1/index.php?option=com_content&view=article&id=142:ab-lerleme-raporlar&Itemid=78 (accessed April 2010).
Gökçe, Feyyat. *Değişme Sürecinde Devlet ve Eğitim*. Ankara: Pegem Akademi Yayıncılık, 2000.
Güven, İsmail, and Canan D. İşcan. "The Reflections of New Elementary Education Curriculum on Media." *Ankara Üniversitesi Eğitim Bilimleri Fakültesi Dergisi* 39, no. 2 (2006): 95–123.
Harris, Suzy. *The Governance of Education: How Neo-Liberalism Is Transforming Policy and Practice*. London: Continuum International Publishing Group, 2007.
Hartley, David. "Personalization: The Nostalgic Revival of Child-Centered Education?" *Journal of Education Policy* 24, no. 4 (2009): 423–434.
Hursh, David. "Neo-liberalism, Markets and Accountability: Transforming Education and Undermining Democracy in the United States and England." *Policy Futures in Education* 3, no. 1 (2005): 3–15.
İnal, Kemal. "AKP'nin Neoliberal ve Muhafazakar Eğitim Anlayışı." In *AKP Kitabı: Bir Dönüşümün Bilançosu*, edited by Bülent Duru and İlhan Uzgel, 689–719. Istanbul: Phoenix Yayınevi, 2009.
Karagöz, Demet, et al. *İlköğretim Sosyal Bilgiler Ders Kitabı 5*. Ankara: MoNE, 2006.
Korkmaz, Isa. "Evaluation of Teachers for Restructured Elementary Curriculum." *Education* 129, no. 2 (2008): 250–258.
MoNE (Ministry of National Education). *İlköğretim Sosyal Bilgiler Dersi (4–5. sınıflar) Öğretim Program*. Ankara: Devlet Kitapları Müdürlüğü Basım Evi, 2004.
———. *İlköğretim (1–5) Sınıf Programları Tanıtım El Kitabi*. Ankara: MONE, 2005.
———. *Sosyal Bilgiler Dersi (4–5) Öğretim Program ve Klavuzu*. Ankara: MoNE, 2009.

Read, Jason. "A Genealogy of Homo-Economicus: Neoliberalism and the Production of Subjectivity." *Foucault Studies* 6 (2009): 25–36.

Robertson, Susan L. "Teachers Matter...Don't They? Placing Teachers and Their Work in the Global Knowledge Economy." 2007. Bristol: The Centre for Globalization, Education and Societies, University of Bristol. http://www.bris.ac.uk/education/people/academicStaff/edslr/publications/22slr/ (accessed March 2009).

TUSIAD (Turkish Industrialists' and Businessmen's Association). "Türkiye'de Eğitim: Sorunlar ve Değişime Yapısal Uyum Önerileri." 1990. http://www.tusiad.org.tr/Default.aspx (accessed March 2010).

Yapıcı, Mehmet, and Ceren Demirdelen. "İlköğretim 4. Sınıf Sosyal Bilgiler Öğretim Programına İlişkin Öğretmen Görüşleri." *İlköğretim Online* 6, no. 2 (2007): 204–212.

Yıldız, Naciye. "Neo-Liberal Küreselleşme ve Eğitim." *D. Ü. Ziya Gökalp Eğitim Fakültesi Dergisi* 11 (2008): 13–32.

6

Learning to FlexLabor: How Working-Class Youth Train for Flexible Labor Markets[1]

Ergin Bulut

The terms of the debate regarding vocational training in Turkey have been discussed in relation to the dichotomy between secularism and religion. This stems from the fact that *Imam-Hatip* schools[2] belong to the category of vocational schools. In a country with such a tense secular-religious divide, the increasing interest of the business world in the field of education is ignored, along with its very political character. Efficiency discourse marginalizes the experience of vocational high school students. In this black-box model of schooling, "the concrete experience of children and teachers—is less important...than more global and macro-economic considerations of rate of return on investment, or more radically, the reproduction of the division of labor" (Apple 1990, 25).

I begin this chapter by addressing the global economic changes and their impact on the Turkish vocational education system. I mostly focus on narratives from fieldwork conducted in a vocational high school in Istanbul. The fieldwork reveals that most of the students come from working-class backgrounds[3] or have families embedded within precarious employment. I argue that school reforms fail to offer the possibility of structural improvement for working-class students but rather prepare them for flexible labor markets that demand flexible personalities, willing to work for unpredictable futures. While schooling is transformed into a space of business-education collaboration, the curriculum is aimed at creating a blue-collar subjectivity, geared toward the creation of a modular human being.

Transformation of Vocational Education in Turkey

Those who have watched the film will remember Charlie Chaplin in *Modern Times*, desperately working on an assembly line. The movie demonstrates how the worker is dominated within the labor process, which does not require very complex skills. Today, skills are only part of the story. We need to love our jobs and be willing to move between careers and reeducate ourselves. It is argued that "at no time in the history of capitalism has the education and training of the workforce assumed such widespread importance as at the present conjuncture" (Ashton and Green 1999, 1). Turkey is no exception.

However, Turkey has its peculiar historicity: its bid to join the European Union (EU) and its desire to become a learning society; the structural transformation of its manufacturing industry since 2001; the desire of capital to integrate with the global economy to produce high-quality products; its young population and the high rate of youth unemployment. Turkish vocational education has always been structurally disorganized. The first serious attempt to organize the system and establish a school-industry partnership took place with the enactment of the apprenticeship law (no. 3308) in 1986.[4] But the problems remained unresolved, and the goals stated by the law led to the Sixteenth National Educational Council (1999), which—only for that year—specifically focused on vocational education.[5] The Council decided that the system would be transformed into a modular one, dismantling the single-skill model, as well as aligning the system with the business world (Tarcan 2001).[6] On the political-economic side of the story, following Turkey's membership in the Customs Union in 1996, there has been an increase in the share of medium- and high-technology manufacturing sectors in aggregate exports. The most influential business organizations, the Turkish Industrialists' and Businessmen's Association (TUSIAD) and the Istanbul Chamber of Commerce (ITO), have prepared extensive reports to make an argument for closing the gap between vocational schooling and the business world (Alpaslan 2007). As a result of the convergence of these political-economic factors, a project called Project for Strengthening Vocational Education (MEGEP) was initiated. The general objective is to develop modern, flexible, and high-quality vocational education with a lifelong learning perspective that can respond to the socioeconomic needs of the country. MEGEP proposes a modular system so as to harmonize Turkish vocational and technical education with the EU in line with flexible labor markets. What does that mean? What is a modular system, and what would a modular human being created by this system look like?

I argue that we are witnessing the creation of the "modular man" (Gellner 1996). The concept of the modular man comes from concept of modular furniture. As opposed to modular furniture, older furniture forces one "to make an irrevocable commitment" (Gellner 1996, 97). In contrast, modular man "is able to combine into a specific-purpose, *ad hoc*, limited association, without binding himself by some blood ritual" (Gellner 1996, 100). Added to this is the concept of lifelong learning. We have to constantly upgrade our skills within the framework of the market. Education becomes socialized, just like work. As it has been argued, within the logic of informational capitalism, that work moves beyond the factory, and life itself becomes a social factory (Hardt and Negri, 2000). In a similar vein, education is no longer confined to the formal space of schooling and the institution. We learn through extra lessons and constantly aim to update our credentials. As Karl Marx once (1990) asserted, labor power is a special commodity, and life in its totality has become a target for maintaining the uninterrupted flow of labor power and the extraction of value. This control is achieved precisely through the chronic unemployment and precariousness that is now the norm in labor markets. No wonder that education has become "a tool in the fetishisation of certificates" (Olssen 2006, 40). We witness the entrenchment of the logic of societies of control (Deleuze 1992) within which we are perpetually controlled and trained; schools are transformed into corporations[7]. However, the discourse of business circles tries to normalize capitalism and hide the intrinsic character of the unemployment it creates, and desires to discipline labor power and wage relations. In the new modular system, "the task of schooling is increasingly subject to the logic of industrial production and market competition" (Ball 1990, 292). The current Justice and Development Party (AKP) government (like its predecessors) and business circles claim that the system will be rational, supraideological, and therefore successful. Yet, working-class students lack the cultural and linguistic capital to express, "market and articulate themselves" within the market. Thus, it is even doubtful whether the project is going to satisfy the demands of capital, let alone provide a good future for these students. I argue that the reform discourse of MEGEP is yet another reproduction of the modernization theory, maintaining the linear relationship between education and development and marginalizing the experience and history of mostly racialized working-class youth in the city.

The dominant agenda aims to establish hegemony over these young people from the lower classes through the discourse of modernization, development, and global competition, as well as by appealing to their desires.

Danville[8] Industrial High School: Selection through Discipline and Brand Loyalty

There are a few private laboratories in the Danville Industrial High School founded through the partnership between the Ministry of National Education and various automobile companies. The first protocol was signed with Company A in 1992–1993, and was followed by Company B, Company C, Company D, Company E, and Company F. As far as the procedure is concerned, the school files an application with the companies to form a partnership. The school provides space to the companies, whereas the companies provide educational support and employment possibilities for the graduates, even though there is no guarantee of employment by the same company. Bearing in mind that attendance problems and discipline records are not rare in vocational high schools, it becomes evident that a student receiving acceptance to a private laboratory is not easy. One of the students, for instance, underlined the notion of being visually presentable. This was echoed by a teacher:

> The candidate student cannot stammer, since he will deal with the customer and perhaps be promoted to the position of service consultant. (O, T., chief teacher in the private workshop, 50, Istanbul).

Representatives of the brands participate in recruitment interviews. The private laboratories undertake the role of a human resources (HR) department, one of the teachers told me. The same teacher maintained that HR departments do not have the opportunity to get to know the employee over a long period of time, whereas the school is the place where the students spend years. Thus, actually, the school in this case begins implicitly (perhaps even explicitly) to act as a human resources department. The teachers working in these private laboratories are excited to become partners with the companies, and try to cultivate brand loyalty among students by taking them to lunch together and having them wear the shirts of each brand or use textbooks with the brand symbol of the company. Then, what are some of the implications of such divisions within the school? How do the private laboratories differ from the "normal" ones?

Educational Differences and Management Discourse

The private laboratories are provided with computer support. Students are supposed to get acquainted with the Internet since engine test equipment is updated not with CDs but over the Internet. Students in those laboratories also have the opportunity to learn vocational English. The students in these private laboratories are also required to read some of the books included in the one hundred essential works of the Ministry so that they can develop their social skills. Students learn how to welcome customers and establish communication, and they learn concepts like "the customer" and "total quality." That is, students are learning to labor emotionally for future jobs. Thus, the most important feature of this kind of education is that it is "brand based." Given the critical literature on how seeing mediates one's subjectivity (Berger 1972, Beller 2006, Rose 2001), we can argue that education actually undertakes a strict aesthetic turn within these circumstances. One of the teachers states:

> The student is motivated in such a way that they assume the brand will go bankrupt were it not for them...A state of belonging is inspired and the message that they are a member of a big family is conveyed. This, of course, directly binds the student. Their shirts are different. Company C or Company D is written on their back. The color is different. They are perceived in a different way at school.

Then, "by what means, mechanisms, procedures, instruments, tactics, techniques, technologies and vocabularies is authority constituted and rule accomplished" (Dean 1999, 31)? How are discipline, efficiency, and brand loyalty maintained in Danville Industrial High School? What kind of techniques do the companies resort to? One of the teachers gives a hint:

> If he has a good score and is also successful in the interview but has written my laboratory as his fourth preference, a student with a lower score but who has chosen my laboratory as his first preference was accepted though the former one was not. *In other words, he will love it. The student will want Company F, Company C, or Company E.* (author's emphasis)

Here, love for the brand becomes the tool for having a privileged identity at school. A student talks about his experience:

> They asked me whether I would go to a distant place if they sent me. They said that my future wife might not like me because of the job I do. It seems that they liked my ideas and accepted me.

The realm of culture—and in this case religion—becomes a terrain through which desire is produced:

> They brought a bag, they brought notebooks. Here, even though other workshops do not give anything to the other workshops, Company C congratulated us on our religious holidays and sent us boxes of candies. They did such a favor. They endorse us.

Another student:

> For instance we didn't pay anything for the shirts, books or notebooks. We had no expenses. They sent a bag, a small bag like a pocket book diary.

Yet Company C has its demands, too:

> They try not to take any money from us, so that we can be [fruitful] to them....Normally, we do not have to attend apprenticeship training next year but they call us for the training. We were not going to have apprenticeship training but it is said that we should.

When a student from Company C was describing their practices, he told me that it is difficult to see the students outside the laboratory. I was told that they can stay in, because there are computers and the teachers let them use the PCs. Even though there is no sharp class difference between the two groups, we can resort to Pierre Bourdieu for an evaluation of why this is so. According to Bourdieu, "Whether students stay in school or drop out, and the course of study they pursue, depends on their practical expectations of the likelihood that people of their social class will succeed academically" (Schwartz 1997, 197). In other words, the technical affordances appeal to the desires of the students and organize the social space.

There is also the opposition between the strict teacher and the friendly boss/teacher. Whereas the teachers of the "normal" workshops are strict and sometimes ruthless toward the students, the teachers of the laboratories are "student-friendly." As the instructor of Company F states, the brand acts as a mechanism for observation since the students of Company F cannot play "long donkey"⁹ in the school due to the fact that "Company F" is written on the shirts they wear. What follows is an example of how the brand image has indeed penetrated into the minds of the youth:

> My father is a taxi driver. The car is a Company F model 1. All the drivers at that taxi station chose Company F. Company F has many advantages .... That's why everybody uses Company F.

When I asked the same student where he was living, he gave the following answer:

> I live in Kuştepe, Danville. And there is Twin-City Automotive where Kuştepe begins. Then comes Savoy, in Zincirlikuyu. There is Mid-West Auto Repairs in Çağlayan. I visit these places, they are nice services.

Similar to total quality management systems that aim to reduce errors to zero, the educational target aims "to integrate the subjectivity of the working individual into the objectives of the organization" (Zeybek 2006, 117).

The superiority of the brand-based training was not always welcomed by "other" students. A student from these normal workshops finds these practices discriminatory, but blames himself and his peers:

> It is because we do not want to study. Yet, we will regret it soon. The problem lies within the students, thinking about other things. They assume they will be happier outside, but they are unconsciously ruining their lives.

On this other side of the coin, it is not total quality management but strict discipline that speaks. Whereas members of the penal colony receive an education of "punctuality, neatness, respect for authority and other elements of habit formation" (Apple 1995, 62), the brand students–they also learn these but not always explicitly–learn how to be flexible, engage in teamwork, and solve problems. This dividing practice of the brands is based on a mechanism through which education as a science establishes truth and produces the knowledge to determine who counts as a legal, desirable subject and citizen.

Conclusion

These narratives reveal that the "human psyche itself has become a possible domain for systematic government in the pursuit of socio-political ends" (Rose 1989, 7). Companies in the school aim to cultivate a particular blue-collar subjectivity without a guarantee of employment. Here, the school becomes accountable to the company and the market. What is more important is that through the selective mechanism, the ideology of meritocracy is maintained. In this respect, an implicit naturalization of the market economy, which entails promoting the failure/success narrative and glorifying the power of the individual to solve problems, takes place (Agostinone-Wilson 2006). The problem is, even though this mechanism provides—perhaps better—employment conditions for future blue collars, "the cost of creating such workers of efficiency will be a loss of autonomy, non-participation in decision making, a denial of democratic freedom, and a lack of personal development through work" (Robertson 2005). For the sake of creating docile, qualified graduates, educators seem to be neglecting the fact that "the power of corporate culture, when left to its own devices, respects few boundaries and even fewer basic social needs, such as the need for uncontaminated food, decent health care, and safe forms of transportation" (Giroux 2000, 100). As an educational reproduction of the modernization paradigm, this reform discourse imposes "a whole set of presuppositions as inevitable: it is taken for granted that maximum growth, and therefore productivity and competitiveness, are the ultimate and sole goal of human actions; or that economic factors cannot be resisted" (Bourdieu 1998, 30). This discourse constructs the ideal of an educational realm where actors are supposedly playing the game on equal terms, as well as marginalizing working class students' personal and collective histories and experience. What we are witnessing is the capitalization of human beings. We require "a critique of all human capitalist social life, the attempt of which pushes to the fore the 'negativity of all passes for the positive in the capitalist society'" (Rikowski 2004, 564). If we fail to unpack the implications of lifelong learning, it might very well be that working-class youth will be the new Chaplins trying to adapt to market forces.

Notes

1. This chapter is a shorter and modified version of an article published by the author in *Journal for Critical Education Policy Studies* (2010, vol. 8,

no. 1), under the title of "Transformation of the Turkish Vocational Training System: Capitalization, Modularization and Learning unto Death." It has been updated in terms of the legal transformations in relation to the broader system. The author would like to thank JCEPS for granting permission to use the article as the basis of this chapter.
2. These schools are designed to train imams, and the conflict stems from the fact that the girls attending these schools—even though they cannot be imams—wear headscarves. It was formerly against the law for them to attend a university, until a recent legal action was taken by the AKP. Also, graduates (both male and female) of *Imam-Hatip* high schools are now treated more equally with graduates of other schools in choosing whatever university they would like to attend. This discourse of "unequal mistreatment" has been skillfully deployed by the prime minister of Turkey, who accused the more secularist political stances of being "ideological" toward *Imam-Hatip* graduates. More recently, the debate has been sparked by an initiative of the government, aiming to restructure the system again. The initiative, which was passed through the relevant commission in the parliament in March 2012, has sparked public criticism. The oppositional parties, the most influential institution for business circles in Turkey (TUSIAD), as well as women's organizations attacked the recent move with the argument that it will strengthen the religious schools and impact girls' education negatively.
3. I want to present some demographic information about the students. I interviewed male students from the engine department. More than 100 students (freshmen and seniors) participated in the questionnaire stage of my fieldwork. I take 100 of them into consideration. Among the students, 43 percent have a family of four people. Sixty-seven percent of them live at their own house. Nearly half of the male parents are primary school graduates, whereas 55 percent of the mothers are primary school graduates. The answers to, "What is your father's occupation?" include doorkeeper, cook, worker, cleaner, retired, artisan, officer, bus driver, driver, worker in an automobile body shop, teacher, policeman, and occupations mostly related to engine repair and maintenance. As for the mothers, 80 percent of them are housewives. Other occupations include cook, cleaner, janitor, administrative chief, and employee at a ready-made clothing shop and textile. These responses reveal that the students mostly belong to working-class families. Moreover, the findings reveal that 60 percent of the students previously worked, mostly in the service sector or blue-collar jobs. In other words, the students can be said to be already accustomed to working before they enter the labor market. More strikingly, they are almost divided as far as their thoughts regarding child labor are concerned. The answers when asked whether children should work or not are as follows. Namely, 47 percent of the participants said children should work, whereas 53 percent were against the idea. As far as failure is concerned, the students either blame themselves or the educational system. While 45 percent of them assume that they are the ones to blame, 30 percent put the blame on the educational system for a person's failure at school.

4. The aim was to integrate those left out of the formal educational system with the education of an apprenticeship, in other words, *to give the students of VT schools the chance to upgrade their skills in the real work environment.* With the Law (no. 3308), we see that "vocational education has begun to function in a dual manner and its relation with the market has reached a structural model" (Aksoy 2005).
5. For a discussion of some of the themes of the Council, see the preparatory documents in Kadi 1998 and Kilic 1998.
6. These decisions materialized with another law, passed as 4702. As I have stated in a previous footnote, more recent transformations paved the way for abolishing the quotient discrimination against the graduates of vocational high schools. This interestingly led to an increase in *Imam-Hatip* high school enrollments. Another recent issue is the increasing collaboration between industry and schools, through which the National Ministry of Education will support the private sector, which will in turn assume the fees per student. These Special Industrial High Schools will function with the logic of a private school, and will be located within Special Industrial Zones, and this raises questions regarding space, subjectivity, and the social reproduction of labor power.
7. For examples of scholarship along these lines, see Tuschling and Engeann 2006; Stoer and Magalhaes 2004; Olssen 2006; Peters, Marshall, and Fitzsimons 2000; Unal, Tural, and Aksoy 2005; McCarthy et al. 2009.
8. Pseudonyms are used for the institutions, the auto brands, and the individuals who participated in the research.
9. A popular game in Turkey, especially among male students.

References

Agostinone-Wilson, Faith. "Downsized Discourse: Classroom Management, Neoliberalism, and the Shaping of Correct Workplace Attitude." *Journal for Critical Education Policy Studies* 4, no. 2 (2006). http://www.jceps.com/index.php?pageID=article&articleID=69 (accessed March 2012).

Aksoy, Hasan H. "Üniversiteye Giriş Sorunu Bağlamında Toplumsal Yeniden Üretim Mekanizması Olarak Mesleki-Teknik Eğitim." *ABECE Dergisi* 226, June. 18–20 (2005).

Alpaslan, Spyhan. "İşsiz Çok Ama İşe Yarayacak Eleman Yok." *İTOVİZYON* 50 (2007): 18–25.

Apple, Michael. *Education and Power.* New York: Routledge, 1995.

———. *Ideology and Curriculum.* New York: Routledge, 1990.

Ashton, David, and Francis Green. *Education, Training and the Global Economy.* Northampton, UK: Edward Elgar Publishing, 1999.

Ball, Stephen. "Management as Moral Technology: A Luddite Analysis." In *Foucault and Education: Disciplines and Knowledge,* edited by Stephen J. Ball, 153–167. London: Routledge, 1990.

Beller, Jonathan. *The Cinematic Mode of Production: Attention Economy and the Society of the Spectacle.* Interfaces, studies in visual culture. Hanover, NH: Dartmouth College Press, 2006.

Berger, John. *Ways of Seeing*. London: Penguin Books, 1972.
Bourdieu, Pierre. *Acts of Resistance: Against the New Myths of Our Time*. Cambridge, UK: Polity Press, 1998.
Brown, Phillip. *Schooling Ordinary Kids: Inequality, Unemployment, and the New Vocationalism*. London: Tavistock Publications, 1987.
Dean, Mitchell. *Governmentality: Power and Rule in Modern Society*. London: Sage, 1999.
Deleuze, Gilles. "Postscript on the Societies of Control." *October* 59 (1992): 3–7.
Gellner, Ernest. *Conditions of Liberty: Civil Society and Its Rivals*. New York: Penguin Books, 1996.
Giroux, Henry. *Stealing Innocence: Youth, Corporate Power and the Politics of Culture*. New York: St. Martin's, 2000.
Hardt, Michael, and Antonio Negri. *Empire*. Cambridge, MA: Harvard University Press, 2000.
Jarvis, Peter. "Globalization, the Learning Society and Comparative Education." In *The Routledge Falmer Reader in Sociology of Education*, edited by Stephen J. Ball, 72–86. London: RoutledgeFalmer, 2004.
Kadı, İbrahim. "Mesleki-Teknik Eğitimin Sorunları ve Öneriler." In *16. Milli Eğitim Şûrası Hazırlık Dökümanı*, edited by MoNE, 56–79. Ankara: MoNE, 1998.
Kılıç, Ruhi. "Bilgi Toplumunda Mesleki ve Teknik Eğitim ve Mesleki Teknik Eğitimde Yeni Yönelimler." In *16. Milli Eğitim Şûrası Hazırlık Dökümanı*, edited by MoNE, 19–26. Ankara: MoNE, 1998.
Marx, Karl. *Capital: Volume 1: A Critique of Political Economy*. London: Penguin Classics, 1990.
McCarthy, Cameron, et al. "Movement and Stasis in the Neoliberal Re-Orientation of Schooling." In *The Routledge International Handbook of Critical Education*, edited by Michael Apple, Wayne Au, and Luis Armando Gandin, 36–51. London: Routledge, 2009.
Olssen, Mark. "Understanding the Mechanisms of Neoliberal Control: Lifelong Learning, Flexibility and Knowledge Capitalism." *International Journal of Lifelong Education* 25, no. 3 (2006): 213–230.
Rikowski, Glenn. "Marx and the Education of Future." *Policy Futures in Education* 2, nos. 3 and 4 (2004): 565–577.
Robertson, Terry. "Class Issues: A Critical Ethnography of Corporate Domination within the Classroom." *Journal for Critical Education Policy Studies* 3, no. 2 (2005). http://www.jceps.com/index.php?pageID=article&articleID=80 (accessed, March 2012).
Rose, Gillian. *Visual Methodologies: An Introduction to the Interpretation of Visual Materials*. London: SAGE, 2001.
Rose, Nikolas. *Governing the Soul: The Shaping of the Private Self*. London: Routledge, 1989.
Schwartz, David. *The Sociology of Pierre Bourdieu*. Chicago: The University of Chicago Press, 1997.
Şimşek, Ali. *Türkiye'de Mesleki ve Teknik Eğitimin Yeniden Yapılandırılması*. Istanbul: TUSIAD, 1999.

Stoer, Stephen, and Antonio Magalhaes. "Education, Knowledge and the Network Society." *Globalisation, Societies and Education* 2, no. 3 (2004): 319–335.

Tarcan, Nurseli. 2001. "Mesleki ve Teknik Eğitim ve Yeni Düzenlemeler." *İşveren*. http://www.tisk.org.tr/isveren_sayfa.asp?yazI_id=359&id=21 (accessed March 2012).

Tuschling, Anna, and Christoph Engemann. "From Education to Lifelong Learning: The Emerging Regime of Learning in the European Union." *Educational Philosophy and Theory* 38, no. 4 (2006): 451–469.

Ünal, Işıl. "Yaşamboyu Öğrenme: Bir Müebbet Mahkumiyet mi?" *Ölçü Dergisi* 12 (2006) :96–103.

Ünal, Işıl, Nejla K. Turul, and Hasan H. Aksoy. "Mesleki Eğitim ve Yaşamboyu Eğitim: Ekonomi Politik Bir Değerlendirme." In *Yaşamboyu Öğrenme*, edited by Sayilan Fevziye and Ahmet Yıldız, 136–152. Ankara: Pegem Yayıncılık, 2005.

Zeybek, Ozan. "Human Enterprise of Global Capitalism and the Golden Collars: Producing the Producer." Master's Thesis, Boğaziçi University, Istanbul, Turkey, 2006.

7

Turkey under AKP Rule: Neoliberal Interventions into the Public Budget and Educational Finance

Nejla Kurul

At the end of 1979, Turkey was facing with an economic slump that was deeply affecting the masses. In the middle of this economic and political crisis, the government, supported by the International Monetary Fund (IMF) and the World Bank (WB), announced an adjustment program on January 24, 1980, that would shape the following years. This neoliberal program was the main component of economic policies in Turkey up to 1988 and was enriched by new measures in time. As Korkut Boratav (2006, 148–149) puts it, this neoliberal program was presented to the masses with a vigorous ideological campaign, as if there was no other way out of the crisis.

However, the program was not new in Turkey or in the world by any means, since it had been suggested during the 1970s to many underdeveloped and/or developing countries by the WB in the name of structural adjustment policies, which consist mainly of market liberalization and reinforcement of the international and domestic capitalist classes against the working class. These developments triggered the capitalist classes in Turkey to take actions against the organized labor movement. In the middle of the economic and political crisis, the so-called January 24 Adjustments, were declared. Since then, the Turkish economy has been integrated into the global capitalist system in a different way. The ruling governments were not able to implement those policies in a democratic way due to the high level of opposition from the labor movement. As a result, a military coup took place in September 12, 1980.

The current ruling Justice and Development Party (AKP) has been fed by the socioeconomic and political conditions created by this military coup. The AKP program is a synthesis of the global neoliberal ideology and new local conservative style.

This chapter aims at analyzing public, especially educational finance policies implemented in Turkey during the AKP era from a critical perspective. A survey of the historical background to clarify the factors that led to the policies of the AKP, and a brief comparison between policies in Turkey and policies worldwide are also included in this chapter's scope.

Main Characteristics of Public Finance and Social Policies during AKP Rule

It was surprising that the AKP became a ruling party the next year after its founding, and more importantly, that it managed to increase the votes it obtained in the 2002 general elections from 34 percent to 46.6 percent in 2007 and to 49.8 percent in 2011. Although proreligious factors have been very effective in the party's obtaining these results, the main element is the "conservative democrat" stance they claim to take and the class interests they claim to represent, namely the great alliance of the new emerging local capital with international finance capital. Attention should also be paid to the period of 1989–2002, in which international finance capital established its hegemony in Turkey, and after which the AKP immediately came to power (Bakırezer and Demirer 2009). This alliance has been ruling Turkey for the last nine years.

The AKP's social policies are based on the encouragement of the capitalist class, which is seen as the engine of the economic growth. The government has implemented liberal tax policies and antilabor social policies, including deunionization and the overlooking of undeclared labor in order to promote the capitalist class, despite its rhetoric of pro-citizenship and human rights. For the AKP governments, low labor costs are necessary for global competition; therefore, they have to be brought down. Although a larger portion of the budget is now allocated to health and education expenditures, the quality of the services have not increased due to commodification and commercialization. Even though the education budget now takes a greater portion of the total budget compared to previous years, most of the allowances are assigned only to employ more teachers. Moreover, the commercialization of education has led to serious differentiation and polarization among schools (Bakırezer and Demirer 2009, 167).

Income and wealth distribution in Turkey has worsened due to new liberal tax and public expenditure policies over the last 30 years. While the global tax burden was reduced to 23 percent from over 30 percent and public services were financed by domestic and foreign public debts, the tax burden has been shifted from the capitalist class onto the working class. For instance, the direct tax burden on a wage earner is between 50 percent and 70 percent, while it is only 28 percent for money-lender or a rentier (it was over 40 percent in 2006). Furthermore, tax revenues have been devoted to capital subsidies and incentives, and military and police expenditures rather than social expenditures that would provide social benefits to the working class and the unemployed. In other words, the masses clearly do not benefit from the total budget increase (Durmus 2010, 42).

With the IMF's and the WB's proposals for stability and structural adjustment programs in the 1980s, the necessity of downsizing the public sector was frequently emphasized. The appeal to cut down on public spending means the regression of social policies, more specifically restriction of the production of collective goods and services such as education, health, and social security. The unavoidability of neoliberal economic policy options was highlighted against the appeal of public service production. Based on this appeal, the opening up to foreign markets, the marketization of public sectors such as health and education, and the shift of research/development activities toward competition and efficiency started in the 1980s. The commodification and commercialization of collective goods and the stripping away of their public nature were accelerated and deepened during the AKP rule.

Educational Finance in the AKP era

The AKP years constitute approximately one-third of the post-1980 period, when neoliberal ideology and policies dominated economic, social, and cultural life in Turkey. Concurrently, due to both external and internal dynamics, neoliberal policies were at the top of the agenda of governments throughout the world. However, the point of view of the AKP's reformist appeal in education is based largely on marketization and aimed at adapting to the globalization process based on neoliberal parameters (İnal 2009). The AKP's influence on education has been in the shape of more solid, applied policies compared to prior governments that started the neoliberal transformation, as outlined:

- School Protection Associations were abolished and replaced with the *Parent-Teacher Association (PTA) Regulation* (no. 25831), which was published in the *Official Gazette* (journal), dated May 31, 2005.
- The enactment of the *Raising the Steps of the Teaching Career Legislation* (no. 25905), dated May 13, 2005, led to differences in wages among teachers doing the same job. According to this regulation, the percentage of specialized teachers within total number of teachers in the education services class is 20 percent, whereas the percentage of head teachers is 10 percent.
- Flexible employment profiles are integrated into the educational field.
- The *Private Education Institutions Law* (no. 5580) was enacted on February 8, 2007.
- Special education (i.e., handicapped education) was privatized with the voucher system.[1]

Although the way to commodifying and commercializing education had been paved prior to the AKP years, the heaviest blow to public education and the strongest boost to the marketization of education were initiated during the AKP years. There was a systematic increase in the share of foreign loans; scholarships and grants; public, personal, and institutional contributions; and PTAs for the funding of education. When the state does not fund and regulate public schools, the result is the commercialization, privatization and commodification of education. Support for private education and the promotion of this sector naturally brought about the rapid privatization and commercialization of education. However, for state schools, privatization in education means that schools turn themselves into a marketplace in order to generate funds, and the private sector and nongovernmental organizations (NGOs) are allowed to enter to schools with profit and charitable motives, respectively.

Financing education through projects that rely on external resources dates back to 1985. WB-supported education loans, European Union (EU)-supported grant projects, and credits provided by the European Investment Bank are some examples. The projects based on agreements between the Ministry of National Education (MoNE) and the WB are as follows: Industrial Schools Project (1985) (US$72.7 million), nonformal Vocational Training Project (1987) (US$71.1 million), the National Education Development Project (1990, $177.2 million), the First Basic Education Project Phase I (1998) (US$337.33 million), the Basic Education Project Phase II (2002, in progress) (US$356.86 million), and the Secondary Education Project (US$270 million). The total size of the WB-supported projects is $US1.285 billion (Yolcu 2007, 116).

The MoNE's inclusion of foreign sources to publicly finance education since 1985 has led to resource diversification and the creation of a project mentality in the education field. The conversion of education finance, including during the AKP period, can be examined in three categories. These are the commodification and privatization of education and knowledge, the commercialization and marketization of education, and the contraction of the education budget due to flexible production and flexible employment.

Commodification and Privatization of Education and Knowledge

It is important to make clear for whom and for what reason the accessibility of education and knowledge has been shifted from the public sector to private sector since the 1980s. For the working class, public education should have continued because it provided benefits to them in terms of a secondary distribution of income. Moreover, schools were safe places to which they could entrust their children during their working hours, and places where the children could secure their future with a good education. The children of the working class are compelled to find work, educated or not, and a good education would increase their chance of employment.

Looking at the matter from the perspective of the capitalist class, firstly the demand by the younger population for better jobs and higher wages was increasing, although the system was unable to meet these demands. The belief that only education and a "diploma" can help youth to get a better job created a high demand for education. This led the capitalist class to realize how profitable the education sector would be. Secondly, the numerical increase in a quality work force due to the popularization of mass education resulted in questions about the amount of resources appropriated to education from public sources. If mass education and schools, which were designed based on the needs of the economy, do not benefit the economy and its interests, then the financing of education should be restructured. Thus, if education is not producing results beneficial to the economy, and thus to the public, and is viewed rather as a human capital investment tool that increases the individual's prospective income, then the financing of education should be provided by individuals, not by the public.

Due to the two reasons given above, the capitalist classes aimed to commodify education. In this regard, education has two advantages as a commodity. Firstly, an individual must fulfill his/her educational needs in order to be able to afford his/her life (use value), and secondly, education as a commodity has a power of exchange among other commodities. The exchange value of education corresponds to the gains to be obtained by the diploma holder in the future and his/her power to access other commodities. The human capital argument, which suggests that higher education leads to higher efficiency and that higher efficiency leads to higher wages (Schultz 1961), illustrates vividly the commoditized and exploited human being who is materialized by the qualities of his/her education.

As there is no need for the popularization of education for the capitalist class in the neoliberal period, then from the profit maximizing point of view, it is important to extract education from its collective nature, to leave quality education to the privilege of the middle and upper classes, to shift the financing of education toward mixed funding whereby parents share the cost of education, to promote private education institutions and privatize the whole system. However, this approach to education necessitated the prerequisite that education services would be considered as means of creating exchange values rather than use values. The most notable example of this is the popular private teaching/tutoring institution sector. Multiple choice exams, which were constituted to meet employment/gain-oriented education demands, led to the establishment of private teaching/tutoring institutions. In fact, private teaching institutions were born out of the education crisis and form an important dimension of education funding.

What is obvious in Turkey today is that education is a commodity. Schools provide education to children or youth that is disassociated from their real learning needs. While the unemployment rate of the educated is increasing, the Turkish education system remains as a system based on elimination, in which diplomas are thought to represent the uncertain professions, jobs, and wages of the future.

Commercialization and Marketization of Education

The commodification of educational services means that these services are produced for their exchange value only. This change in the aim of the production leads to a change in the means and processes of production. Education that motivated by profit and charity converts a school into a competitive marketplace. The impact of marketization on schools and universities can be outlined as follows.

Budget of education is not increased proportional to the increase in need

One of the main factors that decreases the quality of public education is the disproportional share of educational allowances it receives, despite the increasing numbers of students. Budget cuts result in crowded classes, deficiencies in educational equipment, and filthy schools without water, heat, and security. Decreasing quality means decreasing confidence in public schools and teachers. While the MoNE's share of the gross domestic product (GDP) was 2 percent in 1960, it decreased to 1.3 percent in 1975, to 1.6 percent in 1980, and to 1.3 percent in 1985. Moreover, the MoNE's share of the general budget fell from 12.9 percent in 1960, to 11.5 percent in 1980, and to 8.6 percent in 1985 (Yolcu 2007, 100). As illustrated, the share of educational expenditures dropped drastically following the September 12 military coup, leading to further deterioration of the public's confidence about the reliability of public education and its quality. The educational needs of the younger generations have not been met properly, and thus public education was given a bad name through speculation about the low quality of education in public schools due to inefficiency and negligent teachers.

Allowances for both the MoNE and universities mostly decreased under the AKP governments, despite the substantially increasing number of students. The shares of total joint expenditures for the MoNE and universities, including revolving funds in GDP, are as follows (in percent): 4.26 (2000), 4.31 (2001), 4.33 (2002), 4.22 (2003), 4.03 (2004 and 2005), 4.13 (2006), 4.53 (2007), 4.33 (2008), and 4.03 (2009). In the same years, the shares of the MoNE itself in GDP were not regular, reaching the highest share in 2007 (3.05 percent) and decreasing in 2008 and 2009 (2.94 and 2.72, respectively). For university allowances, the figure is 1.04 percent in 2002 (i.e., the year that the AKP came to power), and it decreased to 0.79 percent in

2009. Furthermore, university allowances from the annexed budget also decreased from 0.82 percent in 2007, to 0.78 percent in 2008, and to 0.72 percent in 2009, despite the establishment of new universities (Yılmaz 2009 in İnal 2009, 45). These data prove that the AKP governments have not allocated enough resources to public education, contrary to the generous amounts mentioned in the AKP rhetoric. The aim of the AKP and its neoliberal policies is to minimize public support in collective goods and services such as education and foster commercialization and marketization through a variety of resources for educational funding.

Popularization of governance of education mentality

The concept of good governance has been used as a Trojan horse to encourage the commercialization of public production, and its credibility rose thanks to international organizations such as the WB, the IMF, and the United Nations Development Programme (UNDP) during the 1990s. Through the concept of good governance, the state is reconstructed with a market-friendly approach. In this context, education governance opens up the educational field, schools, and universities to private firms and NGOs, so that public authorities are forced to share their power with the private sector and NGOs. Some reflections about the effects of this process on education are summarized below.

School as marketplace: The trendy notion that schools should create their own funds themselves, together with the insufficient amount of funds allocated to them, despite increases in the numbers of students oblige public school administrations and teachers to come up with new income sources.

Schools compete in the education market with the diplomas they provide at the end of the education process and have become a marketplace of their own where educational materials and equipment are exchanged and subjected to competition. For example, the fact that textbooks are published by several bookstores encourages a competitive attitude in the Board of Education and Discipline, the MoNE, and schools. Private bookstores that publish and distribute books, cafeterias that provide for the nutritional needs of students, companies that offer student transportation, companies that provide school uniforms, and other entities that market complementary goods for education have also been necessary parts of this marketization process. Although these income-creating activities provide school administrations with cash, they form a new power relation, which can lead to power struggles at schools.

In particular, new marketplaces targeting students have been formed inside schools. These commercial markets, which were originally initiated to meet the needs/desires of students, later established a presence in almost all schools as monopolized shops that targeted the pocket money of students and extracted more money from families. For example, students might need to purchase for, an application form, or some other kind of document necessary for their education. Also, it is almost impossible to organize any kind of student activity like a school play, a concert, or a field trip for free of charge. Put differently, these student activities are organized with the aim of raising money. All components of the school are therefore expected to support the income-creating policy within schools.

School as a place of charity: Educational organizations began to be viewed as targets for charitable giving during the AKP era. The Information Management System for Turkish Educational Finance and Expenditures (TEBFIS) is systematically encouraging benevolent and philanthropic persons to provide support, and schools are instructed to raise money through these sources. TEBFIS, financed by the Scientific and Technological Research Council of Turkey (TUBITAK), is a project intended to determine the amount of and sources for money in schools, towns, cities, and regions and to manage these sources and the budget. Philanthropic persons and organizations are classified in this project as: Guardians-Parents/Citizens, Public Institutions, Nongovernmental Organizations, Private Organizations, and International Organizations.

It should be noted that PTAs are regarded as both an autonomous entity from the school administration and a stakeholder. Guidelines for these associations first came into effect in the AKP era. However, the mentality of education governance is pushing for a working structure similar to NGOs. Clause 16 of the National Education Law (no. 1739) was amended in order to establish a legal structure for restructuring PTAs as favorable to education governance. Though the clause states that guardians/parents cannot be forced to make donations to schools, it is a common practice to demand donations from parents during registration for school, and the legality of these donations is never questioned. Having searched for better schools for their children in other neighborhoods, for instance, parents keep quiet and participate in this income-generating process unwillingly. Therefore, donations in cash or in kind at schools should be regarded as compulsory rather than voluntary, shifting the power from PTAs to the school administration in actuality. However, grants-in-aid or donations have the least share in total school incomes. The major income source is obviously the marketization of the services and facilities provided at these places.

Schools as a field of competition: The supply of many social goods including education, health care, social security, and government-supported housing has been taken over by ambiguous NGOs, including private companies. Consequently, public interventions in the supply or financing of these services have decreased drastically. The competition mentality has eliminated all solidarity in education and led to polarization and unbalanced growth between the suppliers of education. Thus, parents have to settle for making obligatory donations and taking responsibility for transporting their child to school, which requires large amounts of time, because schools are in harsh competition, and the neighborhood school cannot always play a part in this situation.

The components of the schools; students, teachers, administraters, and parents, have become competitors due to central exams organized by the governmental bodies. Success in a competitive education system is based on lessons prepared according to the content and format of exams, courses available at schools for additional fees, and a registry for private teaching institutions. What is more, competition among schools is deepening the current inequalities and undermining people's solidarity, which is the main feature of humanity.

Contraction of the Education Budget Due to Flexible Production and Precarious Employment

Flexibility in education consists of the regulation of the production and labor processes like numerical-labor-functional flexibility, and flexibility in relation to time. It also includes flexibility in the production process, in labor organization, and in market conditions. As is known, the major reason for the nonflexibility of the Fordist type of production organization is the nonflexibility of the labor markets, such as higher wage rates, strong trade unions, unemployment insurance schemes, secured employment, and social welfare requirements.

The means of neoliberal flexible education policies, as applied in other public service areas, consist of nonpermanent staff practices, education regions, total quality practice, and strategic planning. First, some of the services that support education, such as school buses, the manufacture of school uniforms, school cafeteria services, and school maintenance, have been subcontracted to private companies. Subsequently, contractual teaching was initiated by the MoNE in the 2003–2004 academic year. The statistics of the MoNE show that teachers have been classified according to employment types since the 2007–2008 academic year. In this respect, the number of contractual teachers was 16.218 at the preschool level, 58.198 at the elementary level, and 7.486 at the secondary level (MoNE 2010). The emergence of precarious and unsecured employment has been due to the AKP's permanent social policies. This regulation aimed at and achieved the end of permanent and secure employment and a reduction in wages.

Conclusion

Capitalism in Turkey today has reached a stage where alienation, the commodification of social life, greed, and violence have been exacerbated by the AKP policies. The social policy of the AKP relies on promoting the capitalist class. The "less is more" approach to areas such as employment, health, social security, public housing, and education, which would fulfill the needs of the masses, is making life unbearable for anyone who falls outside of the capitalist class both in rhetoric and in implemented policies.

The AKP administration is gradually eliminating social structures designed to develop education on the basis of solidarity. The commodification of education, the generation of income through PTAs, the polarization of schools, the manipulation of teacher employment, incentives for private-sector schooling, the violent competitiveness in education, the privatization of special education, the widespread proliferation of charitable giving through school channels are the main transformations that have been effected by the AKP administration in Turkey. The AKP has created major changes in every aspect of education while preserving ownership and power relations.

This process leads to a constant loss of meaning and worth in the educational experience for many students and teachers. Putting an end to this course of events seems possible only through the organized and political resistance of the components of education, and the unification of this resistance through widespread social opposition. Furthermore, the joining of the Turkish opposition with social movements in Europe, the United States, Africa, and the Middle East on common grounds would strengthen the social struggle in Turkey.

Note

1. A neoliberal instrument that suggests that state aid should be delivered directly to parents to increase the variety of possible schools for families and promote competition for efficient services.

References

Bakırezer, Güven and Yücel Demirer. "Ak Partinin Sosyal Siyaseti." In *AKP Kitabı: Bir Dönüşümün Bilançosu*, edited by İlhan Uzgel and Bülent Duru, 153–178. Ankara: Phoneix Yayınları, 2009.
Boratav, Korkut. *Türkiye İktisat Tarihi 1908–2005*. Ankara: İmge Yayınevi, 2006.
Durmuş Mustafa. *Kapitalizmin krizinin yeni aşamasında dünyada ve Türkiye'de ekonomik durum: İstihdamsız büyüme ve adaletsiz bölüşüm*. Ankara: KESK Yayınları, 2010.
İnal, Kemal. "AKP'nin Neo-Liberal ve Muhafazakar Eğitim Anlayışı." *Eleştirel Pedagoji* 1 (2009): 37–50.
MoNE (Ministry of National Education). "Milli Eğitim İstatistikleri 2009–2010." 2010. www.sgb.meb.gov.tr (accessed March 2010).
Schultz, T. "Investment in Human Capital." *American Economic Review* 51, no. 1 (1961): 1–17.
Yolcu, Hüseyin. "Türkiye'de ilköğretim finansmanının değerlendirilmesi." PhD diss., Ankara Üniversitesi Eğitim Bilimleri Enstitüsü, Ankara, Turkey, 2007.

8

External Education Projects in Turkey

Gülay Aslan, Erdal Küçüker, and Ergül Adıgüzel

With the January 24, 1980, decisions in Turkey, the role of the State was defined in accordance with neoliberal policies, and the Turkish economy was restructured (Boratav 1997, Önder 2004, Kazgan 2005). The effects of restructuring the economy were felt deeply in public services, including education. The transformation of the educational system within the framework of neoliberal policies was not achieved at once with the regulations that were put into practice, however. This transformation is the product of a long-term effort, like a marathon, in which the milestones have been laid down with external educational projects.

External educational projects are initiated by the Ministry of National Education (MoNE). A considerable part of the financing of those projects is met by international organizations, and is open to inspection that is directed by the financing institution. External educational projects in Turkey were implemented for the construction of school buildings and for the physical facilities of the existing schools from 1962 to 1980. However, they have been used since the 1980s to transform the whole educational system as a profitable area for the capital owners (Ünal 2002). This process, the commodification of education, is part of the Structural Adjustment Policies (SAPs) used by neoliberalism as a means to penetrate the surrounding countries (Stewart 1995, Güler 1997, Ercan 1998). There are three main transnational organizations that are spreading SAPs all over the world: the International Monetary Fund (IMF), the World Trade Organization (WTO), and the World Bank (WB) (Kweik 2002; Giroux 2008). They employ the neoliberal thesis known as the Washington Consensus

(Williamson 1990, Chomsky 2000) that arose out of the Bretton Woods Conference (Ellwood 2002). Michael Crossley (2000) emphasizes that understanding education without implying that global powers affect educational policy and its practices in any context has become more and more difficult.

External educational projects that direct educational policies in Turkey have been funded by four international organizations: the WB, the European Union (EU), the European Investment Bank (EIB), and Risk Reduction Education for Disasters (Risk RED). Among these, the WB and the EU have played a dominant role in the transformation of the Turkish educational system.

The Justice and Development Party (AKP) government, holding the opinion that external educational projects in Turkey "enlighten the future," defines the role of international finance actors in this transformation:

> Projects enlighten our future .... Our Project Coordination Center... is in successful coordination with many organizations, among which the European Union and the World Bank are in the lead. Projects that we have implemented with the funds and loans obtained from the World Bank, the European Union and various other financial organizations enlighten the future of the Turkish National Education. (Çelik 2007, 3)

Although the opinion about external educational projects "enlightening the future" of Turkey is a relatively "political" piece of propaganda, depending on the perception of what "darkness" is, it is a concrete reality that those projects "shape" the Turkish educational system and its "future." In this context, the purpose of this chapter is to present the effects of the projects implemented between 1985 and 2011. These projects will be examined in terms of their goals, financial structures, implementation results, and observable effects. The chapter will concentrate on the projects implemented during the AKP era, and will try to show that educational projects implemented within SAPs serve to integrate Turkey into globalized capitalism. This chapter also argues that external educational projects implemented in Turkey constitute the implementation tools of neoliberal education policies.

General Features of External Educational Projects

External educational projects have common features in terms of planning and implementation processes. Although those projects seem to be unrelated, the policies actualized through them are similar to and support of each other.

The consistency of those projects in following neoliberal education policies is made possible by the WB's involvement in each phase of the projects. In the planning phase of the projects, a planning team is formed at the central organization of the Ministry, and this team becomes a project implementation team after the project has been approved by the WB. In this way, continuity exists between the planning and the implementation processes of the project. The WB possesses control over both the planning and the implementation teams. Moreover, the Bank also exercises control over procurement processes, which are based on international procurement bidding and are prerequisites to be eligible for a loan. Another prerequisite of the WB is the employment of consultants, who are generally from the United States and are paid by the WB. In this way, the WB increases its inducement and supervision power over the project via consultants who are not native to the country in which they work. Thus, the compliance of those projects with neoliberal education policies, is secured through the planning and implementation carried out under the tight control of the WB.

Effects of Projects on Educational Policies of the AKP Period

External educational projects can be seen as the most effective tools to spread the neoliberal education policies of central countries to surrounding countries. Before discussing the effects of external educational projects, it is important to briefly mention the criticism directed toward neoliberal educational policies in general. The common point underlined by the critiques (see Aslan 2008, Carnoy 2002, Gök 2002) is the loss of the right to education and the deepening of inequality in education in terms of the majority of the population.

Change in Educational Finance: Commercialization

Change in educational finance means privatization and commercialization in the educational system. This change can be formulated as a search for new resources in exchange for decreasing public contributions to educational expenditures, the inclusion of families in educational expenditures, and diversification in financial resources. The increase in educational expenditures by families in the AKP period is a concrete indicator of the change in educational financing. The amount that families allocate to education from their total expenditure increased from 1.3 percent to 2.0 percent between 2002 and 2010, respectively (TUIK 2011).

Increasing the diversity of resources in educational financing is one of the policies suggested by the WB within the SAPs. In a report by the WB regarding Turkey, the need to provide resource diversity in educational financing, and development of the educational enterprise were emphasized (WB 1990). The first example regarding efforts to increase resource diversity in educational financing is seen in the Non-Formal Vocational Training Project (YMEP) that is supported by the WB. One of the aims of this project, implemented in 1987, was to "establish[ing] circulating capital enterprises in 200 institutions" (YMEP 1987). Circulating capital enterprises are commercial enterprises established with the purpose of providing additional income to the institution through the sales of products and services produced at public institutions. This example shows that resource diversity in educational financing means transforming formal and nonformal vocational and technical education institutions into commercial enterprises. The implementation of enterprises that started in two hundred schools/institutions in 1987 has been intensified to all vocational and technical schools/institutions and universities in the AKP period.

Another application regarding resource diversity is the "school-based pilot project" implemented within the Basic Education Project-I (TEP-I). The Improvement Fund was established within this implementation in order to provide financial support to projects prepared by the elementary schools in eight provinces. The aim of this Fund is to transfer resources from the Project to the elementary schools in a way that will also deploy local resources. This application can be seen as an attempt to provide financial diversity by using local resources, and decreasing public educational expenditures. This transformation in educational financing is seen as a dimension of the restructuring of the public financing as a whole.

The importance of contributions by the surrounding area in terms of diversity in educational financing is emphasized continuously. One of the goals of the Secondary Education Project (OÖP) is "to provide contributions and the cooperation of the surrounding area according to regional educational needs parallel to the increase in the quality of education and to the Planned School Development Model [POGM] applications" (OÖP 2006, 16). POGM is a school management model developed within the National Education Development Project

(MEGP). With this model, School Development and Management Teams (OGYE) were established in the schools. OGYE consist of school managers, teachers, support personnel, parents, student representatives, parent-teacher association representatives, and representatives from nongovernmental organizations (NGOs), mukhtar (elected local district or/and village administrators), and chambers of commerce. Representatives from parent-teacher associations (PTAs) and chambers of commerce have a strategic importance in terms of the carrying out of neoliberal educational policies. The model envisions the contribution of parents to the school administrations as flowing through PTAs. However, this discourse about contributions is a deception, because one of the functions of the PTA is "to participate in the development of the financial resources of the school, in the effective and efficient use of these resources, and to make regulations for the provision of financial support by the parents" (*Official Gazette,* May 31, 2005). As can easily be seen, the diversity in educational financing that is emphasized in the projects (e.g., MEGP, TEP-I, OÖP) is intended to include financing by parents through PTAs in an image of democratic participation. Yet at the same time, the inclusion of a representative from the chambers of commerce on the team can be seen as an effort to open the schools to the control of the market.

The diversification of financing in educational institutions has also been supported through the educational planning approach. The strategic planning method employed by the educational planning approach, the frame of which was formed within the MEGP, began to be implemented first in high schools with the OÖP and then in all schools and institutions starting in 2010. The implementation of the strategic planning method in education complies with the localization policies of the WB, and contains two main dimensions: each school/institution will create its own resources and will be able to use these resources for whatever purposes it determines. For this model to work, the schools must move from requiring resources from the Ministry to instead identifying local resources . In other words, they should diversify their resources. This clearly points to a new approach in school management.

Change in Educational Management: Governance

The restructuring of educational management clearly shows the effects of external projects on education. The foundations of this restructuring were laid with the MEGP in 1990. One of the goals of the MEGP, which contains regulations related to the educational system as a whole, is to provide "economy and effectiveness in resource use by improving skills and by the application of management and business administration in the MoNE" (MEGP 1990, 10). Regulations in line with this goal have resulted in the structuring of school administrations within the "governance"[1] approach.

There are two dimensions of the transformation of the management structure of the MoNE within the framework of WB- and EU-supported projects. One of these dimensions is to support the MoNE central organization by establishing new departments that would implement projects "successfully"; and the other is to establish a new "governance" to become the dominant management approach in the schools.

"Independent" departments[2] directly responsible for part of a project have been established in the MoNE central organization within the framework of the MEGP goal that is mentioned above. These departments have functioned as "supreme boards" with some authorizations different from the already existing departments of the Ministry. Each of the newly established departments has moved toward realizing the project goals and employed a management approach different from the traditional bureaucratic functioning in doing this. Later, in almost all the projects implemented (the TEP-I, Strengthening the Vocational Education and Training System Project [MEGEP], the Modernization of Vocational and Technical Education Program [MTEM], the OÖP, the Promotion of Lifelong Learning [HBÖGP]), new departments were established in the Ministry's central organization or in the provinces, and new regulations were made that related to the MoNE's institutional and managerial structure. Interventions related to the transformation of the MoNE central organization were completed with a Legislative Decree approved in 2011. The organizational and management structure established with this Legislative Decree is the structure anticipated in the Green Paper (MoNE 2010a) prepared within the context of the EU-supported Capacity Building Support Project for the MoNE Project (MEBGEP). Thus, the transformation movement that started with the WB project (MEGP) has transformed the Ministry's central organization into a project unit through the EU project (MEBGEP).

The first reorganization related to the restructuring of school administration according to the governance approach in the WB and the EU-supported projects is the POGM, which was tried out in Curriculum Laboratory Schools (MLO) within the MEGP. MLO represent the pilot schools where improvements aimed for within the MEGP are tried out. Trials of new educational programs, management approaches, and technology utilization took place in MLOs within the POGM. All the regulations based on neoliberal policies that applied to the educational system and schools were first tried out in MLOs, and then extended to other schools starting in 1999 (MoNE 1999). Thus, an MLO has the features of a "laboratory'" for neoliberal policies, as its name implies. Intensification of the POGM that was developed in this laboratory has become the goal of the following projects. For example, intensification the effective school approach that employs continuous development and learning organization with POGM applications in all secondary schools was aimed for in the OÖP (OÖP 2006).

The most distinct feature of the POGM is the regulation that is related to the management approach implemented in MLOs and known as Total Quality Management (TQM).[3] TQM, developed to increase the productivity of profit-making enterprises, was accepted as the management method for educational institutions in 1999. Economic concepts, such as customer orientation, continuous improvement, participation, zero-defect, are included in TQM. Moreover, TQM transforms the education administrator into a manager of a profit-making company. This kind of management approach has the potential to transform schools into business organizations. External projects (MEGP, TEP-I, TEP-II, Support to Basic Education Program [TEDP], MEGEP, MTEM, OÖP, Vocational Education and Training [İKMEP], MEBGEP) have played a significant role in financing in-service training programs for the establishment of TQM in schools.

The latest development related to the change in management structure is the Performance Management System (PYS), the trial of which was completed at the end of 2011. The PYS is a control system to evaluate educational institutions and their employees. The most striking aspect of the system is that performance data will be used for the purposes of promotion, career development, career planning, and the rewarding of education employees. The PYS covers only the evaluation of MoNE provincial (city, town, school) organization employees. MoNE central organization employees and inspectors are excluded from the PYS. In the introductory booklet of the PYS, which is planned to be implemented in 2012, it is said that "through the work done within the OÖP context, the competence and skills of the institutions, managers, teachers, and other workers of our educational system are addressed in accordance with today's changing conditions, and a system named 'Performance Management System' has been developed" (MoNE 2011, 8). The main aim of the transformation of the management structure in MoNE central and provincial organizations and in schools and institutions is to guarantee the implementation of a curriculum that supports the changing economic and social structures. The ultimate goal of neoliberal education policies is to facilitate the education and training of individuals according to market needs. This is carried out through changes in curriculum.

Change in the Educational Curriculum: Elasticizing

So far, we have discussed how the education system is being commercialized in Turkey. In this part, we will examine how the curriculum was transformed in accordance with market expectations and the training of manpower (societal labor-power production). The evidence is hidden in the external educational projects implemented by the MoNE.

The structuring of the curriculum and instructional methods are among the issues most emphasized by the external projects. The new elementary school curriculum, developed according to a constructivist approach and implemented in 2005 within the TEDP, has transformed educational content into a form that will respond to market needs (Eğitim-Sen 2005). The new curriculum employs as its economic principles the "realization of sustainable economic development, consideration of regional economic differences in programs, meeting the manpower demands of the economy at sufficient levels, the raising of children with an entrepreneurial spirit, and the prioritization of being production oriented" (MoNE 2005, n.p.). It is not by coincidence that the aim is for students to acquire two of the nine skills listed here through the use of information technologies and entrepreneurship. It is one of the most salient goals in the projects (First Phase of the Education Framework Project-I [EÇP-I], TEDP, MEGEP, MTEM, OÖP, İKMEP) that the curriculum will be elasticized in all education types and at all levels from elementary school to the university so that it will meet market demands rapidly.

Information and communication technologies are seen as "pedagogical saviors"[4] in the process of preparing the society according to market expectations. As Aksoy (2005) emphasizes, with the discourse developed in this way, the view that utilizing the Internet and other educational technology products in education is the key to "quality education" has become a dominant view among families, students, teachers, and education specialists. An examination of the projects (MEGP, TEP-I, TEP-II, EÇP-I, EÇP-II, TEDP, OÖP) demonstrates that a significant portion of resources are allocated for the construction of a computer infrastructure. This would prepare all students for the "informatics" community of the future by making them computer literate. Individuals who have become familiar with computers will become "good" consumers of technology in the future.

Projects related to vocational and technical education aim at shaping education according to the market. These projects (Industrial Training Project, YMEP, MEGEP, MTEM) emphasize the skills required by the market, which must be brought into prominence; the strengthening of the school-market relationship; and the establishment of qualification areas based on vocational standards. The primary dynamic of this transformation is the quality demands of national and international capital and its representatives. The organizational structuring that will bring these demands into practice and direct the curriculum is realized through external educational projects.

The Vocational Qualifications Institute (MYK), an important organization in terms of directing a vocational and technical education curriculum, was established in 2006 within the MEGEP (Law no. 5554).[5] The role of the MYK in the system is "to prepare National Vocational Standards, and to provide structuring of vocational and technical education according to current needs and future trends" (MYK 2011, 8). As Rikowski (2011) emphasizes, this institutionalization, which proposes the structuring of vocational and technical education institutions based on not only knowledge and skills but also attitudes and behaviors required for the performance of a job, indicates that curriculum inspection is left to the market as a whole.

Training manpower according to market expectations is possible with elasticizing of the curriculum and through modular programming. Elasticizing of the curriculum and organizing it with a modular approach are the main aspects of the projects (MEGEP, MTEM, İKMEP, HBÖGP). The Vocational Education and Instruction Draft Strategy Document 2010–2013 developed with the MEGEP and revised with İKMEP (MoNE 2010b) proposes moving to a modular curriculum system and training teachers for the advertising of this system. The success of the projects depends largely on teachers, and teacher-training programs in line with the new curriculum are emphasized. These projects, while directing in-service training programs to provide help teachers adjust to the new curriculum concept, directly interferes with the higher education programs in terms of training teachers who will enter the system.

Conclusion

This chapter has examined the impact of external educational projects, implemented in Turkey since the 1980s, on the educational system and educational policies. This investigation shows that projects presented with the term "reform" serve neoliberal ideology and play an important role in articulating education to the market rather than meeting the education needs of the society.

Within this framework, neoliberal education policies have directed project goals, implementation processes, and project outcomes. Radical changes have been made in educational financing, educational management, and educational programs through these projects. These changes have two main purposes. The first purpose is the commodification of the educational system by weakening the public attitude and opening the market to international competition, and the second purpose is to create a society that consists of individuals who have the perception that there are no classes, borders, or inequalities.

The educational policies implemented during the AKP period show that the AKP is a loyal follower of, rather than a force for breaking with, the previous period in terms of external educational projects. However, this chapter contends that as the negative effects of neoliberal education policies on schools and students especially in poor communities become obvious, reactions to the AKP's policies will be inevitable.[6] In other words, educational policies of the AKP will result in a struggle between poor communities and the AKP in the near future.

Notes

1. The term "governance," derived from the word "government" and used for the first time in the report related to the development of Africa by the WB in 1989, have been used within the frameworks of "democratic" management concepts such as "transparency," "participation," and "rendering of account." The formation of a management structure according to the institutional regulations necessary for the implementation of the YUP programs lies behind the development of the WB concept of governance and the expression of it as "good governance" (Zabcı 2002). According to the *Governance Report* prepared by the WB in 1994, based on the experiences

obtained from the 455 development projects implemented in three regions, governance is "the implementation style of the power in the management of the economic and social resources of a country toward the purpose of development" (Bayramoğlu 2002). This power is becoming more and more centralized. Gill deciphers this type of power as an "attempt 'to issuing the constitution of a single global economy' as mentioned by the authority names of the WTO" (cited by Zabcı 2002, 156).
2. Units established within the MoNE central organization in the context of the NEDP are the Project Coordination Center, the Educational Research and Development Directorate, and the Management Evaluation and Development Directorate.
3. See Aslan and Küçüker (2011) for evaluations regarding the suitability of TQM, examined in the CLS model and then intensified in all of the schools, for the educational institutions.
4. See Apple (1989) regarding the concept of "pedagogical redeemer."
5. The Central Executive Board (ÇSGB), a related institution of the Ministry of Labor and Social Security, is a public institution that has a public entity, financial and administrative autonomy, and a special budget. The responsibility of the ÇSGB is to accredit, evaluate, and document the vocational and technical educational institutions and their programs. Thus, the MoNE has become open to the inspection of the ÇSGB, an institution that functions under market conditions, for the assessment and evaluation of its graduates.
6. One of the most striking results of the educational financing policies that have been insistently implemented by the AKP since 2002 is the resignation of fourteen school heads and ten deputy heads in Silvan, Diyarbakır, at the beginning of 2011, who "claim[ed] the inadequacy of the allocation provided and the lack of attendance in schools" (*Hürriyet* January 25, 2011).

References

Aksoy, Hüseyin H. "Orwell ve Huxley'in gelecek tasarımları çerçevesinde bir değerlendirme." *Eğitim Bilim Toplum* 3, no. 11 (2005): 54–67.
Apple, Michael W. *Teachers and Texts: A Political Economy of Class and Gender Relations in Education*. New York: Routledge, 1989.
Aslan, Gülay. "Türkiye Üniversitelerinde Neoliberal Değişim: Öğretim Üyelerinin Kavram ve Uygulamalara Ilişkin Değerlendirmeleri." PhD diss., Ankara University, Ankara, Turkey, 2008.
Aslan, Gülay, and Erdal Küçüker. "Türkiye'de Toplam Kalite Yönetimi Modelinin Eğitimin Kamu Hizmeti Niteliğine ve Eğitim Öğretim Süreçlerine Uygunluğu." *G.Ü. Sosyal Bilimler Araştırmaları Dergisi* 6, no. 2 (2011): 202–224.
Bayramoğlu, Sonay. "Küreselleşmenin Yeni Siyasal Iktidar Modeli: Yönetişim." *Praksis* 7 (2002): 85–116.
Boratav, Korkut. "Yapısal uyum ve bölüşüm: Uluslararası bir bilanço." In *Türk-İş 1997 yıllığı 1990'ların bilançosu*, 31–45. Ankara: Türkiye İşçi Sendikaları Konfederasyonu, 1997.

Carnoy, Martin. "What Does Globalization Mean for Educational Change? A Comparative Approach." *Comparative Education Review* 46, no. 1 (2000): 1–9.
Çelik, Hüseyin. *Proje Günlüğü: Ortaöğretim projesi bilgilendirme materyali*. Ankara: MoNE, 2007.
Chomsky, Noam. *Halkın Sırtından Kazanç*. Translated by Barış Zeren and Deniz Hakyemez. Istanbul: OM Ekonomi-Politik, 2000.
Crossley, Michael. "Bridging Cultures and Tradition in the Reconceptualisation of Comparative and International Education." *Comparative Education* 36, no. 3 (2000): 319–332.
Eğitim ve Bilim Emekçileri Sendikası. *Yeni Ilköğretim Müfredatının Değerlendirilmesi*. Ankara: Eğitim-Sen, 2005.
Ellwood, Wayne. *Küreselleşmeyi Anlama Kılavuzu*. Istanbul: Metis, 2002.
Ercan, Fuat. *Eğitim ve Kapitalizm Neoliberal Eğitim Ekonomisinin Eleştirisi*. Istanbul: Bilim, 1998.
Giroux, Henry A. *Eleştirel Pedagojinin Vaadi*. Translated by Umre D. Tuna. Istanbul: Kalkedon, 2008.
Gök, Fatma. "Eğitimin Özelleştirilmesi." In *Neoliberalizmin Tahribatı 2: Türkiye'de Ekonomi, Toplum ve Cinsiyet*, edited by Neşecan Balkan and Sungur Savran, 94–110. Istanbul: Metis, 2002.
Güler, Birgül A. "Yapısal Uyarlanma Reformları ve Devlet." In *Türk-İş 1997 Yıllığı 1990'ların Bilançosu*, 74–84. Ankara: Türkiye İşçi Sendikaları Konfederasyonu, 1997.
Hürriyet. "Silvan'da 12 Okul Müdürü Görevinden İstifa Etti." October 25, 2011.
Kazgan, Gülten. *Türkiye Ekonomisinde Krizler (1929–2001) "Ekonomi Politik" Açısından Bir İnceleme*. Istanbul: Bilgi Üniversitesi, 2005.
Kwiek, Marek. "Yüksek Öğretimi Yeniden Düşünürken Yeni Bir Paradigma Olarak Küreselleşme: Gelecek İçin Göstergeler." *Kuram ve Uygulamada Eğitim Bilimleri* 2, no. 1 (2002): 133–154. Translated by Emrah Akbaş.
MoNE (Ministry of National Education). *MEB Projeler Koordinasyon Merkezi Başkanlığı Stratejik Planı 2010–2014*. Ankara: MoNE, 2009.
———. *Mesleki Eğitim ve Öğretim Taslak Strateji Belgesi 2010–2013*. Ankara: MoNE, 2010b.
———. "Milli Eğitim Bakanlığı Müfredat Laboratuar Okulu Uygulamalarının Yaygınlaştırılmasına Ilişkin Yönerge." *Tebliğler Dergisi* 2506 (1999): 16–25.
———. *Performans Yönetim Sistemi Taslak Kitabı*. Ankara: MoNE, 2011.
———. *Program Tanıtımı*. Ankara: MoNE, 2005.
———. *Yeni Yönetişim Modeli Yeşil Belge II. Taslağı*. Ankara: MoNE, 2010a.
MYK (Vocational Qualifications Institute). *2011–2015 Stratejik Planı*. Ankara: MYK, 2011.
Official Gazette. "Okul-Aile Birliği Yönetmeliği." May 31, 2005.
Önder, İzzettin. *AKP Karanlığında Ekonomi, Siyaset, Dış Politika ve Eğitim: Türkiye Nereye Götürülüyor?* Istanbul: Dünya, 2004.
Rikowski, Glenn. *Marksist Eğitim Kuramı ve Radikal Pedagoji*. Translated by Cumhur Atay. Istanbul: Kalkedon, 2011.

Stewart, F. "Eğitim ve Uyum: 1980'lerin Deneyimi ve 90'lar İçin Bazı Dersler." In *Piyasa Güçleri ve Küresel Kalkınma*, edited by Rene Prendergast and Frances Stewart, translated by İdil Eser, 167–204. Istanbul: Yapı Kredi, 1995.
TUIK (Turkish Statistical Institute). *Hane Halkı Tüketim Harcamaları Anketi*. Ankara: TUIK, 2011.
Ünal, L. Işıl. "Eğitimin Yapısal Uyumu." *Özgür Üniversite Forumu* 17 (2002): 125–133.
WB (World Bank). "Staff Appraisal Report" No. 8328-TU. 1990. http://web.worldbank.org/external/projects (accessed May 2011).
Williamson, John. "What Washington Means by Policy Reform." In *Latin American Adjustment: How Much Has Happened?*, edited by John Williamson, 7–38. Washington, DC: Peterson Institute for International Economics, 1990.
Zabcı, Filiz Ç. "Dünya Bankasının Küresel Pazar İçin Yeni Stratejisi: Yönetişim." *Ankara Üniversitesi Siyasal Bilgiler Dergisi* 57, no. 3 (2002): 151–179.

9

The New Stream of Trade Unionism: The Case of Eğitim-Bir-Sen in Turkey

Duygun Göktürk, Gökçe Güvercin, and Onur Seçkin[1]

Under the onslaught of global neoliberal policies, the fissure between the public and private spheres has deepened and resulted in deep structural changes in public employment regulations. The economic decisions of January 24, 1980, which laid the foundations for the market economy in Turkey, initiated a new structuring process by replacing public administration with a public management system (Köroğlu 2005). Thus, the nature of being a public employee began to alter. Concepts related to private employment, like flexibility, performance-based evaluations, and contractual and temporary personnel hiring, have been brought into public employment policies.

In the late 1980s, the Islamic political parties' rise to power benefited from new political openings, and they started to integrate their indigenous networks into the state (Öniş 1997). The origins of the present-day conservative-moderate Justice and Development Party (AKP) can be traced back to those years. The overwhelming majority of the population voted for the AKP in the 2002, 2007, and 2011 general elections, and the party solidified its rule in those elections.

The neoliberal attack on the state during the AKP period cannot be considered as "a single monolithic manifestation" (Steger and Roy 2010, 11). Along with the AKP period, the party put extreme faith in disseminating its ideological maxims through education. In this context, teacher's unions can be considered as the active sites for legitimizing and perpetuating the party's ideological credo in the field of education. With respect to this, we have also witnessed dramatic changes in the area of trade unions. The trade union of teachers, *Eğitim-Bir-Sen*[2] (Union of Unity of Educators), established in 1992, has become as one of the largest public employees' institutions in Turkey. During AKP rule (2002–present), the unpredictable increase in the number of *Eğitim-Bir-Sen* members drew a great deal of attention. While in 2002 the number of *Eğitim-Bir-Sen* members was 18,028, it then increased rapidly to 195,695 in 2011 (see Table 9.4), corresponding to a 985 percent increase. On the other hand, the number of members of *Eğitim-Sen* (Union of Education and Science Laborers) decreased by 22 percent, and number of members of *Türk-Eğitim-Sen* (Education, Teaching and Science Professions Public Employee Union of Turkey) increased by 42 percent. While other trade unions showed limited progress during this historical period, such a massive bounce in the number of *Eğitim-Bir-Sen* members is unusual and needs to be examined. In 2011, based on its having the highest ratio of membership, *Eğitim-Bir-Sen* has become a nationwide authorized union that has the right to carry out collective bargaining meetings with the government in the field of education and science.

In this chapter, we intend to describe the presence of the trade union *Eğitim-Bir-Sen* in its multiple dimensions. The role assigned to and attained by *Eğitim-Bir-Sen* will be examined with a particular focus on the agenda of the union's regular meetings. Analysis of the meetings mainly tends to reify in what ways the Union engages in neoliberal policy regulations and collaborates with AKP policies while at the same framing its agenda as one of opposition.

Trade Unionism in the Field of Education

The roots of teacher's unions in Turkey go back to the Ottoman Empire period. The first teachers' association *Encümen-i Muallimin* (Board of Teachers) was established in 1908 and was followed by *Türkiye Muallimler ve Muallimeler Cemiyetler Birliği* (Confederation of Female and Male Teachers Community)—from 1921 to 1935—as the first central organization of teachers in the country.

With the establishment of the republic in 1923, the Republican People's Party was formed and stayed in power until 1950. The period between the years of 1923 and 1950 is described as a single-party era that created a new political and economic agenda in Turkish society. According to Altunya (1998), the regulations and laws issued during this era enforced a strict autonomy between trade unions and the state. As a key example, with the *Law of Takrir-i Sükun* (Maintenance of

Order Law) organizing by teachers in any community was limited only to the membership in *Halk Evleri* (People's Houses), social assistance foundations, and local teachers' associations (Altunya 1998).

The historical and polity routes available to unions in Turkey have changed tremendously with military interventions. In Turkey's political history, military interventions can be considered as one of the most essential historical contexts that have generated a convoluted relationship between the state and trade unions. The country has weathered four military coups: May 27, 1960; March 12, 1971; September 12, 1980, and the "postmodern coup" of February 28, 1997. With the constitutional change that resulted from the 1960 coup, public employees' right to establish trade unions gained a legal basis. This right was later rescinded by the 1971 coup, which removed the right to establish a union and become a member (Altunya 1998). Subsequently, instead of unions, the government offered legitimacy to associations in Turkish society. The political and economic climate was altered by the third military coup in 1980, which promulgated structural adjustments in policies in accordance with the neoliberal agenda of globalization. Putting an extreme faith in the market economy was not in collaboration with the union movement in Turkey, and the governments in this period instituted bans on the activities of associations and arrested active members of those associations. In short, teachers were prohibited to be either a member of a trade union or an association, which, in the meantime, became an ideological decision. The 1990s paved the way for the resurgence of the union movement. Firstly *Eğitim-İş* (Union of Education and Science Profession Public Employees) and *Eğit-Sen* (Union of Education and Science Laborers) were established, and then they were united under the name of *Eğitim-Sen*. In 1992, two additional teacher's unions were founded: *Türk-Eğitim-Sen* and *Eğitim-Bir-Sen*.

Trade Unions during the AKP Period

The AKP has been in power since 2002. It came to power as a single-party government in the last three nationwide elections. During the AKP years, unionization ratios increased from 29.9 percent (2002) to 52.5 percent (2011), and from 47.9 percent (2002) to 63.7 (2011) percent among all public employees, and among public employees who have the right to become a union member, respectively (Devlet Personel Dairesi Başkanlığı 2001). Following the implementation of the Public Employees Unions Law in 2001, the Ministry of Labor and

Table 9.1 Unionization rates between 2002 and 2011

Status of Public Officers/Years	2002	2005	2008	2011
Number of public employees*	21,79,150	20,99,368	21,54,789	22,74,041
Number of public employees who have the right of being a union member**	13,57,326	15,84,490	16,91,299	18,74,543
Number of union member public employees***	6,50,770	7,47,617	9,30,397	11,95,102
Unionization ratios among all public employees (%)	29.9	35.6	43.2	52.5
Unionization ratios among public employees who have the right of being a union member (%)	47.9	47.2	55	63.7

Source: *Official Gazette* (Journal) 2002, 2005, 2008, 2011; DPB 2011.
*State Personnel Presidency Statistics.
**Numbers given in the *Official Gazette*.
***Numbers given in the *Official Gazette*.

Social Security began to keep records of official statistics. According to the "Public Workers/Employees Records" in 2011, the number of employees hired in public institutions was 2,274,041. But due to legal regulation, judges, prosecutors, local authorities, military officers, and police forces cannot be members of unions (see Table 9.1[3]). In the following part, we will present some of the fundamental statistics related to the AKP years.

The total number of members in three prominent public employee confederations[4] was greater than one hundred thousand in Turkey in 2011. Table 9.2[5] lists the names of those three confederations with the statistical values.

Based on the statistical information in Table 9.2, the number of *Memur-Sen* members has shown a very large increase over the past decade, as the ratio of members was 6.4 percent out of all members in 2002, and then it reached its highest ratio in 2011 with 43 percent.

Table 9.3 shows membership rates of the public employees who work in the education and science fields. Table 9.4 shows the most prominent unions and confederations.

In 2002, there were only five teacher trade unions; that number increased to 23 in 2011. The largest three teacher unions in Turkey are dependent on the three largest confederations.

So, in what ways can we interpret these statistics? The increasing numbers of union members cannot only be interpreted as a sign of the democratization process in society, but on the contrary, can also be

Table 9.2 Statistics for confederations between 2002 and 2011

Name of the Confederation/Years	2002	2005	2008	2011
KESK (Public Laborers Unions Confederation)	2,62,348	2,64,060	2,23,460	2,32,083
%	40.3	35.3	24	19.4
TURKIYE KAMU-SEN (Turkey Public Employees' Unions Confederation)	3,29,065	3,16,038	3,57,841	3,94,497
%	50.6	42.3	38.5	33
MEMUR-SEN (Public Employees' Unions Confederation)	41,871	1,59,154	3,14,701	5,15,378
%	6.4	21.3	33.8	43.1
Others*	17,486	8,365	34,395	53,144
%	2.7	1.1	3.7	4.5
Total	6,50,770	7,47,617	9,30,397	11,95,102

Source: Official Gazette (Journal) 2002, 2005, 2008, 2011.
*Numbers of members of other confederations and independents.

Table 9.3 Membership rates of public employees

Years/Membership	2002	2005	2008	2011
Number of public employees who have the right of being a union member	6,53,962	7,62,728	8,13,657	9,09,168
Number of public employees who are in the meantime a member of union	2,95,235	3,28,174	4,01,482	5,24,484
Ratio %	45.1	43.03	49.34	57.68

Source: Official Gazette (Journal) 2002, 2005, 2008, 2011.

considered as a rendering of the union movement as into something uniform, homogeneous, and static. In the following part, we will discuss this further.

According to the AKP party programs, democratization efforts were resumed under the AKP regime and entrenched in the party program of 2011 under the subtitle of "Democratization and Civil Society." The program clarifies that the AKP "will re-determine the status of the public employee and take the unionization and union rights of public employees in hand again" (AKP, 2011). Also, the part titled "Public Employee Administration" formulates that the AKP will "abolish obstacles to trade unions and political rights, and avoid

Table 9.4 Unions within confederations

Confederation	Union	2002	2005	2008	2011
Türkiye Kamu-Sen	Türk Eğitim-Sen	125863	127846	146127	179300
		42.6	39	36.4	19.72
KESK	Eğitim-Sen	149383	139429	112366	115949
		50.6	42.5	28	12.75
Memur-Sen	Eğitim-Bir-Sen	18028	58372	119046	195695
		6.1	17.8	29.7	21.52
Others		1961	2527	23943	33540
		0.7	0.8	6	3.68
Total		295235	328174	401482	524484
		45.1	43.03	49.34	57.7

Source: *Official Gazette* (Journal) 2002, 2005, 2011.

the unnecessary interventions of politicians in trade unions and their members" (AKP n.d.). Under "Working Life," as one of the significant parts that portrays the implementations, the party indicates that "freedom of the organization will lead up to it, unionization will be promoted, and changes in regulations will be done to provide union rights to public employees, which includes strike and collective bargaining rights and freedom" (AKP n.d.). In their proclamation for the national election in June 2011, the AKP claimed that the party had provided collective bargaining rights to public employees through partial changes in the constitution, and would abolish obstacles for unionization and collective contracts, and that unionization rates and utilization rates from collective contracts would be increased to the European Union average level (AKP 2011).

In 2010, partial changes in the constitution were one of the most debated issues in the context of union rights. After the constitutional referendum in September 2010, the changes in the collective contract right of public employees was accepted, but legal regulations have not been actualized yet. The government and confederations discussed the new law, and a draft proposal of the law, which consisted of limited rights of collective bargaining for public employees, was conveyed to the cabinet. However, the draft contained no item related to the right to strike (*Memurlarsitesi.net* 2011).

Despite the "positive" incentives offered in official documents and party programs, the party's formula for trade unions has been extensively criticized. According to the International Trade Union Confederation's (ITUC) *Annual Survey of Violations of Trade Union Rights 2011* in Turkey, in 2010, many workers were forced to resign from the union of their choice to join management friendly organizations. The worrying trend of judicial harassment of trade unions continued, and many workers were laid off due to their union membership. The Constitution was partially amended in 2010 to grant more freedoms; however, trade union rights remain excessively restricted by law. (ITUC 2011, n.d.)

The ITUC report also states that "the public sector union KESK has in general been hit very hard by systematic judicial harassment" (ITUC 2011, n.d.). The *2010 Progress Report* for Turkey, published by European Commission, declares that in spite of the fact that constitutional amendments have broadened trade-union rights in public service areas, trade-union rights are not in line with European Union (EU) standards and International Labor Organization (ILO) conventions. According to this report, "Lack of consensus among social partners and the government is an obstacle to the adoption of new legislation. The constitutional amendment package did not introduce the right to strike for civil servants" (European Commission 2010, 29). The report *Regulations Related to Working Life and Loss of Rights in the AKP Period (2003–2011)*, published by *Basın-İş* (Press and Graphic and Packaging Industry Workers' Union), (2011) also argues that violations of trade-union rights have increased during the AKP period. The report also asserts that the AKP has established trade unions in conformity with the government, and that these unions have compelled workers to leave their own trade unions and become members of these unions that have close relations with the government, citing the example of *Memur-Sen*.

The Case of Eğitim–Bir–Sen

Eğitim-Bir-Sen was established in the early 1990s by Mehmet Akif Inan and his colleagues. Inan can be considered as one of the prominent figure in the union's history, who began chairing the confederation *Memur-Sen* in 1995, and chaired both *Eğitim-Bir-Sen* and *Memur-Sen* until his death in 2000. The union's history of its presidency indicates that the professional backgrounds of the majority of the presidents are affiliated with religious studies. Before we engage in a discussion of how the union frames and spins its messages to attract an attention and public support, it is important to address the following information in this context. This chapter does not aim to expand the personal histories of the union presidents, but affirms that it is in tension with mobilizing unions' constituents and with the framing of the unions' messages.

One of the attributes of *Eğitim-Bir-Sen* echoes nationalist ideology. The logo of the union, with its lectern, laurel branches, and torch, can be interpreted as a signifier of traditional education through the lectern, peace through the laurel branches, and modern national education through the firebrand (İnce and Battal, 2004). According to a report written by two union administrators, the characterization of union politics was framed within the meaning system of the East and preserved in this statement: "The Eastern model of seeking rights" (İnce and Battal, 2004). The report also clarifies that the union aims to cherish the ideal of nationalism and legitimizes this order through its messages, potential constituents, and members.

Promoting the union's political agenda and influencing policy makers require what Tarrow (1994) calls a legitimate "repertoire of contention." In this vein, the questions of How does the union translate its ideas into practice? How can we interpret the Union's repertoire of contention? Is it confrontational, conventional, or any other form? need to be examined. In the first place, in reference to İnce and Battal (2004), the debate about the union's collective-action approach diverges from the concepts of a "Marxist approach," an "ideological approach," and a "class-based approach." In other words, *Eğitim-Bir-Sen* is not centering its struggle on the "logic" of structural strains and the advocates who say that that this type of unionism has disrupted the labor peace of employees instead of protecting their rights, and has caused employees to remain distant to trade unions. From the standpoint of *Eğitim-Bir-Sen*, trade unions are regarded as nongovernmental organizations (NGOs), and NGOs are institutions that direct government activities (İnce and Battal 2004). This most clearly takes the form of emerging nonconfrontational interaction between the state and unions, which enables the state (or governments) to interrupt the repertoire of contention.

On the other hand, *Eğitim-Bir-Sen* states that, "keeping the union always away from ideological and political structuring in every place" and "treating all political parties equally" (*Eğitim-Bir-Sen*, n.d.) are two of their major principles, which is in contradiction to their course of action, as outlined below. In this respect, *Eğitim-Bir-Sen* has been extensively criticized on the grounds of its developing a close relationship with the AKP. For instance, in the last national election on June 12, 2011, many administrators of *Memur-Sen* and especially the affiliated trade union *Eğitim-Bir-Sen* resigned from their positions to be deputy candidate of the AKP, for which resignation was a requirement in order to be candidate. The General Secretary of *Eğitim-Bir-Sen* was the deputy candidate of the AKP in the 2011 national election. Although he could not be elected as a deputy, he was appointed to be the deputy minister of Labor and Social Security.

The union's triennial meeting of the General Assembly can be considered as a place in which the extension of the governments' role in the union movement and the political agenda of the Union are formulated. Since its establishment, four assembly meetings have been held, and they were a composite of representatives from the government and various public institutions.

During these assemblies, ministers of the Ministry of National Education (MoNE) highlighted the ongoing negotiations between the principles of neoliberalism and the union movement, with a particular focus on a "new" stream of trade unionism. Through the marginalization of other teacher trade unions, the ruling party has rendered a new form of trade union movement (*Eğitim-Bir-Sen* 2011a). This ideological context suggests us to revisit Manfred B. Steger and Ravi K. Roy's definition of the neoliberal agenda of globalization, which perpetuates itself through three intertwined manifestations: "(1) an ideology; (2) a mode of governance; (3) a policy package" (Steger and Roy 2010, 11). Based on this, we argue that the neoliberal restructuring of Turkish society produced a new vision of a struggle that should develop intimate ties with the ruling party's ideological stance, mode of governance, and policy package in order to validate itself. The most visible impact of this nonconfrontational interaction defines "new" functional requirements that trade unions must adhere to in order to function and find validation. This ideological function establishes and maintains itself through persuasive frames. In this vein, we apply Hank Johnston's (2010) conceptualization of "framing" in our reading of *Eğitim-Bir-Sen*. According to Johnston, framing is a process by which to maximize the public's attention to a "movement," and its qualities can be listed as follows:

- Frame alignment refers to how social movements can make their frames more attractive and persuasive.
- Frame resonance and idea capture the degree to which potential constituents find the movement's framing compelling.
- Master frames are more general cultural currents and ideas that are popular and effective. (Johnston 2011, 80)

By deploying Johnston's model of framing, we argue that the prime minister's, the Ministry of Education's, and the president of the Higher Education Council's attendance at the union's meetings; their appreciation of the union's framing of the headscarf ban issue and coefficient practice;[6] their willingness to collaborate with *Eğitim-Bir-Sen* and *Memur-Sen;* their focus on how an ideal union should be, with the indication that unions should advocate for rights and freedom rather than struggle against ideological oppression, all contributed to generate interest in and sympathy for the union (*Akhaberci* April 16, 2011). As a clear affirmation of this process, during the Eighteenth National Education Council, 220 proposed decisions were accepted as advisory jurisdictions for the future policies of the MoNE. Two of the accepted proposals in particular are important, and are in line with conservative nature of *Eğitim-Bir-Sen*. One of the decisions concerned their giving in to allow Islamic divinity students to start school beginning in the fifth grade. The other one provided for a continuation of compulsory religious courses in primary and secondary school, which does not address and is not in accordance with the constitutional right to religion, which is defined as providing elective religious education opportunity to parents who are willing to send their children to those schools (*Eğitim-Bir-Sen* 2011b, *Eğitim-Bir-Sen* 2011c). Similarly, these cases support our arguments.

Conclusion

Deriving from these analyses, with the increasing power of the AKP governments in Turkish society, there is considerable pressure not only to reformulate the sphere in which education is carried out but also to constrain and devalue the forms of organized struggle in society.

Through an attempt to consolidate an alternative understanding of collective action, the AKP governments have been trying to transform the teacher's unions. This transformation has been perpetuated through the rationalization of policies in education with an increasing complexity of the social division of labor. In addition, such a transformation does not come through "collective action" performed on the streets, or through strikes and petitions but mostly as a result of "silent action" that engages in and is supported by governmental policies and that collaborates with the ruling powers.

The practice of organized struggle in *Eğitim-Bir-Sen* indicates that some forms of collective action cannot be properly understood unless a union's organizational structure and policies (administration-related policies and intraorganization regulations and implementations) and its interaction with the actors in the political realm are examined together. In this respect, this chapter argues that *Eğitim-Bir-Sen* engages in consensual overlapping with the ruling powers and articulate its endeavors as part and parcel of this kind of political engagement. In a larger context, such an articulation serves to perpetuate the interests of neoliberal policies and the involvement of the teacher unions as forms of collective struggle in the neoliberal model of education.

As the meetings and speeches demonstrate, *Eğitim-Bir-Sen* structures and constitutes its agenda in collaboration with the state in general and the AKP government in particular. This collaboration cannot be regarded as a guarantee of the democratic rights of employees and members but rather as fetters upon the potential attitudes that can challenge the relations of domination and, in the meantime, it shifts the emphasis away from a concentration on the multivocal political realities and heterogeneous structures of society.

Notes

1. *Authors' names are listed alphabetically.*
2. Rather than use the English form of the word for "trade unions" in Turkey, e.g., the Union of Educators (UE), we prefer to use the Turkish version (*Eğitimciler Birliği Sendikası* or *Eğitim-Bir-Sen*). This approach will be applied to other trade union names and abbreviations as appropriate at the beginning of this paper.
3. Compiled and calculated from various statistical data published in the *Official Gazette* (Journal) 2002, 2005, 2008, 2011, and DPB 2001.[4] The notion of "repertoire of contention" developed by Charles Tilly frames "the whole set of means that a group has for making claims of different kinds on individuals or groups" so it is therefore "not only what people do when they make a claim; it is what they know how to do and what society has come to expect them to choose to do from within a culturally sanctioned and empirically limited set of options" (Tarrow 1993:283). According to Tarrow (1993:289), "the most important contribution of Tilly's concept of the repertoire is to help us disaggregate the popular notion of protest into its conventional and less conventional components."
4. Confederations are umbrella organizations for trade unions in different service branches, in the same way as are worker and employer confederations.
5. Compiled and calculated from various statistical data published in the *Official Gazette* (Journal) 2002, 2005, 2008, and 2011.
6. The coefficient practice was put into effect during the February 28 period in the late 1990s, when the military forced the elected pro-Islamic government at the time to resign. Critics say the practice was designed to hold

back graduates of *Imam-Hatip* high schools from entering universities. When the AKP came to power in 2002, attempts were made to end the coefficient practice a number of times. The attempts were first blocked by former president Ahmet Necdet Sezer and the Council of State. Another amendment in 2010 was not a complete solution to the problem either. The law was also amended to solve the coefficient problem so that future blocks by the Council of State will be averted (For details, see: http://www.hurriyetdailynews.com/default.aspx?pageid=438&n=yok-to-lift-8216coefficient8217-practice-return-fees-of-the-past-2011-09-15).

References

Akhaberci. "Başbakan Erdoğan Memur-Sen Genel Kurulunda Konuşması." April 16, 2011. http://www.akhaberci.com/siyaset/basbakan-erdogan-memur-sen-genel-kurulunda-konusmasi-video-izle (accessed June 2011). AKP. "Declaration of General Election of JDP." 2011. http://www.akparti.org.tr/upload/documents/beyanname2011.pdf (accessed June 2011).

———. "Başbakan Erdoğan Memur-Sen Genel Kurulunda Konuşması." April 16, 2011. http://www.akhaberci.com/siyaset/basbakan-erdogan-memur-sen-genel-kurulunda-konusmasi-video-izle (accessed June 2011). AKP. "Parti Programı." n.d. http://www.akparti.org.tr/site/akparti/parti-programi (accessed October 2011).

Altunya, Niyazi. *Türkiye'de Öğretmen Örgütlenmesi 1908–2008*. Ankara: Ürün Yayınları, 1998.

Apple, Michael W., and Susan Jungck. "You Don't Have to Be a Teacher to Teach This Unit: Teaching, Technology, and Gender in The Classroom." *American Educational Research Journal* 27, no. 2 (1990): 227–251.

Başbakanlık. "Kamu Görevlileri Sendikalari Kanunu." 2001. http://mevzuat.basbakanlik.gov.tr/Metin.Aspx?MevzuatKod=1.5.4688&sourceXmlSearch=&MevzuatIliski=0 (accessed October 2011).

Basın-İş. "AKP Döneminde (2003–2011) Çalışma Yaşamına Dair Düzenlemeler ve Hak Kayıpları Raporu." 2011. http://www.basin-is.org/arastirma/arastirmalar.html (accessed September 2011).

Devlet Personel Başkanlığı. "Kamu İdarelerindeki Kadro ve Pozisyonların Yıllara Göre Dolu Kadro Dağılımı." 2011. http://www.dpb.gov.tr/dpb_istatistikler.html 9 (accessed September 12, 2011)

Eğitim-Bir-Sen. "İlkelerimiz." n.d. http://www.egitimbirsen.org.tr/sendika.php?cid=33 (accessed October 2011).

———. "Tarihçe." n.d. http://www.egitimbirsen.org.tr/sendika.php?cid=32 (accessed June 2011).

———. "İlkelerimiz." n.d. http://www.egitimbirsen.org.tr/sendika.php?cid=33 (accessed October 2011).

———. "4. Olağan Genel Kurulumuz Yapıldı." 2011a. http://www.egitimbirsen.org.tr/detay.php?id=138481&cid=52&keyword=Genel%20Kurul (accessed June 2011).

———. "18. Milli Eğitim Şurası ve Sendikamız." 2011b. http://www.egitimbirsen .org.tr/detay.php?id=137951&cid=52&keyword=%FEura (accessed October 2011).

———. "220 Kararın Alındığı Şura'ya Damgamızı Vurduk." 2011c. http://www .egitimbirsen.org.tr/detay.php?id=137888&cid=52&keyword=%FEura (accessed October 2011).

European Commission. "Turkey 2010 Progress Report." 2010. SEC(2010) Brussels. November 9, 2010. http://ec.europa.eu/enlargement/pdf/key_documents/2010/package/tr_rapport_2010_En.pdf (accessed June 2011).

İnce, Tahir, and Erol Battal. *Öğretmen Örgütlenmeleri ve Eğitim-Bir-Sen.* Ankara: *Eğitim-Bir-Sen* Yayınları, 2004.

ITUC (International Trade Union Confederation). "Annual Survey of Violations of Trade Union Rights." 2011. http://survey.ituc-csi.org/Turkey. html?lang=en#tabs-1 (accessed October 2011).

Johnston, Hank. *States and Social Movements.* Cambridge, UK: Polity Press, 2011.

Köroğlu, Özlem. "Kamu İşletmeciliği Anlayışı ve Kamu İstihdamına Etkileri." PhD diss., Ankara University, Ankara, Turkey, 2005.

Memur-Sen. *Gündoğdu: Toplu Sözleşme Yasası, Seçimden Önce Çıkmalı.* 2011. http://www.memursen.org.tr/haberdetay.php?fide=2197 9 (accessed October 2011).

Memurlarsitesi.net. *4688 Sendikalar Kanunu Değişiklik Tasarısı Taslağı.* 2011. http://www.memurlarsitesi.net/4688-sendikalar-kanunu-degis iklik-tasarisi-taslagi-h63903.html (accessed November 2011).

Official Gazette. "Kamu Görevlileri Sendikaları ile Konfederasyonların Üye Sayıları, İstatistikleri." No. 27987. July 7, 2011.

———. "Kamu Görevlileri Sendikaları ile Konfederasyonların Üye Sayıları, İstatistikleri." No. 26935. July 13, 2008.

———. "Kamu Görevlileri Sendikaları ile Konfederasyonların Üye Sayıları, İstatistikleri." No. 25868. July 7, 2005.

———. "Kamu Görevlileri Sendikaları ile Konfederasyonların Üye Sayıları, İstatistikleri." No. 24808. July 7, 2002.

———. "Kamu Görevlileri Sendikaları Kanunu." No. 24460. July 12, 2001.

Öniş, Ziya. "The Political Economy of Islamic Resurgence in Turkey: The Rise of the Welfare Party in Perspective." *Third World Quarterly* 18, no. 4 (1997): 743–766.

Steger, Manfred B., and Roy Ravi K. *Neoliberalism: A Very Short Introduction.* New York: Oxford University Press, 2010.

Tarrow, Sidney. *Power in Movement: Social Movements, Collective Action and Politics.* New York: Cambridge University Press, 1994.

III

The AKP and Neoliberal-Conservative Reconstruction in Education

10

The Marketization of Higher Education in Turkey (2002–2011)

Nevzat Evrim Önal

The neoliberal transformation of higher education is a process that has been occurring across an area far wider than Turkey, especially in the last decade. The most dramatic example of this is the Bologna Process administered by the European Union (EU) but covering 49 countries[1] under European Higher Education Area (EHEA), of which Turkey is a member. This makes it impossible to analyze and criticize the neoliberal phenomenon within a framework that takes into account the prominent Islamic element in the politics and ideology of the Justice and Development Party (AKP) as the main determinant of the transformation of Turkish higher education system. Such an approach would have to view the transformation in a country-specific light and would fail to explain the reason for the similarities between the policies proposed by international actors and those policies carried out by the AKP.

This article asserts that the transformation of Turkish higher education is a result of neoliberalism, which the author of this article sees as the current political economy of imperialism. This transformation is carried out by the AKP in line with the policies suggested by imperialist institutions and the Turkish bourgeoisie according to their respective needs. The Islamist ideology stands out during the whole process; however, it reflects the political-ideological needs of the AKP as the ruling party as well as the need to use coercion in effecting a social transformation, which is definitely against the interests of Turkish society as a whole, particularly the working class.

Prominent Trends of Neoliberalism in Higher Education

Critical writings on the neoliberal transformation of higher education use a wide variety of definitions: commodification (Noble 2002), commercialization (Bok 2004), capitalization (Münch 2010), and so forth. This article uses the term "marketization" in a similar context to that used by Levidow (2002), meaning the overall transformation of higher education, which subordinates it to the needs of the capitalist market.

Higher education holds a dual purpose in the capitalist society: It provides the bourgeoisie with a necessary amount of properly skilled labor, and it reproduces and disseminates the ideology of the ruling class to the educated strata of the public.

The Keynesian welfare state (or its developmental counterpart in developing countries) rested on the sacrifice of some of the immediate material interests of the bourgeoisie in order to create a state apparatus that seemed neutral and acted as a mediator in the class struggle. In this model, state education was an important public good, and the place of universities outside the market gave them an important credibility as ideological apparatuses. Obviously, this concept of higher education was incompatible with neoliberalism, and even more so after the collapse of socialism in the Eastern Bloc, since in the absence of a real socialist alternative, coercion rapidly took the place of consent and a "neutral," inclusive university that served as part of the ideological apparatus was no longer needed (Readings 1996, 40). In this context, the neoliberal transformation of higher education can be summarized as a "realignment" of the higher education system to meet the contemporary needs of the bourgeoisie.[2] This realignment has to be brought about with substantial change. The transformation of Turkish higher education, which is part of the transformation of European higher education, is largely the result of this process.

This process was dramatically coined as the term "the death of universities" by Terry Eagleton (2010), who correctly stresses that the problem runs "much deeper than tuition fees." This chapter points in the same direction and defines three dominant, interlinked characteristics of this transformation. These characteristics will be abstracted here from policy documents produced by World Bank (WB), as that the views of the WB can be considered as representative of the views of neoliberal imperialism. To illustrate:

> The reform agenda of the 90s, and almost certainly extending well into the next century, is oriented to the market rather than to public

ownership or to governmental planning and regulation. Underlying the market orientation of tertiary education is the ascendance, almost worldwide, of market capitalism and the principles of neoliberal economics. (Johnstone et al. 1998, 5)

Privatization: The first prominent trend in the transformation of higher education is the privatization of higher education. This means a shift in the behavior of higher education institutions so that they become similar to, and in time indistinguishable from corporations.

This is brought about by neoliberal policies that cut off government funding. Indeed, universities in developed countries that enjoyed substantial government grants under Keynesian-type policies began to lose this funding in the neoliberalization process of the 1980s. As tax cuts shrank government budgets, the WB announced that "higher education [is] in crisis" (WB 1994, 1). After four years, it claimed that "an increasing reliance on tuition, fees, and the unleashed entrepreneurship of the faculty may be the only alternatives to a totally debilitating austerity" (Johnstone et al. 1998, 5).

Therefore, the private universities, which emerged as an important aspect of the privatization of higher education, are not the only "private" institutions in higher education. Under neoliberal economic policies, public universities too had to act like corporations, so they became "more 'private' than the stereotype of 'public,' even if they remain[ed] state owned, substantially tax-supported, and avowedly 'public' in their mission" (Johnstone et al. 1998, 5).

All this transformation goes hand in hand with the talk about institutional autonomy. However, the autonomy frequently mentioned in this context is autonomy from government, not from capital. The neoliberal university is autonomous from the government in the sense that it has to create and manage its own revenues (WB 1994, 10), but not from its new financiers. Indeed, by the agents of capital see any attempt at scientific autonomy as "professorial" and "elitist" (Johnstone et al. 1998, 5).

The privatization of higher education, accomplished by means of economic policy, is enshrouded in an ideological fog according to which students and the companies that will employ them are "stakeholders" in higher education, and therefore the university should be accountable to them. Implications of the accountability to bourgeois employers who would be employing the graduates would be dealt with further in this chapter. Accountability to students and parents, on the other hand, only means the transfer (and therefore, the privatization) of a sizable amount of the cost of higher education "to parents and students, who are the ultimate beneficiaries of higher education" (Johnstone et al. 1998, 5).

This "beneficiary" identification is one of the main elements of neoliberal ideology as it concerns education, particularly higher education, and it should be properly criticized. Neoliberal ideology contends that the student gains access to higher-paying jobs through his/her education; therefore, the cost burden of the education should be borne by him/her. The high unemployment ratio of the educated worldwide belies this, but as the competitive and consumerist ideology of this proposition takes hold, tertiary education becomes the necessary qualification to "employability," not even "employment" (Levidow 2002, 3).

All the ideological content of the WB aside, it is obvious that when the costs of education are transferred to the people who are being educated, the rate of tertiary education enrollment will fall dramatically unless those people are provided with a means of payment. Therefore, a system that provides long-term debts to students is suggested (WB 1994, 13; Johnstone et al. 1998, 7).

Open adherence to the labor needs of the bourgeoisie: It has been mentioned previously that after the collapse of the Eastern Bloc, the ideological role of higher education in capitalist society lost its prior importance, and the only important outcome of education for the bourgeoisie became the vocational skills a worker gains from it.

However, the costs of education are reflected in wages. Therefore, the bourgeoisie always prefer short, job-oriented forms of education.[3] What is more, the price of labor-power, like any commodity, decreases where there is excess supply, so the "reserve army of labor" formulation of Karl Marx (1867)[4] applies to every subcategory of skilled labor.

The university of the Keynesian era, instead of catering to the immediate labor needs of the bourgeoisie, served its historical interests in the class struggle. Now that this function is no longer considered to be needed, the university designed to this end is seen as a burden by neoliberal capitalism. This burden is shaken off in a simple "quantity over quality" model: (1) the programs are redesigned to be "vocationally relevant" and as short as possible, with each course consisting of "modules" corresponding to specific vocational skills; and (2) the access rate to the tertiary education is greatly increased through "massification."

An important concept in this regard is "diversification," which means devising new, vocational and shorter types of higher education.

This creates a "trend towards community colleges, polytechnics, adult and continuing education programs, and distance learning programs" (Johnstone et al. 1998, 3). The adult education aspect of this is reflected in the term "lifelong learning," which is seen as an alternative path of education whereby the individual postpones attending tertiary education after graduating from secondary school and takes vocational courses later in life to further his/her career. Distance education, on the other hand is presented, particularly to low-income countries, as a cheaper alternative to increased access to tertiary education:[5] "[In countries] where the growth of higher education lies mainly ahead, and where the massification of higher education simply cannot occur with the physical campuses...cost-effective, technologically-mediated instruction, with opportunities for self-paced learning must remain high on the reform agenda" (Johnstone et al. 1998, 27).

Another outcome of diversification is the separation of research and education. The marketization of research is not within the scope of this chapter, but it should be noted that this separation is one of the key causes of the "death of universities." When those who teach are distanced from research, they are distanced from contemporary issues in their field, thus becoming mere instructors who transfer standardized course content to students. However, regardless of the problems it poses, this is precisely what the bourgeoisie wants from higher education: delivery of standardized, vocation-oriented modules compatible with their labor market expectations (WB 2002, xix). Moreover, this process will produce a form of higher education in which quality-assurance systems will be implementable and effective (Johnstone et al. 1998, 6). This, in turn, transforms the academic staff into "putative experts in standardized quantitative methods of performance" (Levidow 2002, 4). Indeed, the new higher education system increasingly relies on experts from corporations to teach, particularly in more market-oriented programs like lifelong learning (WB 1994, 75).

Proletarianization of the academic staff: The conversion of skilled professionals into wage laborers has always been a natural trend of capitalist development.[6] However, this trend did not work for academic staff in the Keynesian period. On the contrary, academic staff enjoyed a considerable personal autonomy as well as tenure in public universities so that they were easily considered as part of the middle class.

The neoliberal transformation of higher education is stripping away these privileges, and those who are directing the transformation are very open about what will happen: "Radical change, or restructuring, of an institution of higher education means either fewer and/or different faculty, professional staff, and support workers. This means lay-offs, forced early retirements, or major retraining and reassignment" (Johnstone et al. 1998, 24).

The main drive behind this process is the new, exclusively job-oriented nature of higher education. This brings about, as mentioned before, standardized curricula that leave no room for critical thought, and all of the qualities of academic teaching are reduced to quantifiable "outputs." The students gain nothing "universal" from university programs, only very limited job-related skills. The academician, on the other hand, becomes outmoded, even anachronistic, since this education can be delivered by almost anybody, and an instructor that has job experience is far more efficient than a professor, no matter how knowledgeable the latter is. So the fact that a professorship is mentioned almost with disdain in the WB documents concerning this issue is no surprise: "Such technology gives rise to possibilities such as: multi-way interactive video capability for synchronous distance education.... Some are predicting the end of the university as we have known it, and the virtual irrelevance of such familiar elements as... the tenured professor" (Johnstone et al. 1998, 26).

Before Bologna and the AKP: The Marketizing Impact of 1980

The neoliberal transformation in general was put into effect in Turkey during the years of military repression following the coup of 1980. Universities, which had become turbulent centers of revolutionary thought and action in the 1970s, were paid particular attention by the military dictatorship, and a special government body, the Council of Higher Education (CoHE), was established to administer them.

CoHE has been the driving force behind the transformation of higher education ever since, particularly so because its authority over the higher education system is nearly absolute. The president of the CoHE is the immediate superior of all the university presidents, he appoints all the faculty deans at all universities, and presents three candidates to the president of Turkey when a new president is to be appointed to head a university. When a new university is to be established, the CoHE is the institution that approves it before the establishment process comes to the parliament.[7] The CoHE also controls the

Student Selection and Placement Center (OSYM), the national body that tests and places students in higher education institutions; therefore, all student access to higher education is through the CoHE.

Although the CoHE is a council, the president of CoHE (who is also the immediate superior of all the council members) holds all the decision-making power, and is answerable only to the president of Turkey; therefore, the CoHE is a body that is synonymous with its president (Okçabol 2011, 12). This is why the actions of İhsan Doğramacı, the first president of the CoHE, who held the position for almost eleven years (the normal presidential term is four years), are very important and explain the nature of the CoHE and the processes it directs.

The first important step was to make higher education subject to tuition. The *Higher Education Law* (no. 2547)[8] passed on April 11, 1981, declared that higher education, which had previously been provided completely free, was henceforth "subject to tuition" (Article 43).

The next step was to make private higher education possible. Article 120 of the Turkish constitution of 1961 expressly forbade the establishment of private higher education institutions. Article 130 of the new Turkish constitution, passed on October 18, 1982, under the military dictatorship, states that: "Institutions of higher education, under the supervision and control of the state, can be established by foundations in accordance with the procedures and principles set forth in the law provided that they do not pursue lucrative aims."[9] This article was formulated by Doğramacı himself (Kongar 2011). Not coincidentally, he became the founder of Bilkent University, the first private university in Turkey, in 1984, while he was still in office as the president of the CoHE.

The synchronicity in those years between reaction and marketization was striking. The CoHE, which emerged as the ultimate product of this reaction, continued to be the primary force behind marketization.[10] This process speeded up considerably with Turkey's entrance into the Bologna Process and the AKP's coming to power.

Between AKP Rule and the Bologna Process: The Transformation of Turkish Higher Education

Before examining the three dominant trends of neoliberalism in Turkish higher education, it is necessary to present a snapshot of the system. Table 10.1[11] provides this snapshot, using the total program quotas and entry rates of the 2010 university entrance process.

Table 10.1 Overview of Turkish higher education (2010 university quotas and entry rates)

		Public	Private	% Private	Entry Rate Public	Entry Rate Private
Number of universities		106	53			
4-Year BA or equivalent: Total (excluding Open University)	Quota	299404	44179	12.86	96.14	79.46
	Placement	287857	35104	10.87		
4-Year BA or equivalent: Second (evening) Education	Quota	92091	0	0	98.05	–
	Placement	90293	0	0		
4-Year BA or equivalent: Distance Learning	Quota	2226	0	0	99.10	–
	Placement	2206	0	0		
4-Year BA or equivalent: Open University	Quota	N/A	N/A	N/A	–	–
	Placement	104731	N/A	N/A		
2-Year Associate Degree: Total (excluding Open University)	Quota	276917	32063	10.38	79.14	42.63
	Placement	219271	13668	5.87		
2-Year Associate Degree: Second (evening) Education	Quota	81932	4671	5.39	82.65	53.09
	Placement	67715	2480	3.53		
2-Year Associate Degree: Distance Learning	Quota	6900	930	11.88	76.55	26.67
	Placement	5282	248	4.48		
2-Year Associate Degree: Open University	Quota	N/A	N/A	N/A	–	–
	Placement	97.782	N/A	N/A		

Source: CoHE and ÖSYM.

Privatization: The need for and intent to generate more widespread privatization of Turkish higher education has been stated by almost all the actors in the transformation process. The common-sense perspective involves imposing the costs of education to students, while at the same time creating long-term loan opportunities (CoHE 2007, 204; TUSIAD 2003, 26; WB 2007, 25). A study done by the State Planning Organization (DPT) goes further to suggest that students, who are already paying 4 percent of the expenses for an education at public universities, should pay 50 percent of these costs (Türkmen 2009, 36–37).

However, everybody is smart enough to realize that such a plan is impossible to implement without damaging the massification agenda. Therefore the WB stresses that "a high priority of Turkey in the short run is to design an appropriate public/private financing plan" (WB 2007, 6). Furthermore, the Turkish higher education system is already a quite private system as it is. Aside from the presence of private universities, which enrolled 11 percent of four-year applicants and 6 percent of two-year applicants (the overall enrollment rate of private universities was 5 percent in 2005), the tuitions of the diversified programs in public universities are not easily affordable for people with an average income,[12] either. Average yearly tuition for second (evening) education (30 percent of total public enrollment) in public universities is US$750. The CoHE itself (2007, 65) calculates that students in second education are financing 50 percent of their education. Distance-education programs, which were first constructed in public universities, charge similar tuitions. Open university students (more than 25 percent of four-year and 30 percent of two-year public enrollees in 2010) pay approximately US$300 per year (and finance 34 percent of their education) (CoHE 2007, 65). Therefore, it is not consistent with reality to claim that higher education in public universities is completely subsidized.

In any case, the rate of private education will surely rise in the years to come. The AKP's "Target 2023" program clearly states, "More Private Universities!"[13] in the sense that the massification agenda will be pursued not by establishing new public universities but by licensing more private institutions in the future. What is more, the proportion of Open University and distance learning courses in higher education, which are clearly more self-financed, is bound to rise.[14] However, the hardships of setting up a student borrowing system in a country that already has a massive amount of household debt, high unemployment, and a draft military service for all male graduates will not be easily tackled.

Open adherence to the labor needs of the bourgeoisie: Under this heading, too, the capitalist actors voice a consensus: The curricula of programs in Turkish higher education are not labor market-oriented, the system needs to be massified, and the primary objective of programs should be to provide students with necessary vocational skills (WB 2007, 3–4; CoHE 2007, 186; TUSIAD-EUA 2008, 22; MUSIAD 2007, 34).

An important step in this direction has been the expansion of higher education. Between 2002 and 2011, the AKP governments have established 50 new public universities and authorized 39 private universities; this has doubled the gross enrollment rate of tertiary education.[15] However, the "vocational relevance" issue remains unresolved. According to the Turkish bourgeoisie,[16] higher education is still "abstract" (TUSIAD-EUA 2008, 22). The solution proposed is intensification of capital-university interaction (WB 2007, 20). One important attempt at cutting this Gordian knot was the CoHE's proposal (2007, 186) to establish advisory boards within public universities. This scheme was developed further by the Turkish Industrialists' and Businessmen's Association (TUSIAD), which suggested that these boards should include representatives of the stakeholders in higher education (read: employers), take the boards of trustees in private universities as a model, and balance the power of the president and the academic senate, which only represent faculty members (TUSIAD-EUA 2008, 22 and 103). When the proposal was finalized by the CoHE and sent to universities, the need for advisory boards was justified through Bologna Process, and the proposed advisory boards included the chairpersons of the local chambers of industry and trade (CoHE 2009). In the end, the project did not materialize, particularly because of serious protests, but it still remains on the agenda.

Proletarianization of academic staff: The tenure of the academic staff in public universities has become challengeable with the transformations that have take place in the last decade. This is most openly voiced by the bourgeois actors, who display an almost open disdain for the job security of academic staff in public universities. According to TUSIAD, tenure results in suppression of innovative teaching and research in favor of extra teaching for overtime pay (TUSIAD-EUA 2008, 116), and universities should be autonomous in their personnel policies, that is, they should be free to expel or differentiate payments between members of their staff (TUSIAD-EUA 2008, 69).[17]

The WB also suggests that staff salaries in public universities should be differentiated according to performance (Hatakenaka

2006, 24), but more importantly, it points to another constraint that is related to the massification agenda: the PhD requisite for teaching in undergraduate programs. The WB report defines this as a bottleneck to the expansion of higher education and adds that in institutions where the main objective is teaching, a PhD and publications are not good criteria for evaluating the performance of academic staff (Hatakenaka 2006, 23). Moreover, this report also states that the income of academic staff will fall due to massification, and that they will "no longer be a small group of elite but a large group of professionals" (Hatakenaka 2006, 24). In general, the working conditions of academic staff are moving in this direction. A serious contributing factor is the presence of private universities, which hire staff either on a yearly basis or teaching hour-based payment.

The quality and quantity problem of scientific research and publishing in Turkey is closely related to the working conditions of the academic staff, but will not be solved by privatization, since private institutions do not offer better working conditions or lighter teaching loads. On the contrary, the points made by the WB prove to be correct: as system becomes massified, the academic lecturer becomes a vocational teacher who delivers standardized modules. This person is not different from a skilled worker, and can be replaced just as a skilled worker can be. So, the WB's emphasis on the lack of differentiation in the Turkish higher education system is worth attention. The WB states that "most public institutions in Turkey have been developed as though they are or will be research universities" (WB 2007, 10), and it points to institutions that will focus only on teaching. This emphasis is echoed in the statements made by the president of the CoHE, who maintains that some universities should focus on research and become "super universities" (*Sabah* October 30, 2009), while teaching institutions should have a narrower focus and become "boutique and thematic" universities (*Sabah* December 29, 2009).

Conclusion

This chapter attempted to present an overview of the neoliberal transformation that has accelerated considerably in the last decade. This transformation has seriously eroded the academic quality of Turkish higher education, as it has in other countries. To show the similarities between this process in Turkey and what has been happening in other countries, this chapter presented snippets from the general framework built by the WB and matched the points in this framework with elements in the Turkish experience.

This framework, which can be analyzed as a "marketization" agenda, transforms universities into corporations, faculties into departments, university presidents into managers, and academicians into workers. However, this new type of educational institution does not serve its students; it serves the bourgeois employers, who will employ the students, by teaching the students only vocational skills, for which they will hire students once they graduate . This piecemeal teaching (called modular teaching) is contrary to the notion of the university because it has nothing whatsoever "universal" in it, as it only improves the labor power of the individual, not the individual her/himself. All of the subcategories and aspects of the transformation of higher education in Turkey contribute to bourgeois interests (and therefore are contrary to the interests of the working class), and they are almost completely translated from policies designed internationally by the WB and the Europe-wide by Bologna Process.

Notes

1. Forty-nine countries at the time this article was written. www.ehea.info/members.aspx (accessed January 2012).
2. Indeed, the similarities between the patterns of the transformation of higher education in countries that have different cultures, economic means, and so forth (Johnstone et al. 1998, 1) show that the homogenizing factor of neoliberal imperialism is the main driving force behind this transformation.
3. "the shorter the time required for training up to a particular sort of work, the smaller is the cost of production of the worker, the lower is the price of his labor-power, his wages" (Marx 1847). www.marxists.org/archive/marx/works/1847/wage-labour/ch04.htm (accessed January 2012).
4. www.marxists.org/archive/marx/works/1867-cl/ch25.htm#S3 (accessed January 2012).
5. It should also be noted that distance education is much more marketable than conventional higher education (Levidow 2002, 4).
6. "The bourgeoisie has stripped of its halo every occupation hitherto honored and looked up to with reverent awe. It has converted the physician, the lawyer, the priest, the poet, the man of science, into its paid wage laborers" (Marx and Engels 1848). www.marxists.org/archive/marx/works/1848/communist-manifesto/ch01.htm#007 (accessed January 2012).
7. In Turkey, higher education institutions are established by parliamentary legislation.
8. This was also the law that established the CoHE.
9. The "foundation" identity of private universities soon became a sham since all the foundation universities acted like private corporations from the start,

while enjoying all the tax exemptions of foundations. Today, foundation universities are identified as private universities by every actor that has defined policies in the field, i.e., the WB (2007, 10), the CoHE (2007a, 168), (CoHE 2007b, 9), and so on.
10. For example in 1992, it introduced "second education," which is evening education in universities where tuition fees are considerably higher.
11. Compiled and calculated from various statistical data at the websites of the CoHE (yok.gov.tr) and the OSYM (osym.gov.tr); accessed January 2012.
12. The current minimum wage is US$370 per month in Turkey.
13. www.akparti.org.tr/site/hedef/397/daha-fazla-ozel-universite (accessed January 2011). This is curiously absent in the English version, which only states a target of "more Turkish universities abroad."
14. This is another change the bourgeoisie have been advocating for a long time (TUSIAD 2000, 28).
15. www.tuik.gov.tr/VeriBilgi.do?tb_id=14&ust_id=5 (accessed January 2012).
16. In this chapter, reports issued by the two prominent associations of the capitalist class in Turkey will be taken as the representative of the views of the Turkish bourgeoisie. Of these, TUSIAD represents the top level of the bourgeoisie, most of whom have been around since the Second World War. MUSIAD represents the more "Islamic" segment of the bourgeoisie, which mainly became prominent the AKP came to power.
17. Since the cited report is commissioned by TUSIAD for the European Universities Association (EUA), it is safe to assume that the EUA, a central partner in the Bologna Process, shares this opinion.

References

Bok, Derek. *Universities in the Marketplace: The Commercialization of Higher Education*. Princeton: Princeton University, 2003.

CoHE (Council of Higher Education). *Türkiye'nin Yükseköğretim Stratejisi*. Ankara: CoHE, 2007a.

———. *Vakıf Üniversiteleri Raporu*. Ankara: CoHE, 2007b.

———. *Yükseköğretim Kurumlarında Danışma Kurulları Kurulması Konusunda Yönetmelik Taslağı*, Official communiqué to all rectors dated September 25, 2009.

Eagleton, Terry. "The Death of Universities." *The Guardian* December 17, 2010. www.guardian.co.uk/commentisfree/2010/dec/17/death-universities-malaise-tuition-fees (accessed January 2012).

Hatakenaka, Sachi. "Higher Education in Turkey for the 21st Century: Size and Composition." 2006. worldbank.org/EXTECAREGTOPEDUCATION/Resources/444607–1192636551820/S._Hatakenakas_report_on_Higher_Education_in_Turkey_for_21st_Century_Nov_2006.pdf (accessed January 2012).

Johnstone, D. Bruce, Alka Arora, and William Experton. *The Financing and Management of Higher Education: A Status Report on Worldwide Reforms*. Washington DC: World Bank, 1998.

Kongar, Emre. "Üniversite Hocaları Kahraman Olmak Zorunda Değildir." *Cumhuriyet*, November 3, 2011.
Levidow, Les. "Marketizing Higher Education: Neoliberal Strategies and Counter-Strategies." oro.open.ac.uk/5069/2/LL_Marketising_HE.pdf (accessed January 2012).
Marx, Karl. *Capital* Vol. 1. [1867] www.marxists.org/archive/marx/works/1867-c1 /index.htm (accessed January 2012).
———. *Wage Labor and Capital*. [1847] www.marxists.org/archive/marx/works /1847/wage-labour (accessed January 2012).
Marx, Karl, and Friedrich Engels. *Communist Manifesto*. [1848] http://www.marxists.org/archive/marx/works/1848/communist-manifesto (accessed January 2012).
Münch, Richard. "Bologna, or the Capitalization of Education." *Eurozine*, January 7, 2010. www.eurozine.com/articles/2010-07-01-munch-en.html (accessed January 2012).
MUSIAD (Independent Industrialists and Businessmen's Association). *Türkiye'de Mesleki ve Teknik Eğitim: Sorunlar-Öneriler*. Istanbul: MUSIAD, 2007.
Noble, David F. "Technology and the Commodification of Higher Education." *Monthly Review* 53, no. 10 (2002). monthlyreview.org/2002/03/01/technology -and-the-commodification-of-higher-education (accessed January 2012).
Okçabol, Rıfat. "YÖK ve Bologna Süreci." In *Bolonga Süreci Sorgulanıyor*, edited by Nevzat Evrim Önal, 11–39. Istanbul: Yazılama, 2011.
Readings, Bill. *The University in Ruins*. Cambridge: Harvard University, 1996.
Sabah. "Özel Üniversite Kurmak için Anayasa Değişikliği Gerekir." December 29, 2009. www.sabah.com.tr/Egitim/2009/12/29/ozel_universite_kurmak_icin_ anayasa_degisikligI_gerekir (accessed January 2012).
———. "Süper Üniversite Geliyor." October 30, 2009. www.sabah.com.tr/ Gundem/2009/11/30/super_universite_geliyor_834613356250 (accessed January 2012).
Türkmen, Fatih. *Yükseköğretim Sistemi İçin Bir Finansman Modeli Önerisi*. DPT Pub. No. 2787. Ankara: DPT, 2009.
TUSIAD (Turkish Industrialists' and Businessmen's Association). *Yükseköğretimin Finansmanı: Yasal Düzenleme İçin Öneriler*. Istanbul: TUSIAD, 2000.
———. (Turkish Industrialists' and Businessmen's Association). *Yükseköğretimin Yeniden Yapılandırılması: Temel İlkeler*. Istanbul: TUSIAD, 2003.
TUSIAD-EUA (Turkish Industrialists' and Businessmen's Association - European Universities Association). *Türkiye' de Yükseköğretim: Eğilimler, Sorunlar, Fırsatlar*. Istanbul: TUSIAD, 2008.
WB (World Bank). *Constructing Knowledge Societies: New Challenges for Tertiary Education*. Washington DC: The World Bank, 2002.
———. *Higher Education: Lessons of Experience*. Washington DC: The World Bank, 1994.
———. *Turkey: Higher Education Policy Study* Vol. 1: *Strategic Directions for Higher Education in Turkey*. Washington DC: The World Bank, 2007.

11

Neoliberalization and Foundation Universities in Turkey

Ömür Birler

The Turkish higher education system is composed of a two-tier structure: state (public) universities and nonprofit foundation (private) universities.[1] This dual structure was established based on changes in the *Higher Education Act*, following the 1980 military coup. The military intervention not only radically restructured the political arena by leading to the forming of a new constitution (1982), but also made the necessary policy arrangements for the integration of the Turkish economy integration into the global market system (Ercan 2005). One of the most important aspects of these policies was the transformation of the higher education system. This chapter provides an analysis of the emergence and the development of foundation universities (FUs) and examines their role in the neoliberalization of the higher education system in Turkey. To that end, the chapter is divided into three parts: first, a brief history of FUs in Turkey will be presented. Then, part 2 will analyze the first phase of the rise of FUs, which is the period between 1984 and 1999. Here, the basic characteristics of the first generation of FUs and the mechanisms employed for their integration into the neoliberal market system will be examined. The third part will focus on the second phase, the expansion period since 2000. The analysis of the second generation of FUs is crucial not only because it reveals that FUs are now irreversibly incorporated into the market economy but also because it displays the impact of the ruling Justice and Development Party (AKP), the AKP regime, and its role in the neoliberalization of higher education.

History of Private Higher Education Institutions in Turkey

The first private higher education institutions in Turkey started to appear in 1965 with the First Article of the *Private Education Institutions Act* (no. 625) (Yalçıntan and Thornley 2007). Established in the form of fee-paying academies and four-year vocational schools, these institutions quickly became popular, and by 1971 their numbers had climbed to 41, with more than fifty thousand students enrolled (Mızıkacı 2010). However during those six years, as an emerging and rapidly growing sector, these institutions failed to reach the required standards for higher education. Many were established in apartment and office buildings and lacked the proper infrastructure for research and academic human resource development.[2] Faced with such serious problems, the Constitutional Court canceled the Act in 1971.

Following the 1980 military coup, the higher education system in Turkey was completely restructured. In 1981, in accordance with the new *Higher Education Act* (no. 2547), the entire system became centralized, and all higher education institutions were tied to the Council of Higher Education (CoHE). The transformation of all higher education institutions into universities was one of the first items on the CoHE's agenda. Following the implementation of this Act, the CoHE introduced the centralization of the application procedure to universities and required all candidates to take a central university exam that would place successful students at their desired universities.

Although article 130 of the 1982 constitution gives the state the right to establish universities, in 1984 with a minor amendment in the article, foundations were also allowed to establish nonprofit private higher education institutions. The legitimation of the amendment was achieved on the basis of two arguments: Turkish higher education institutions were inefficient and globally uncompetitive. The existing universities, it was argued, could not satisfy the increasing demand for higher education. Nor could they compete with the rising standards of the global era (CoHE 2007). Therefore the establishment of the private FUs, with the legal constraint that preserved their nonprofit character, was beneficial for both the society and the existing institutions.

In line with this argument, Bilkent University became the first FU established on the basis of this legislation in 1984.[3] However, the formation of FUs was not welcomed at the social level. Two important criticisms were raised against the privatization of higher education. First, this plan was seen as being against the principle of education as a public good, which should be for all and free of charge. The involvement of the private sector in higher education can lead to social injustices that can have a negative impact on public university students, who are mostly from middle- and lower-income families. Second, the public subsidies available for FUs were causing a fundamental inconsistency. If the state universities were no longer sufficient to meet the demands of the higher education standards, the decision to allocate public revenues for the establishment of private FUs instead of improving these public institutions could only be explained as a political choice that favored the free-market system. Moreover, the first examples of FUs showed that they benefited heavily from not only from public subsidies but also land appropriations.[4] Clearly, the state has been supportive of the privatization of higher education and thus prioritized the establishment of FUs through policies based on state subsidies and land appropriations (Ercan 2005, Yalçıntan and Thornley 2007, Şenses 2007).

Nevertheless, FUs are not completely autonomous in their research activities and curriculums. The *Higher Education Act* requires all FUs to be subject to the same regulations as public universities in terms of their structural organization. Additionally, the CoHE still determines the rankings in the central university exam. However, despite the CoHE's strict regulation in the fields of academic, administrative, and educational matters, FUs enjoy greater autonomy with regard to financial issues (CoHE 2007). Although the amount of state subsidies allocated to an FU is determined by a number of criteria defined by the CoHE,[5] the two major income sources of FUs, namely contributions from the foundation and tuition fees, are not subject to any regulation by the CoHE.

It is plausible to argue that the relative financial autonomy given to FUs is one of the clearest reasons behind the increasing number of private higher education institutions. Since 1984, the number of FUs has rapidly increased. While their expansions were rather gradual during the 1990s, a sharp rise occurred with the turn of the millennium.[6] Today there are 62 FUs with a growing share of 7.8 percent of the entire higher education at the undergraduate level; 10.4 percent at the master's level, and 11.9 percent at the doctoral level.[7] However a deeper analysis of the past three decades of FUs is necessary in order to understand their relationship to the emerging neoliberal policies.

The First Generation of Foundation Universities: 1984–1999

Following the establishment of Bilkent University, FUs slowly began to multiply. During the 1990s, 19 private higher education institutions were established.[8] Slowly increasing their enrollment rates, FUs grew both in research and education capacities. Between 1984 and 1999, the total number of faculty rose from 67 to 2,624, while the total number of students enrolled in undergraduate and associate degree programs climbed from 426 to 27,367 (CoHE 2007). Although these numbers indicate a significant escalation in the staff and enrollment of FUs, these institutions still remain very limited compared to public universities. Nonetheless, the irreversible transformation of the higher education system is clearly marked with the first generation of FUs. A closer look to the characteristics of FUs reveals the critical relationship between the features of private higher education and the neoliberal market system.

Mark Olssen and Michael A. Peters portray the characteristics of the neoliberal private higher education system in eight different categories (Olssen and Peters 2005). Among them, three traits are crucial so as to understand and to trace the transformation of the higher education system: research, pedagogy/teaching, and accountability. According to Olssen and Peters, the field of research, which was traditionally linked to teaching and undertaken by curious individual academics, is now mostly externally funded in line with the necessities of the domestic or the international market, and is consequently isolated from teaching. The neoliberal higher education system requires control over universities' research facilities by governments or external agencies, such as university ranking institutions, rather than the universities themselves. This control system regularly measures academics' performances and reflects its findings on the performance indicators of individuals' academics. Similarly, while the traditional teaching system of higher education followed full-year courses with a limited number of students for the purpose of disseminating knowledge for its own sake, private higher education institutions have introduced mechanisms of semesterization, modularization, and distant learning, which emphasize vocational knowledge in order to increase the efficiency of mass education. Finally, the accountability of universities is no longer scrutinized on the basis of peer-review and facilitation, but rather on performance indicators of the institutions' financial outputs (Olssen and Peters 2005).

A closer examination of FUs in Turkey with regard to the crucial areas mentioned above, namely research, teaching, and accountability, reveals traces of neoliberalization during the period of transformation. In the field of research, the most visible outcome of this orientation is the ranking of academic publications. According to the CoHE's *Report on Foundation Universities*, the top three institutions, as based on publications per faculty member, (SCI+SSCI+AHCI) are FUs (CoHE 2007).[9] Overall there are nine FUs among the top 20 institutions listed.[10] However, this impressive ranking is completely reversed when we simply look at the total number of publications (SCI+SSCI+AHCI). There are only three FUs that made it into the top fifty institutions listed.[11] The remaining 16 FUs constitute the bottom rankings of the list.

The principle cause of such contradictory figures is the size of FUs. Compared to extensively established, state universities that serve the public, FUs are smaller in size and have less experience.[12] By 1999, the total number of faculty working at FUs was close to a mere 8 percent of the total number of academics (CoHE 2007). Consequently, it is no surprise that any assessment taking overall figures into account would reveal the research activities of FUs as weak and underdeveloped. However, as the ranking based on the number of publications per faculty demonstrates, a few FUs indeed maintain a considerable level of research activity.

In order to make sense of this outcome, it is worthwhile to remember the significance of publications as criteria for faculty appointments and promotions, as well as a performance indicator for the university ranking agencies. On the one hand, it would be a reductionist analysis to argue that the research orientations of academics affiliated with FUs originate purely from meeting the required number of publications. On the other hand, it is clear that a prioritization of research in terms of the quantity of publications rather than in terms of the quality of scholarship has become the working principle of some FUs. The choice of quantity over quality inevitably leads to the commodification of scientific research. In this regard, the first generation of FUs has paved the way for a redefinition of both research and the researcher. Insofar as faculty members' research activities are evaluated as annual performances and reflect on their academic prospects, research results, discoveries, and creative contributions are no longer public goods or integral parts of the "general quest for knowledge" but are instead pieces of "intellectual property" that are rated by external agencies (Kezar 2004).[13]

Similarly, the role of the faculty started to change with the first generation of FUs. As Gary Slaughter and Sheila Rhodes argue, the neoliberal university emphasizes the role of the faculty not as educators, researchers, or members of a larger community, but as entrepreneurs (Slaughter and Rhoades 2004). The redefinition of the faculty's institutional role is accomplished in part through the rewards structure of the university. Burton R. Clark notes that there has been an increasing prevalence of financial rewards for faculty in accordance with their contribution to the publication pool (Clark 1998). This reward system is clearly reflected in faculty salaries. Varying across academic positions and institutions, the first generation of FUs have offered superior salary packages to their full-time faculty members. While monthly salaries could reach up to ten thousand or more TRY (US$6,000) at top-ranking research-oriented universities, the average payment is around 5,000–7,000 TRY (US$2,800–4,000).[14]

No doubt, changes in the approach to conducting scientific research have been reflected in the teaching facilities of FUs. Since their establishment, FUs have attracted prospective undergraduate students by following two basic strategies: first, by granting scholarships to the top one hundred or two hundred students on the admissions exam, and second, by requiring lower entrance scores than public universities.[15] In order to increase their competitiveness vis-à-vis the public institutions, all first-generation FUs adopted English as their teaching language and emphasized their determination to prepare the younger generations for better employment opportunities and internationality.

Just as with the redefinition of the research activity, the first generation of FUs recreated the purpose of education. Institutions of higher education principally claim that they are creating the next generation of employees (Aronowitz 2000, Giroux 2005). What is unique about the neoliberal institution's approach to this goal is the explicit manner in which it is undertaken. To this end, the curriculum is explicitly structured to meet the needs of capital, while desired student development and educational outcomes are defined by job training and career development.

According to Murat C. Yalçıntan and Andy Thornley, almost 40 percent of the students studying at FUs are enrolled in programs related to economics, management, and administrative studies (2007, 829–830). This percentage is considerably lower in the public universities, which cannot adapt to market needs quickly or do not function according to market principles and have different priorities. Therefore, graduates of FUs are most likely to become professionals who will generally aim to work for multinational companies and banks that can afford to pay high salaries.

Alongside the traditional four-year undergraduate institutions, the first generation of FUs provide vocational training to a large number of students. Due to their minimal eligibility criteria[16] and the possibility of lateral transfer to a four-year undergraduate program for successful students, vocational schools have gained popularity and in some cases they accommodate the majority of students. Among the first generation of FUs, only four universities do not offer two-year vocational training programs.[17] The rate of student enrollment in vocational schools varies from 3 percent to 53 percent in the remaining institutions (CoHE 2007).[18] These high rates also indicate that for the first generation of FUs, the function of teaching is aligned with the neoliberal transformation of the higher education system.

Another striking feature of the first generation of FUs is their choice of location. Of the 20 universities established between 1984 and 1999, 19 of them are found in two metropolitan cities of Turkey, that is, Istanbul and Ankara[19]. Although the regulations pertaining to FUs aimed to prevent their establishment only in metropolitan areas by requiring them to obtain comparable levels of research and educational capacities with the public universities in their locality, the unspecified criteria of comparison render the regulation weak and have led to a major concentration of FUs in large cities (Yalçıntan and Thornley 2007). This choice of location also shows us that for the first generation of FUs, the concentration of capital and the market mechanisms play a vital role. The desire to be in the center of capital not only increases their competitiveness in terms of attracting prospective students, but also adds to their reputation as their graduates become a part of the same market.

Clearly the relationship of FUs to the market is best seen in the composition and the functioning of their administrative and financial units. Although regulated by the CoHE, FUs are autonomous in forming their own administrative structure. The decision-making system in FUs is run by a board of trustees, which is responsible for appointing the faculty (including the president)[20] and managing the university budget. Lacking in public universities, such autonomy creates an opportunity for FUs to develop a free academic environment.

However, a closer look to the formation of the board of trustees and its approach to administrative and financial issues would reveal quite the opposite. The first generation of FUs has been mostly founded through the initiatives of financially powerful corporations.[21] These corporate ties are reflected in the composition of the board of trustees. In all FUs, while the chairman of the board of trustees is the founder of the originating foundation, the president of the university appears as a mere executer of decisions taken by the board. Therefore, it is difficult to argue that FUs have academic autonomy.

Clearly the decisions made by the board are also influenced by the funding capacities of the university. According to the CoHE's *Report on Foundation Universities*, 16 out of 20 FUs have been receiving at least 80 percent of their total income from student tuition fees (CoHE 2007, 25).[22] However, the rate of annual expenses per student is actually very low considering the high-priced tuition fees. The *Report on Foundation Universities* states that annual expenses per student range between 4,000–7,000 TRY (US$2,300–4,000) (CoHE 2007, 26). Therefore, it is plausible to argue that the decision-making system of FUs is heavily influenced by its financial outputs. Although these institutions are nonprofit by law, the continuation of FUs rests on their financial stability and the reproduction of market mechanisms within the higher education system. As we will discuss in the next section, the inclination to utilize neoliberal strategies for the commodification of higher education has expanded even further during the second generation of FUs.

Second Generation of Foundation Universities: Post-2000s

With the turn of the millennium, the number of FUs escalated greatly. However, the real boom came with the start of AKP rule. Since 2003, an additional 39 FUs were established, and the total number of FUs has increased to 62. Such an immense growth in quantity has naturally resulted in the further commodification of higher education. While maintaining a concentration in metropolis areas, FUs have started to emerge in periphery urban areas, such as Gaziantep, Kayseri, Konya, Trabzon, Samsun, Bursa, Alanya, and Antalya.[23] The forces that rendered this quick proliferation of FUs are hidden in the successful neoliberalization policies of the preceding decades as well as the AKP regime's support for the establishment of additional universities. However, the most influential policy change that eased the establishment of FUs occurred in 2008, whereby the prerequisite of founding a faculty of sciences or humanities was eliminated.

Following this change, an additional 26 FUs were established in less than four years.

The increase in the quantity of FUs was naturally reflected in their administration. The transformation of research, teaching, and accountability continued to further adapt to market mechanisms. In this respect, while the number of publications remains as the fundamental tool for measuring the success of research facilities and faculty performance, external funding agencies began to be a major source for research projects. Among these, the European Union Framework Programs and the Scientific and Technological Research Council of Turkey (TUBITAK) research and development project funding began to accept research proposals in 2000 and paved the way for both the internationalization of research funds and the intensification of market-oriented project agendas.[24]

Similarly, the teaching facilities of FUs have further oriented themselves to the requirements of the market. With the elimination of the requirement of a science or humanities faculty, many FUs became more liberal in only establishing the desired faculties. This led to a soaring number of profession-oriented universities. The number of FUs centered on medical training has increased from three to thirteen since 2000. Likewise, the volume of vocational schools has grown immensely with the newly established FUs. However, the signature of the AKP period is the establishment of faculties of theology in FUs. Founded by cabinet decree, three FUs began offering degrees in 2010.[25] The emergence of theology faculties clearly demonstrate that during the AKP regime, FUs have become not only an integral part of the commodification of the higher education system but have also started to contribute to the agenda of political conservatism/Islamism that accompanies the neoliberal hegemony in Turkey.

Another indicator of the increasing role of Islamism in FUs is the growing involvement of Islamic foundations in the private higher education system. Since 2000, while the composition of the board of trustees has remained mainly intact, the most visible change has occurred with the introduction of FUs established by Islamic foundations. Emphasizing their commitment to Islamic values in their strategic plans, these FUs do not differ in terms of their reliance on student tuition fees and the accountability of their financial outputs. In this regard, they represent the hegemonic formula of neoliberalism: political conservatism combined with market liberalism.

One final issue must be stated before concluding this chapter. As mentioned earlier, the internationalization of research facilities has become a common element of the second generation of FUs. However, the takeover of Istanbul Bilgi University by a for-profit company, namely Laureate Education, in 2006 marks the beginning of a major transformation for the future of FUs in Turkey.[26] The introduction of a for-profit company signals that the commodification of higher education services that started under the existing system of FUs could transform into the privatization of the universities in the near future.

In conclusion, the FUs have been active in transitioning to a neoliberal higher education system since the 1990s. Although the first generation of FUs demonstrated only minor changes in terms of the commodification of research and teaching facilities, they definitely laid a strong foundation for the next generation. Under AKP rule, the second generation of FUs completed their integration into global markets through research funds, accreditation systems, ranking agencies, and the introduction of a global for-profit higher education company. In this sense, the AKP regime has certainly reinforced the role of FUs in the neoliberalization of higher education.

Notes

1. It might be useful to explain the term "foundation" in the Turkish context. Foundations as semipublic institutions have a long history. Originally established as charitable institutions to which Muslims could donate, they became widespread during the Ottoman period for the purpose of preserving property, which was otherwise not recognized as a legal right. Today their public benefit continues, but now with different individual advantages, such as tax exemption, making abolishment of the property difficult, and maintaining the founders' influence.
2. Saner gives some striking examples from their marketing slogans: "Your diploma is ready at the seaside" or "Pay the money, get the diploma" (Saner 2000).
3. Following its establishment, the Constitutional Court decided that the formation of FUs should be regulated by an act and abrogated the exiting regulation. The resolution on the legal status of Bilkent had to wait until 1992, when Act 3785 was promulgated. Nevertheless, the university continued its regular activities during these years.
4. The first three examples of FUs (Bilkent, Koç, and Başkent) appropriated their lands with the decision of the Council of Ministers at no cost, on the condition that the land would be used for education and research.
5. Those criteria include the number of faculty and research assistants, the number of available student scholarships, and the growth rate of the university.
6. While the total number of FUs established during the 1990s is 20, this number has tripled during the first decade of the 2000s.
7. Calculated by using the figures in COHE (2007, 28) and COHE (2007a, 88).

8. The distribution of the number of FUs respective to the years in which they were established are as follows: 1992, 1; 1994, 2; 1996, 5; 1997, 8; 1998, 3; 1999, 3.
9. These are Işık, Başkent, and Koç Universities.
10. These are Bilkent, Çankaya, Doğuş, Atılım, Sabancı and Fatih Universities.
11. These are: Başkent, #16; Bilkent, #23; and Yeditepe, #50.
12. Figures show that 60 percent of the faculty members working at FUs are lecturers, and that 40 percent have titles of assistant professor or higher (CoHE 2007, 30). Not surprisingly, the opposite picture emerges in state universities: 40 percent of the employed staff are lecturers, and the remaining majority holds tenured positions (CoHE 2007a, 94).
13. Among the first generation of FUs, Bilkent University has been ranked among the "World's Best Universities" by Times Higher Education and Quacquarelli Symonds consistently since 2009. Likewise, Koç University has been ranked among the top 100 universities by the Financial Times.
14. The average monthly salary for full-time professors working at public universities is 3,800 TRY (US$2,200).
15. Placement at a private or a public institution solely depends on the results of a ranking system produced by the central university examination scores. The score determines the university that students will attend and the subjects they will study, according to their preferences.
16. Vocational schools require very low scores on the central university exam.
17. These are Koç, Sabancı, Işık, and Atılım Universities.
18. Student enrollment rates in vocational schools: Beykent, 53 percent; Maltepe, 32 percent; Bahçeşehir, 32 percent, Fatih, 27 percent, İstanbul Kültür, 23 percent, İzmir Ekonomi, 20 percent; Kadir Has, 18 percent; Bilkent, 8.8 percent; Çağ, 7.6 percent; Bilgi, 6.1 percent. Figures taken from CoHE (2007, 28)
19. The only exception is Çağ University, located in Mersin.
20. The election of candidates and the appointment of the president are finalized by the board of trustees in FUs and then approved by the CoHE; whereas, the president is appointed at state universities (CoHE 2010)
21. When we analyze the founding capital behind FUs, there appear to be three industrial sources: funding from private secondary education or private tutoring institutions (Yeditepe, Istanbul Kültür, Çankaya, Bahçeşehir, and Doğuş Universities), the construction sector (Beykent, Maltepe, and Atılım Universities), and a powerful bourgeoisie (Sabancı, Koç, Kadir Has, Çağ, and Okan Universities). The exceptions to industrial capital are Bilkent, Baskent, Ufuk, and Fatih Universities. It is striking that three of these (except Bilkent) were established around a school of medicine.
22. Tuition fees vary between 12,000–30,000 TRY (US$6,800–17,200).
23. The distribution of FUs at the end of 2011 was as follows: 33 in Istanbul; 11 in Ankara; 5 in Izmir; 2 each in Mersin, Konya, Gaziantep, and Kayseri; 1 each in Antalya, Alanya, Trabzon, Bursa, and Samsun.
24. It is no surprise that Bilkent, Koç, and Sabancı Universities are among the top ten universities benefitting from TUBITAK funds.
25. These are Fatih, Fatih Sultan Mehmet, and Istanbul 29 Mayıs Universities.
26. For an excellent analysis of the takeover process, see Arslan and Odman 2011.

References

Aronowitz, Stanley. *The Knowledge Factory: Dismantling the Corporate University and Creating True Higher Education.* Boston: Beacon Press, 2000.
Arslan, Hakan, and Aslı Odman. "İstanbul Bilgi Üniversitesi'ndeki şirketleşme ve Sendikalaşma Süreci." In *Metalaşma ve İktidarın Baskısındaki Üniversite,* edited by Fuat Ercan and Serap Korkusuz Kurt, 593–632. İstanbul: Sosyal Araştırmalar Vakfı, 2011.
Clark, Burton R. *Creating Entrepreneurial Universities: Organizational Pathways of Transformation.* New York: Pergamon, 1998.
CoHE (Council of Higher Education). "Bologna National Report." 2009. http://bologna.yok.gov.tr/ (accessed December 2011).
———. "The Higher Education System in Turkey." 2010. http://www.yok.gov.tr (accessed December 2011).
———. "Türkiye'nin Yükseköğretim Stratejisi." 2007a. http://www.yok.gov.tr (accessed December 2011).
———. "Vakıf Üniversiteleri Raporu." 2007. http://www.univder.org/vakif_rap.pdf (accessed December 2011).
Ercan, Fuat. "Neoliberal Eğitim Politikaları Anlamak." *Sivil Toplum* 3, no. 12 (2005): 17–37.
Giroux, Henry. *The Terror of Neoliberalism: Cultural Politics and the Promise of Democracy.* Boulder, CO: Paradigm Publishers, 2005.
Kezar, Adrianna J. "Obtaining Integrity? Reviewing and Examining the Charter Between Higher Education and Society." *The Review of Higher Education* 27, no. 4 (2004): 429–459.
Levy, Daniel C. "The Enlarged Expanse of Private Higher Education." *Die Hochschule* 2 (2008): 13–14.
Mızıkacı, Fatma. "Isomorphic and Diverse Institutions among Turkish Foundation Universities." *Education and Science* 35, no. 157 (2010): 140–151.
Olssen, Mark, and Michael A Peters. "Neoliberalism, Higher Education and the Knowledge Economy: From the Free Market to Knowledge Capitalism." *Journal of Education Policy* 20, no. 3 (2005): 313–345.
Saner, Ali Ihsan. *Devletin Rantı Deniz.* Istanbul: Iletişim Yayınları, 2000.
Şenses, Fikret. "Uluslararası Gelismeler Isıgında Türkiye Yükseköğretim Sistemi: Temel Egilimler, Sorunlar, Çeliskiler ve Öneriler." *ERC Working Papers in Economics,* 2007.
Slaughter, Sheila, and Gary Rhoades. *Academic Capitalism and the New Market Economy: Market, State and Higher Education.* Baltimore: John Hopkins University Press, 2004.
Yalçıntan, Murat Cemal, and Andy Thornley. "Globalisation, Higher Education, and Urban Growth Coalitions: Turkey's Foundation Universities and the case of Koç University in Istanbul." *Environment and Planning C: Government and Policy* 25 (2007): 822–843.

12
The *Dershane* Business in Turkey

Ayhan Ural

The Republic of Turkey is a state that constitutionally secures its social character. The constitution guarantees equal opportunities in education to each citizen. The governments in this respect have adopted a policy aimed at meeting the educational needs of the citizens through public schools. On the other hand, the regulations enabling the private sector to invest in education have also been effective since the 1960s. The *dershane* (private tutoring courses) business, which is the focus of this research, constitutes an example of private investment in education. The purpose of this chapter is to provide information and a critical perspective on the current situation regarding Turkey's *dershane* business.

The Concept of the *Dershane* Business

The notion of private tutoring courses known as *dershane* in Turkey is expressed differently in different societies. Entrepreneurs who create formal establishments for tutoring commonly call them centers, academies, or institutes. In Japan, tutoring centers that supplement the school system are known as *juku*, and in the United Kingdom, such institutions are called crammers (Bray 1999).

Dershane, a concept that has concerned the entire society in Turkey in the last three decades, is defined in the dictionary as a private institution that, as a supplement to regular school, gives lessons to students for a fee (TDK 2011). In a similar vein, in the documents of the Ministry of National Education (MoNE) the concept of the *dershane* is defined as a private teaching institution that aims to guide students and graduates in the courses that they want to be successful, to prepare them to the entrance exams of higher schools and of public and/or private institutions, to encourage them making research and analysis (MoNE 2005a, MoNE 2008).

The definition of *dershane* shows that expectations from the *dershane* and the public schools are completely overlapping. In other words, the institution named as *dershane* shows no different characteristic addressing a new structure or action than the notion of school. The whole functions determined in the definition of *dershane* are the same as the expressions defining the primary and secondary schools in the education law (MoNE 2011a). This situation openly reveals that the activity known as private tutoring in Turkey is not different from public schools but is a commercial business made besides school. This chapter focuses on the commercial character of *dershane*, and argues that the *dershane* as a business activity is identified with the commercial nature and turns into the notion of *dershane* business.

Historical Development of *Dershane* Business

The *dershane* business in Turkey first obtained a legal status in 1965 with the adoption of the Law (no. 625). In this law, private schools, private courses, motor vehicle driving schools, student study education centers and *private dershanes* are specified as private education institutions. In Turkey's education system, the *dershane*, which also existed before the legal regulation of 1965, along with supporting the courses of students in formal education, carried out courses of short duration generally for adults in fields like foreign language, art, commerce and home economy (Duman 1984).

From the 1970s, the *dershane* has been attributed along with its traditional functions, a new function consisting of preparing students for centralized exams. However, they harmed the equal opportunities in education which drew the *dershane* into debates. These debates had lasted for years and were influential in the non-enforced decision of closing the *dershane* in 1983 with the Law (no. 2843). In the period following this year, every debate over the *dershane* in Turkey constantly brought up the above-mentioned "non-enforced decision on closing" and the reasons for it. According to these reasons, which still mostly have currency and validity, the *dershane* (Akyüz 2008):

- creates unequal opportunity in education,
- makes excessive profits,

- weakens schools by taking on teachers from public schools,
- by transmitting the knowledge in form of blocks, makes test acrobatics as if decoding,
- puts public schools in trouble,
- does not achieve any educational activity,
- harms the prestige of the profession of teacher,
- by forcing the learning capacity, causes various damages to students.

The numbers of *dershanes* in Turkey, the numbers of enrolled students and working teachers are as follows according to the selected years (see Table 12.1[1]).

As can be understood from the increase in the numbers of *dershanes* in Table 12.1, the concept of the *dershane* in Turkey has been considered as a profitable investment by entrepreneurs. Besides, it is argued that the number of *dershanes* in Turkey is higher than what is reflected in official statistics. The number of the so-called unregistered, illegal or pirate *dershane* is said to be between one thousand (*Hürriyet* July 5, 2011) and fifteen thousand (*Milliyet* 2009).

The Conditions Generating the *Dershane* Businesses

Before the 1980s, small numbers of *dershane* businesses were able to meet the demand for educational support of students. Today, in order to meet the mass demand, *dershane* businesses turned into big

Table 12.1 The change in the *Dershane* business with figures

Years	Number of Dershanes	Number of Students	Number of Teachers
1965	74	–	–
1975	157	45,582	1,383
1980	174	1,01,703	3,826
1990	762	1,88,407	8,723
1995	1,292	3,34,270	10,940
2000	1,864	5,23,244	18,175
2001	2,122	6,06,522	19,881
2002	2,568	6,68,673	23,730
2003	2,984	7,84,565	30,537
2005	3,928	9,25,299	41,031
2007	3,986	10,71,827	47,621
2009	4,262	11,74,860	50,432
2011	4,099	12,34,738	50,209

Source: MoNE 2011d, ÖZDEBİR 2011.

businesses with their rapidly increasing numbers. This reality basically results from the change in the educational policies of Turkey after the 1980s. During this process, the resources allocated to education have been far from meeting the social demand for education in terms of quantity and quality.

As a result, the philosophy of offering education as a public service has been abandoned. And the understanding of equal opportunity—preeminent from the beginning of the republic—being set aside, violations of the right to education have increased. Consequently, with the claim of giving equal opportunity in education (ÖZDEBİR 2011), the *dershane* business, in its effort for legitimization, could find an adequate environment to grow and develop. Put forward with its function of supporting public schools, the sector of *dershane* benefited in fact from the incapability of the public schools.

The decline in the quality of the public education has transformed the *dershane* business into a profitable investment. Especially in the period after 1980, the schooling rates did not meet the demand and therefore, as a solution, the examination system based on elimination was preferred. As a result of this, the *dershane* business in Turkey turned to be a mass phenomenon. In this period, the number of *dershane* in Turkey increased especially in parallel with the adoption of "the concept of competitive education" (Ural 2004).

According to Kavak (2011), the persistent problem of the supply-demand disequilibrium in higher education as the most critical subject on the agenda in Turkey, has led to the increase in the number of *dershanes*. Similarly, the Council of Higher Education (CoHE) (2007) has also attributed the excessive growth of the *dershane* sector to the fact that secondary education is not being offered successfully and homogeneously. There are many reasons for the excessive increase in the number of *dershanes* in Turkey. A general list of these reasons, based on some of the research carried out in this field (e.g., Akyüz 2008, ATO 2005, CoHE 2007), follows below:

- an inadequate number of schools,
- a lack of qualified teachers and an insufficient number of teachers,
- a dual education system—two groups are taught in one day in the same school,
- the high number of students per classroom,
- the lack of equipment and facilities,
- outdated educational programs,
- the inequality in the distribution of teachers,

- the students' success in previous schools/classes is not evaluated when they enter a new school,
- the consideration of academic success as the sole criterion,
- the creation of school types, which leads to discrimination,
- the limited number of schools—school types—that accept students with competitive examination,
- the difference between the evaluation of success in schools and the school entrance examination,
- the increase in the number of the school entrance examination,
- society's positive opinion of the *dershane*,
- the increase in differences among schools of the same type and level.

The Consequences of the *Dershane* Business in Turkey

After the 1980s, the education system in Turkey became exam-oriented. The phenomenon of competition in education, which is a result of the orientation toward exams, is largely due to the system's inability to provide sufficient schooling for students. In particular, the capacities of public schools in secondary and higher education are not sufficient to meet the demand. This limitation in the schools' quotas has also made the selection of students inevitable. From this perspective, the eliminatory central exams related to selection force students to take supplementary lessons outside of regular school. The *dershane* business, created in view of meeting such demand, paved the way for drawing public education into market relations. The fact that the *dershane* is seen as an economic investment by Turkish society also supported the opening of new ones. The loss of quality in public schools due to a lack of governmental support, has implicitly paved the way for private schools and *dershanes*. Private tutoring especially, as a result of a mass demand for the *dershane*, has become an important sector that influences the social and economic life in Turkey.

Turkey adopted the principal policy of resolving the problems facing education with an exam-based competitive education concept. This situation, which may be termed "exam mania" has penetrated every level of the education system. A study carried out on this subject (Eğitim-Sen 2008) has determined that a student takes a total of 739 exams from elementary school until graduation from a university.

Public schools, which are said to be also supported by the *dershane* in Turkey (ÖZDEBİR 2011), are not successful enough in achieving the goals of the Turkish education system, as international research and reports on education have also revealed (OECD 2011a, OECD 2011b, UNDP 2011).

The Program for International Student Assessment (PISA) is the most concrete example of this. The PISA research, in which Turkey took part in 2003, 2006, and 2009, indicated that the results concerning Turkey did not reveal any significant change. Indeed, the inefficiency of the public elementary education system was considered to be a long-lasting problem. According to the research related to these three periods of time, students in Turkey do not have the necessary skills in the fields of science, mathematics, and reading comprehension (MoNE 2005b, MoNE 2007, OECD 2011b). The reason for this may be due to the approach to education that results from private tutoring, which has developed independently and has been accepted in parallel with public education since the 1980s.

The approach that is defined as the "concept of competitive education" (Ural 2004) has put forward its goal as aiming for an individual to be able to use his/her difference, capacity, and opportunity to express his/herself. Its implicit goal is, however, that the individual learns to move forward by taking advantage of the others' lack of ability. The basic characteristic that would destroy the concept of competitive education in Turkey is the development of fundamental human values, such as asking questions, understanding, giving meaning, being curious, creating, criticizing, trusting, imagining, wanting, and sharing. In this way, the concept of competitive education, which is presented under the guise of supporting individualism, may be considered not only as a means to destroy individualism but also as a great obstacle to socialization.

The system of elementary education in Turkey may also be defined according to the definition of capitalism in relation to education: everyone has the social responsibility to protect and watch out for the individual, as opposed to the Mario educational model (Ural 2011), which makes everyone dependent on the commands and actions of authority. The exam-centered approach aims at attributing all the negative aspects of the educational process and system to the students in Turkey, and tries to portray those who design and implement the system as quite innocent.

For instance, by including information on the "number of applicants without a calculated point" (OSYM 2011) in the results of a nationwide central exam, a perception of those students who "score zero" is created in the public mind. The fact that there are many problems in education is attributed to the mistakes of students, not the errors of the system. However, this illusion does not eliminate the reality that the real persons "scoring zero" are the policy makers and implementers. Kühn (2007) especially attributes the failure of students, who have turned to *dershane* because they are considered as unsuccessful in school, to the inefficiency of the school/education system.

In Turkey, almost 17 percent of the population lives below the poverty level, and 18 percent is at risk of living below the level (TUIK 2011), so costs of the *dershane* have a significant impact on a family's way of life. According to Mehmet M. Akgündüz (2009), the yearly costs per student in Turkey vary from $1,000 to $10,000. In particular, the fact that families from low-income groups spend most of their income for *dershane* (Ekinci 2009) clearly shows the dimensions of the problem.

Another issue related to this subject is employment in the field of the *dershane* business. There are major problems concerning the work conditions of employees in the *dershane* business in Turkey. *Dershane* administrators, in particular, who tend to benefit financially from the excess numbers of teachers, force newly graduated teachers to work uninsured and with a much busier weekly schedule than is the standard in regular schools. Moreover, it is common for *dershane* administrators to hire as teachers, individuals who have graduated from the departments of basic sciences at universities even though they are not certified as teachers.

The common characteristic for both groups is that they are openly exploited. This situation is turned into an economic opportunity by *dershane* administrators. Especially in the 2000s, with the rapid transformation in the private tutoring sector, the rights legally guaranteed to *dershane* teachers have often been violated, their working conditions have become more severe, and their wages have decreased (Sosyal-İş Sendikası 2011, Türk Eğitim-Sen 2011). It turns out that, based a study carried out on this subject (Yılmaz 2009), *dershane* teachers are dissatisfied with their working conditions.

Inspections carried out according to sector by the Social Security Institute show that unregistered employment in *dershane* businesses has become a extremely common. The inspections revealed that in 2007, 70 percent, in 2008, 48 percent and in 2009, 87 percent of the *dershane* personnel that were interviewed were employed as unregistered workers (*Radikal* December 11, 2008). A similar inspection carried out by Tez Koop-İş trade union reveals that personnel in *dershane* businesses are kept in a system in which they are deprived of their legal rights and are exposed to professional and human deprivation (Gök 2005).

Beyond being an important economic activity in Turkey, private tutoring is also used by religious organizations in a dangerous way "to recruit people" (Önder 2011). This situation shows that the door that was shut with the "understanding of unifying education" (MoNE 2011b), which was seen as a basic necessity in the creation of the Turkish republic, has been inched open by the *dershane* business.

According to Gök (2005), the customary existence of *dershane* affects education at all levels. By doing so, it prevents Turkish society from realizing that efficient education is one of the most important public responsibilities. In Turkey, the education system, which was unable to meet the demand of students at all levels, suggested after 1980 that a solution could be an eliminatory approach based on elitism. Within this period, numerous examinations were created. In an education system in which ranking and elimination are dominant, it was inevitable that private tutoring would develop so extensively. A study of TED (2005), according to which 60 percent of students and 68 percent of parents think that it is not possible to succeed in school without *dershane*, openly shows the social support that private tutoring has won.

The effect of attending the *dershane* on the individual's—the student's—mental health may also be considered as another aspect of this discussion. The literature contains some statements that assert that the *dershane* especially prevents children and youth from experiencing a happy childhood. Doğan Cüceloğlu (1993) has pointed out that the level of anxiety that students face when they are about to take the university entrance exam in Turkey is higher than that of patients about to undergo an operation. Ayhan Ural (2008) has argued that the exams in the Turkey's education system and the *dershane* that promote these exams constitute an important assault on childhood.

By calling his list of suggestions to students taking the university entrance exam with words like "pilfer prunes, caress basil, run in railways," Yılmaz Özdil (2009) has drawn attention to the problems that may be created when the exams are made to be the centre of students' life. Such a huge growth in the *dershane* business is expressed by Dogan Kuban (2011) as a form of corruption, revealing the collapse of the Turkish educational system.

The efforts of substituting schools with the *dershane* are quite odd. It is obvious that the *dershane* will continue to be defined as businesses, based on their economic functions, and not as substitute schools (Ural 2006), however high their enrollments might be. However, offices related to public administration in Turkey have developed plans to change the structure and functions of the *dershane* businesses in the near future.

The Ninth Development Plan prepared by the State Planning Organization (DPT) (2011) and the strategic plan by the MoNE (MoNE 2011c), covering the years 2011–2014, aim to transform the *dershane* into private schools. As can be deduced from this offer, the *dershane* in Turkey have been considered as a veiled tool in the legitimization of the gradual transformation of education into a system based on payment. The word "transformation," which is widely used in the privatization of services provided by the public sector in Turkey, has also been adapted to this process by aiming to win public support for this transformation.

As a consequence, in the process of adapting capitalism to education and the school system, the phase "opening the system to the market invasion" (Hirtt 2004) has also been employed in the field of education. As a result of all this, the *dershane* in Turkey, as Derya K. Demirer (2011) also pointed out, has become a milieu in which the commoditization of education has spread to every social segment. Marie H. Roesgaard (2006) and Mark Bray (1999) argued that the private tutoring systems they defined as "shadow education" are coming into being due to the insufficiency of the formal education systems in each country. However, it is observed, as in Turkey, that the *dershane* is transformed into a mechanism that postpones the problem of unequal opportunities in education, by deepening the problem rather than solving it.

Demirer (2011) rightly compares the *dershane* to a place of transition in which hot social problems are left to cool down, and he regards it as a safety valve with a high explosive potential. The European Union (EU), aware of this danger, has considered the commercialization of education outside school as a concept that increases inequality, and it has initiated action to warn its member countries about this problem (European Commission 2011).

In countries where social justice is insufficient, as in Turkey, equal opportunity in education is vital. According to a study that examines the level of social justice in Organization for Economic Cooperation and Development (OECD) countries (Bertelsmann-Stiftung 2011),

Turkey is the OECD's least socially just country. The inequalities in access to education play an important role in the reasons why Turkey occupies last place, according to the study.

These types of studies also demonstrate the necessity of offering education as a public service and one that is available to all social groups. In this framework, the *dershane* business in Turkey should be discussed in all its aspects as a concept that affects the social, cultural, and economic life of all social groups, and its actions to weaken public education should be prevented.

Conclusion

This chapter discussed the reasons, the developments, and social effects of the *dershane* business, which is a widespread commercial field of activity in Turkey, as in some other parts of the world (Bray 2009). With their increase in market share, *dershane* businesses have been generalized so that the efficiency of public schools is now questioned. Critics of the *dershane* business have raised such issues as these businesses' creation of unequal opportunities in education, their ability to weaken the public educational system by employing qualified teachers from public schools, their high rate of profits, their role as a substitute for public schools, their lack of social and cultural activities, their pedagogical approach of transmitting knowledge in the form of blocks, and their focus on tests.

In conclusion, the concept defined as *dershane*:

- has come into being as a complement to inefficient public education-state schools,
- has developed with through claim that it can overcome the inefficiency of public schools,
- has grasped that it needs to maintain the inefficiency of public schools at a proper level in order to support its own existence,
- has created public opinion that insures its survival,
- has made the public opinion dependent on itself,
- has spread over a vast geographical location
- has become very differentiated from public schools and tried to transform the meaning of it
- has become an uncontrolled power.
  Therefore:
- The concept of competitive education has emerged and developed.
- Collaboration, solidarity, and sharing have been destroyed.
- The childhood and adolescence of the individual have been stolen.

- The freedom and uniqueness of the individual have been destroyed.
- The rights to education and equal opportunity have been destroyed.
- Education has been marketized.
- School has been made into a commercial place.

The way to eliminate the *dershane* is not to close them, but rather to remove the reasons that have caused their emergence. Believing that this is possible and trying to achieve it, may be a small step for societies that claim a view of social justice. However, it will be a large step for the individual, using one of the fundamental human rights, namely his/her right to education.

In order to resolve this problem and similar ones, the concept of competitive education should be excluded from the Turkey's education system.

Note

1. Compiled and calculated from various statistical data at the websites of MoNE and ÖZDEBİR (accessed December 2011).

References

Akgündüz, Mehmet M. "Ankara İli Çankaya Ilçesindeki Lise Öğrencilerinin Görüşlerine Göre Dershanelerin İşlevlerinin Değerlendirilmesi." Master's thesis, Ankara University, Ankara, Turkey, 2009.

Akyüz, Yahya. *Türk Eğitim Tarihi*. Ankara: Pegem Akademi Yayınları, 2008.

ATO (Chamber of Commerce, Ankara). "Dershaneler Dosyası." 2005. http://www.atonet.org.tr/turkce/ bulten/bulten.php3?sira=272 (accessed December 2011).

Bertelsmann-Stiftung. "Social Justice in the OECD." 2011. http://www.sgi-network.org/pdf/SGI11_Social_Justice_OECD.pdf (accessed December 2011).

Bray, Mark. "Confronting the Shadow Education System: What Government Policies for What Private Tutoring?" 2009. Paris: UNESCO International Institute for Educational Planning IIEP.www.unesco.org/iiep/eng/publications/recent/abstracts/2009/Bray_Shadoweducation.htm (accessed December 2011).

———. "The Shadow Education System: Private Tutoring and Its Implications for Planners." 1999. Paris: UNESCO International Institute for Educational Planning IIEP. www.iiep.unesco.org/information-services/publications/searchiiep-publications/economics-of-education.html (accessed December 2011).

CoHE (Council of Higher Education). *Türkiye'nin Yükseköğretim Stratejisi*. Ankara: YÖK Yayınları, 2007.

Cüceloğlu, Doğan. *İnsan ve Davranışı*. Istanbul: Remzi Kitabevi, 1993.

Demirer, Derya K. "Eğitimde Metalaşmak ve Emek Sömürüsü: Bir Meşrulaştırma Alanı Olarak Dershaneler." In *Metalaşma ve İktidar Baskısındaki Üniversite*, edited by Fuat Ercan ve Serap Korkusuz-Kurt, 439–459. Istanbul: Sosyal Araştırmalar Vakfı, 2011.

DPT (State Planning Organization). "Dokuzuncu Beş Yıllık Kalkınma Planı." 2011. http://ekutup.dpt.gov.tr/plan/plan9.pdf (accessed December 2011).

Duman, Tayip. "Türkiye'de Özel Dershaneler ve İşlevleri." Master's thesis, Ankara University, Ankara, Turkey, 1984.

Eğitim-Sen. "Sınava Endeksli Eğitim Öğrencilere Değil Dershanelere Fayda Sağlıyor." 2008. www.egitimsen.org.tr/icerik.php?yazI_id=260 (accessed November 2011).

Ekinci, C. Ergin. "Türkiye'de Yükseköğretimde Öğrenci Harcama ve Maliyetleri." *Eğitim ve Bilim* 34, no. 154 (2009): 119–133.

European Comission. "The Challenge of Shadow Education: Private Tutoring and Its Implications for Policy Makers in the European Union." 2011. www.fundatiadinupatriciu.ro/ uploaded/the-challenge-of-shadow-education-1.pdf (accessed December 2011).

Gök, Fatma. "Üniversiteye Girişte Umut Pazarı: Özel Dershaneler." *Eğitim, Bilim, Toplum* 311 (2005): 102–109.

Hirtt, Nico. "The Three Axes of School Merchandization." *European Educational Research Journal* 32 (2004): 442–453.

Hürriyet. "Dershanelerin Yüzde Yirmisi Kaçak." July 5, 2011. http://www.hurriyetegitim.com/haberler/05.07.2011/dershanelerin-yuzde-20si-kacak.aspx (accessed August 2011).

Kavak, Yüksel. "Türkiye'de Yükseköğretimin Görünümü ve Geleceğe Bakış." *Yükseköğretim ve Bilim Dergisi* 1 (2011): 55–58.

Kuban, Doğan. "Dershane mi Istersiniz, Öğretim mi?" *Cumhuriyet Bilim Teknoloji Dergisi* 1282 (2011): 2–21.

Kühn, Lotte. *Schulversagen*. München: Knaur Tashenbuch, 2007.

Milliyet. "Kaçak Dershaneler Kayıtlının Dört Katı." February 10, 2009. http://www.milliyet.com.tr/Guncel/HaberDetay.aspx?aType=HaberDetay&Kategori=guncel&KategoriID=24&ArticleID=1057765&Date=10.02.2009&b=Kacak%20dershaneler%20kayitlinin%20dort%20kati (accessed August 2011).

MoNE (Ministry of National Education). "Milli Eğitim Temel Eğitim." 2011a. http://mevzuat.meb.gov.tr/html/88.html (accessed May 2011).

———. "Özel Dershaneler Yönetmeliği." Ankara: Resmi Gazete (no. 25883), 2005a.

———. "Özel Öğretim Kurumları Genel Müdürlüğü." 2011d. http://ookgm.meb.gov.tr/kategorigoster.asp?id=198 (accessed December 2011).

———. "Özel Öğretim Kurumları Yönetmeliği." Ankara: Resmi Gazete (no. 26810), 2008.

———. "PISA 2003 Uluslararası Öğrenci Değerlendirme Projesi, Ulusal Nihai Rapor." Ankara: Eğitim Araştırma ve Geliştirme Dairesi Yayınları, 2005b.

———. "PISA 2006 Uluslararası Öğrenci Değerlendirme Projesi, Ulusal Ön rapor." Ankara: Eğitim Araştırma ve Geliştirme Dairesi Yayınları, 2007.

———. "Strateji Raporu." 2011c. http://sgb.meb.gov.tr/ Str_yon_planlama_ V2 /MEBStratejikPlan.pdf (accessed December 2011).

———. "Tevhid-i Tedrisat Yasası." 2011b. http://mevzuat.meb.gov.tr/ html/110 .html (accessed December 2011).
OECD (Organization for Economic Cooperation and Development). "Education at a Glance 2011: OECD Indicators." 2011a. www.oecd.org/document/2/ 0,3746, en_2649_39263238_48634114_1_1_1_1,00.html (accessed November 2011).
———. "Programme for International Student Assessment–PISA" 2011b. http://www.oecd.org/document/61/0,3746,en_32252351_32235731_46567613_1_1_1_1,00.html (accessed November 2011).
Önder, Mustafa. "Dershane Salgını." *Yeniçağ Gazetesi*, October 13, 2011. http://www.yg.yenicaggazetesi.com.tr/yazargoster.php?haber=20105 (accessed August 2011).
OSYM (Student Selection and Placement Center). "Öğrenci Seçme ve Yerleştirme Merkezi." 2011. http://www.osym.gov.tr/belge/1–4843/ossye-iliskin-sayisal-bilgiler. html (accessed November 2011).
ÖZDEBİR. (Union Association of Private Courses). 2011. http://www.ozdebir.org .tr/ (accessed December 2011).
Özdil, Yılmaz. "Erik Arakla Fesleğen Okşa Raylarda Koş." *Hürriyet*, June 14, 2009. http://hurarsiv.hurriyet.com.tr/goster/haber.aspx?id=11861897&yazarid=249 (accessed August 2011).
Radikal. "Türkiye'deki Çalışanların Çoğu Kayıt Dışı." December 11, 2008. http://www.radikal.com.tr/Radikal.aspx?aType=RadikalHaberDetayV3&ArticleID =912237&Date=11.12.2008&CategoryID=101 (accessed August 2011).
Roesgaard, Marie H. *Japanese Education and the Cram School Business: Functions, Challenges, and Perspectives of the Juku*. Copenhagen (Denmark): Nias, 2006.
Sosyal-İş Sendikası. "Milli Eğitim Bakanlığına Bağlı Dershanelerde Çalışan Öğretmenler İçin." 2011. www.sosyal-is.org.tr/yayinlar/dershane_brosur _18_06_2010.pdf (accessed December 2011).
TDK (Turkish Language Association). 2011. http://tdkterim.gov.tr/bts/ (accessed December 2011).
TUIK (Turkish Statistical Institution). 2011. http://www.tuik.gov.tr (accessed December 2011).
Türk Eğitim-Sen. "Öğretmen Istihdam Politikamız." 2011. www.turkegitimsen. org.tr/ haber_goster.php?haber_id=13830 (accessed December 2011).
Ural, Ayhan. 2011. *Hafif Ağır Denenceler*. Ankara: Detay Yayıncılık, 2006.
———. "Mario Eğitim Modeli." *Eleştirel Pedagoji* 13 (2011): 18–29.
———. *SBS üreticilerine*. *Alternatif Çocuk Gazetesi* 1(2). Ankara: Gazi Üniversitesi İletişim Fakültesi Yayınları, 2008.
———. "Yarışmacı Eğitim Anlayışının Eleştirisi." *Üniversite ve Toplum* 4, no. 1 (2004). http://www.universite-toplum.org/text.php3?id=178 (accessed March 2004).
Yılmaz, Kürşad. "Özel dershane öğretmenlerinin örgütsel güven düzeyleri ile örgütsel vatandaşlık davranışları arasındaki ilişki." *Kuram ve Uygulamada Eğitim Yönetimi* 15, no. 59 (2009): 471–490.

13

The Growth of Islamic Education in Turkey: The AKP's Policies toward *Imam-Hatip* Schools

Mustafa Kemal Coşkun and Burcu Şentürk

The Justice and Development Party (AKP) emerged out of the Welfare Party (RP), which was a political Islamist party, and came to power in 2002. The AKP's politics and discourse are characterized by conservative democracy, which claims to combine the traditional lifestyle inspired by Islam with the Western liberal values that are based on the free market and globalization. The AKP's orientation, which is based on the contradictory attitudes of Islam and the West, is quite different from traditional Islamic discourse. After the political victory of the AKP, the debates about the relationship between Islam and the functions of *Imam-Hatip* schools (IHSs) significantly increased. IHSs, which were founded as a control mechanism of the state over religion, turned out to be a vote-hunting tool of the populist right-wing, and after the 1970s, these schools became the sources of the grassroots of Islamist parties.

This study will discuss the AKP's policies toward IHSs. The main argument of this study is that, under the AKP government, the function of IHSs was redesigned as an instrument to create new modern, conservative intellectuals by articulating the AKP's discourse and contributing to the dispersion of its ideology, and that IHS students are inspired by the AKP's political discourse.

This study is based on data obtained through 217 questionnaires conducted in three IHSs. The schools are chosen on the basis of their location in order to have as homogenous a sample as possible in terms of the socioeconomic status of students in Ankara in 2009. The authors visited classes with the teachers and explained the research to the students. The students were asked whether they were willing to take part in the questionnaire, and none of them refused to participate. The questionnaire was composed of sections on demographic questions; the choice of school; the choice of profession; attitudes on modernity, science, community and religion; the position of women in social life; the choice of newspaper and television programs; and the major problems of Turkey.

A Brief History of IHSs

The establishment of modern Turkey in 1923 opened a new chapter in the history of the Turkish people. The reforms carried out in the nation-building process were designed to cover the entire restructuring and transformation of the society in accordance with the scheme of what is imagined as a modern and secular society/nation. The Republican People's Party (CHP), who were the founders of the republic, aimed at, by means of educational reforms, "fostering...secular and nationalist values" (Özdalga 1999, 419), and they saw education "as the source of modern citizenship" (Pak 2004a, 325). The state took up the responsibility of training religious clergy, rather than handing this job over to the civil society, through IHSs, which were founded as vocational schools in 1923 in 29 different locations (Tanilli 1994). In the first decades of the modern Turkish republic, the main discourse justifying the opening of the IHSs was concerned the cultivation of "enlightened" *imams* (prayer leaders) and *hatips* (preachers), in other words, religious leaders who preached loyalty to a secular nation-state. Since large numbers of Turkish people disapproved of the CHP government due to its repressiveness and stringent control over religion, the introduction of multiparty politics in 1946 and the lively competition for votes made Islam a burning issue. In 1950, the Democratic Party (DP), which was opposed to the secular-modern nation-state ideology of the CHP, came to power and facilitated the resurgence of Islam, especially at the popular level. At that point, IHSs became an element of its populist policies for winning the support of the masses. The successor right-wing parties displayed this attitude of the DP toward IHSs until the 2000s.

IHSs and the Increase in Islamic-Oriented Political Parties

The greatest and the most significant political Islamist movement in Turkey was the National Outlook movement, which was initiated by

Necmettin Erbakan in the late 1960s. He established first the National Order Party (MNP) in 1970, and then the National Salvation Party (MSP) as its successor in 1972. Both parties were condemned for being antilaic, and were closed down after the military interventions in 1971 and 1980, respectively. In 1983, Erbakan established the RP.

The general elections in 1995 resulted in a prominent victory of the RP, which won 21.4 percent of the votes, and in 1996, Erbakan became the prime minister. Political Islam peaked in the 1990s, and the Islamist discourse expanded and competed with the secular ideology, as political Islam was perceived as a prominent challenge and threat for the present system. In this period, the RP enjoyed strong support from the *cemaat*[1] (religious community), to which *Imam-Hatip* students and their families belonged. A large portion of deputies, mayors, and grassroots activists of the RP consisted of IHS graduates. With the rise of political Islam, the debates on IHSs both in academia and at the policy level took place between two camps. The first camp saw the IHSs as a vehicle of Islamic renewal and rejuvenation, while the second camp believed that these schools had been educating antisystemic and fundamentalist individuals. According to them, IHSs were a potential threat to the secular principles of the republic.

The Turkish Armed Forces (TSK) as well as the secular political elites and the secular elements of the population were not comfortable with this rise of political Islam, and they were in the second camp of the debates on IHSs. On February 28, 1997, the TSK initiated a meeting of the National Security Council and took a series of decisions related to the rising power of political Islam in Turkey. It was declared that the possibility of an installment of sharia was the major threat facing Turkey. The decisions taken in this meeting directly affected Islamic education and IHSs.

First of all, Koran courses were subjected to control by the Ministry of National Education; children under the age of 12 years were not allowed to attend these courses. Female university students were forbidden to wear headscarves in class. The scoring system of the university exam was changed, and for IHS students, it became nearly impossible to enter departments other than theology programs at a university. In an implicit way, IHS graduates were prevented from being employed in some state institutions, such as the army, the police force, and nonreligious jobs such as medical doctors/physicians, lawyers, engineers, and so forth. The duration of compulsory education was increased to eight years (from five years) and therefore the junior high school level (i.e, secondary school level) of IHSs was closed. The result of preventing IHS students from working in nonreligious jobs and the closing of the junior high school level of IHSs was a significant decrease in both the number of the IHSs and IHS students. Consequently, by means of the policies implemented between 1997 and 2002, the state increased its control over religion in the public sphere, and this obstructed the IHSs' growth.

Following the ban on the RP by the Supreme Court, the RP's deputies established the Virtue Party (FP), which was also closed down in 2001 since the Supreme Court had concluded that the FP had engaged in antilaic activities. This marked a turning point for the Islamist movement; a division appeared between the advocates of National Outlook and the younger generation in the Islamist movement. The former established the Felicity Party (SP), and the latter the Justice and Development Party (AKP) in 2001. The AKP, in contrast to the RP, FP, and SP, adopted a globalist view and emphasized incorporation into the global system both on a domestic and an international level. The AKP defined itself as conservative democratic, launched a pro–European Union (EU) policy, and detached itself from the traditional political Islamist discourse that assumed a contradiction between Islam and the West. It did not have an antilaicist perspective, which had usually been taken by former Islamic-oriented parties. On the other hand, the AKP successfully addressed the religious segment of the society through its promises to solve the problems of the headscarf and the admission of IHS students to the university. In 2002, in the first general elections in which the AKP participated, it got 34 percent of the votes and came to power.

IHSs and the Educational Politics of the AKP

With the AKP's rise to power, regarding the promises of the AKP about the *Imam-Hatip*s and the covering of women's heads (the headscarf issue), it seemed inevitable that one of the main contentions to be brought into the political limelight was going to be the role of religion in education (Pak 2004b, 322).

In the context of the AKP's policies toward IHSs, debates concerning IHSs arose both on the level of policy making and of public debate, with respect to two aspects. The first one is about the status of IHSs. Are the IHSs vocational schools that are supposed to educate religious clergy, or do they mainly target religious education? The presence of female students, even their outnumbering of male students, is considered a key issue in this debate. In Islam, women are not allowed to occupy the professions of *imam* and *hatip*

(Eyüboğlu 1979, 77), yet even the name of these religious schools is *Imam-Hatip* schools. Therefore, female students cannot work as an *imam* or a *hatip* after their graduation. Their only professional opportunity is to work as religion teachers in schools. However, the vacancies available in these departments are far less than the number of female graduates. Since the existence of female students is neither widely discussed in public debates nor tackled on the policy-making level, it can be concluded that the public does not perceive IHSs as vocational schools. Accordingly, it can be suggested that these schools are not considered vocational schools even by female students of IHSs and their families, since the major factor in female students' choice of this type of school is to fulfill the will of their families.

Our research indicates that 63.1 percent of female IHS students in the sample would like to have nonreligious jobs, for which the IHSs are not designed. Moreover, this perception of IHSs is not restricted only to female students. Sixty-two percent of all IHS students would like to have professions (i.e., doctor, teacher, and lawyer) that do not have any connection to their high school education, whereas the ratio of students who choose IHSs in order to acquire a job (i.e., *imam*, *hatip*) that is compatible with their high school education is only 38. This attitude of IHS students goes hand in hand with the AKP government's perception of IHSs. The AKP government also proved that they did not perceive IHSs as vocational schools by shifting their status from vocational schools, to "Religious Education Intensive Regular High Schools" in 2009 (Official Gazette, July 31, 2009).

It was their families' will that was the prominent reason for 42 percent of IHS students choosing IHSs, implying that a significant portion of these students did not choose these schools on their own. Considering that these schools are no longer vocational schools, it can be suggested that IHSs' main function was formerly to train clergy to carry out religious services, and that in the meantime they have been transformed into "more mainstream educational institutions that cater primarily to the children of conservative and religious parents... and communities wanted to guide children's lives in accordance with their religious beliefs and to create a new generation of devout Muslim" (Pak 2004b, 333).

The second aspect of the debate involved which departments in universities should accept IHS students. When these institutions were legally recognized as vocational schools, their students were only admitted to the theology departments. Although IHSs offer the same

Table 13.1 Statistics of IHSs

	Number of the Schools	Total Number of Students
2001–2002	558	77,389
2002–2003	536	71,100
2003–2004	452	84,898
2004–2005	452	89,914
2005–2006	453	1,08,064
2006–2007	455	1,20,668
2007–2008	456	1,29,274
2008–2009	458	1,43,637
2009–2010	465	1,98,581

Source: Ministry of National Education (2011).

curriculum as before, since their status was transformed to that of "regular high schools," their students' choice of university departments is no longer restricted to theology departments. Therefore, the students of IHSs now have access to nonreligious professions such as medicine, law, teaching, and engineering. Consequently, it is not unexpected that the number of IHS students increased as it is shown in Table 13.1.[2]

IHS Students as Organic Intellectuals

The AKP initiated a new era in the relations between the IHSs and the right-wing party in power. It considers the IHSs as an instrument for educating what Antonio Gramsci calls "organic intellectuals," whereas previous right-wing populist parties perceived the IHSs as a tool for populist policies. Thus these schools have become an instrument for creating a *cemaat* that is loyal to the AKP's rule. IHS graduates will be the organic intellectuals of the *cemaat*, who harmonize modern urban life with an Islamist and conservative lifestyle. On this point, enabling IHS students to have access to any departments in universities, implying that they can be employed as professionals, is critical. In this sense, the general aim of the AKP in changing the status of IHSs is to create new public officers and civil servants who have a conservative-Islamist ideology. Put differently, an Islamist orientation and discourse would be installed among public administrative staff. Henceforth, IHSs are institutions intended for educating the organic intellectuals as well as the members of the *cemaat* who are familiar with positive science and also have a strong religious background and conservative upbringing. In this sense, these schools are considered as a tool for the inculcation of social behavior required for a person to become a member of the *cemaat*.

The *cemaat* stands for a civil society that is shaped and reproduced by the AKP's policies, mostly through the media instruments inspired by the Gülen Movement[3] and the intellectual proponents of the AKP. Based on the findings of our research, it can be suggested that the IHS students follow these media instruments. For example, 47.8 percent of IHS students read the newspapers *Zaman* and *Yeni Şafak*, which are known to be the media organs of the Gülen Movement and to reflect the AKP's policies and ideas. Moreover, 19.9 percent of students read the newspapers *Vakit* and *Milli Gazete*, which have an Islamist orientation and are close to the perspective of the SP (or that of Necmettin Erbakan as the founder of National Outlook). In this context, 68 percent of IHS students read the Islamist newspapers, although the political parties and ideas are slightly different from each other. The section of the questionnaire on the choice of television channels, shows that 51.2 percent of students watch the Islamic-oriented channels like *Samanyolu, Meltem, Kanal 7*, which mostly broadcast religious programs and are owned by the religious communities.

Given that a large number of IHS students in the sample declare that they read the newspapers that not only share the same political-ideological perspective with the AKP and Gülen Movement, but also function in spreading their political views, this chapter suggests that IHS students are highly influenced by the AKP's discourse and ideology. For example, for the AKP and the Gülen Movement, the problem of the headscarf issue was among the major problems of Turkey, which becomes a powerful instrument in the discourse of the AKP during election times.

When the IHS students in our sample were asked to write down the three major problems of Turkey, 32.3 percent of IHS students stated the ban on the headscarf as the major problem of Turkey. Unemployment, economic problems, and terrorism are mentioned as the major problems of Turkey by, respectively, 22.4 percent, 11.8 percent, 7.5 percent of students in the sample. Moreover, environmental issues and problems in education are considered to be major problems.[4] This finding also shows that the perceptions of IHS students are mostly shaped by the political agenda and discourse of the AKP, in the sense that students take the agenda of the AKP as the agenda of all of Turkey. Therefore, the AKP was quite successful in fulfilling its goal of creating a new *cemaat* whose members are educated and articulate in its policies, loyal to its political agenda, and consider the political agenda and the atmosphere of Turkey through the party's perspective. In this sense, it is not surprising that the IHS students perceive the ban on the headscarf as a major problem and generalize it to the whole population, where other problems such as unemployment and the economic situation, from which the majority of the population suffers, are outnumbered.

The AKP has overemphasized that many members of the party, including the prime minister, AKP deputies, mayors, and party members graduated from IHSs. In this way, it has identified the rise of the AKP's power with the expanding opportunities for IHS students in terms of choice of university departments, which directly affects them in their future occupations. During the AKP's rule, education in IHSs provides a privilege in a certain part of the society. This opens up a new space for the construction of the identity of alumni of the IHSs. Therefore, being educated in IHSs becomes part and parcel of the identity of the alumni and students of these schools. The speech given by the Prime Minister Erdoğan in a meeting organized by the Alumni Association of IHSs perfectly corresponds to these features of their identities.

> Today, rather than addressing you, I am addressing myself among you.... Being a graduate of an IHS has been a source of pride for myself for my whole life. I am also proud that all my sons and daughters graduated from IHSs. They have never disappointed me. I shall always remain proud of being a graduate of *Imam-Hatip* until the end of my life.[5]

Combining Modernity with Islam

One of the central points of the debates between Islamists and secularist-modernists has concerned the status of woman. Both in the nation-building process of the CHP and in the recent revivalist period of Islam, the aim was to create a new type of society in which the issues of woman and family were emphasized, since "women, both as mother and as spouse, [were seen] as the heart of the society" (Esposito 1991, 205), and women are mostly constructed as the "the cultural and the biological reproducers of the nation and the carriers of the national values" (Yuval-Davis 1997, 21). While the unveiling of women in the public sphere was represented as a proof of an achievement of the modern nation-state by the republicans, from an Islamist and antilaic perspective, veiled women, whose aspiration is not to be visible in the public sphere, are highlighted as the "carriers of tradition" (Yuval-Davis 1997). In this sense, the issues of the presence of women in the public sphere and politics, and the headscarf have been hotly debated in terms of the representation of women throughout the history of the modernization of Turkey.

With the combination of modernism and the conservative-religious life style advocated by the AKP, a new ideal woman, who is visible in the public sphere with her headscarf as a symbol of tradition and Islam, appeared (Seçginelgin 2011, 143). The students' attitudes toward an "ideal woman" (Table 13.2), suggests that IHS students consider that a woman's place is her home, but she is allowed to be educated and to work, which implies being visible in public sphere. These attitudes of students illustrate the way in which they combine the modern promises for women in terms of participation in public life with traditional lifestyles, which are mainly based on the gendered segregation of the public and the private. Furthermore, promoting women's visibility in

Table 13.2 Percentages of agreement with statements* about women's status

	Agree (%)	Neither Agree nor Disagree (%)	Disagree (%)	Total (%)
Women should work	69	14.5	16.5	100
Women can talk with other men	47.2	18.1	34.7	100
Women can talk only with their husband	27.7	14.4	57.9	100
Professional education is unnecessary for women	7.6	5	87.4	100
Women's heads should be covered in public places	82.6	10	7.4	100
Women can travel alone	36.4	18.1	45.5	100
A woman's place is her home	44.9	14.3	40.8	100

*These statements were "Likert-type" statements: "strongly agree" at one end, and "strongly disagree" at the other end of each statement. The table presents percentages of "strongly agree and agree" combined as "agree" responses, and "strongly disagree and disagree" combined as "disagree" responses to the statements.

the public sphere is neither inspired by the ideals of women's freedom nor by the unveiled female icon of republican ideology. Women, who are allowed to study and work, are supposed to balance their public visibility with the traditional and Islamic way of life, in which they are forbidden to travel alone and to socialize with men, and are required to wear a headscarf. This attitude of students confirms that they attempt to harmonize the modern life and the Islamic lifestyle, as this harmony is also promoted through the AKP discourse.

The attitudes of IHS students toward Islam and the Islamic and modern lifestyles was assessed through a set of questions on the role and influence of religion in daily and social life. Table 13.3 illustrates that for *Imam-Hatip* students, a life that lacks a religious perspective is not compatible with their understanding of morality.

First of all, the students believe that a concept of morality independent from religion is not possible at all, while faith is a must for a decent life for 98 percent of them, and less than half of them think that an atheist can be a good person. This perception of morality is significantly related to the AKP's discourse, which emphasizes the relationship between Islam and morality. The prime minister recently declared that Turkey needs a religious generation for the country's moral superiority, and that this generation will be created by the AKP. He replied to the critic of his declaration, saying the following: "Rather than a religious generation, shall we aim at upbringing a *tinerci*[6] generation? Is it acceptable that the AKP with its conservative democratic identity should bring up an atheist generation?" (*Evrensel Gazetesi*, February 1, 2012). Based on his speech, it is especially clear

Table 13.3 Religion and culture relations*

	Agree (%)	Neither Agree nor Disagree (%)	Disagree (%)	Total (%)
Faith is a must for a dignified life	98	1	1	100
All the aspects of our culture should be adapted to the modern age	48.2	26.7	25.1	100
An atheist can be a good person	39.1	21.3	39.6	100

*These statements were "Likert-type" statements: "strongly agree" at one end, and "strongly disagree" at the other end of each statement. The table presents percentages of "strongly agree and agree" combined as "agree" responses, and "strongly disagree and disagree" combined as "disagree" responses to the statements.

that the opposite of a "religious generation" might be only either a *tinerci* or an atheist, which implies that the only decent lifestyle is one inspired by religion and one in which there is no room for a morality without religion. Secondly, nearly half of the students think that the culture should adapt to the modern way of life. It can be suggested that IHS students agree with the AKP's main discourse, which is based on a combination of traditional values and modern life.

Conclusion

While the role of religion in the society has always been an element of a crucial debate since the early years of the modern Turkish republic, religious education has also created hot debates and political clashes since education is a key instrument in shaping society in a way that ensures that a religious sect and the clergy internalize the secular features of the new republic and cannot challenge it. IHSs emerged on a political agenda in which the state needed to take a strong control over religion. After 1950, these schools turned out to be the political instrument of right-wing parties' populist policies. With the appearance of Islamic parties and political Islamic movements in the 1970s, these movements and parties established more direct and organic relations with IHSs. IHSs status in this era changed from that of a "political instrument of popular policies" to a grassroots element of the Islamic-oriented political parties. On this point, with this crucial change in their roles, they started to be regarded as a potential threat to the secular and modern features of the Turkish state. Therefore, IHSs became a centerpiece of the policies that sought to protect secularism from the rise of political Islam in the late 1990s.

The organic relations of IHSs with the Islamic-oriented political parties became even more obvious in the era of the AKP governments. Additionally, IHSs in this era began to be considered as an instrument through which a *cemaat*, which is an alternative to a secular social formation, is maintained. This *cemaat* is supposed to follow and support the AKP's policies, and it is a community that harmonizes the religious way of life with modern life. This is also apparent in our research, which indicates that the majority of IHS students follow the voices of the media that support the AKP and the issue that they perceive as the major problem of Turkey, namely, the ban on the headscarf, which is what the AKP presented as a significant problem and attempted to resolve.

Given that the AKP took 49.8 percent[7] of the votes in the general election in June 2011, the AKP has the enough power to expand its *cemaat* and increase the number of its organic intellectuals. While our research touched upon to what extent the perspective of IHS students is shaped by AKP policies, it might prompt future research on the central position of IHSs in the AKP's period in governmentand policies. Moreover, examining the relationship between IHSs and the AKP in future studies might contribute to a proper understanding of the large public support that the AKP has gained during the past nine years.

Notes

1. In its general meaning, *cemaat* refers to "community" in Turkish, and its narrow meaning is a group of people who belong to the same religious group. Throughout this article, *cemaat* will be used in its narrow meaning, "religious community."
2. Compiled and calculated from various statistical data at the websites of MoNE (accessed March 2011).
3. Fethullah Gülen is a religious scholar who is the inspiration behind the movement, as a moderate Muslim. This is a movement that is growing in the Turkish diaspora around the world as well as in Turkey, and it is well funded (For details, see Ebaugh 2010).
4. The section about the problems of Turkey in the questionnaire comprised of an open-ended question to which students are asked respond by writing down the major problems of Turkey. The reason for not providing choices and for designing this part as open ended is to be able to understand the way in which students conceptualize, perceive, and express the major problems of Turkey.
5. www.samanyoluhaber.com.tr. December 5, 2010.
6. *Tinerci*, which literally means "thinner addict," is used for the street children who are addicted to thinner, and this concept has negative connotations in terms of criminality and morality.
7. This was a remarkable success of the AKP, since from the beginning of the multiparty era of Turkey, which started in 1946, none of the political parties were able to gain such a large portion of the votes in general elections.

References

Akşit, Bahattin. "Islamic Education in Turkey: Medrese Reform in Late Ottoman Times and Imam-Hatip Schools in the Republic." In *Islam in Modern Turkey*, edited by Richard L. Tapper, 145–170. London: IB Tauris, 1991.
Ebaugh, Helen R. *The Gülen Movement: A Sociological Analysis of a Civic Movement Rooted in Moderate Islam*. New York: Springer, 2010.
Esposito, John. *Islam: The Straight Path*. New York: Oxford University Press, 1991.

Evrensel Gazetesi. "Erdoğan: Dindar Gençlik İstiyorum." February 1, 2012. http://evrensel.net/news.php?id=22269 (accessed February 5, 2012).
Eyüboğlu, İsmet Z. *Alevilik-Sünnilik: İslam Düşüncesi*. Istanbul: Hür yayınları, 1979.
Hermann, Rainer. "Political Islam in Secular Turkey." *Islam and Christian-Muslim Relations* 14, no. 3 (2003): 265–276.
MoNE (Ministry of National Education). "Önceki Yıllarda Yayınlanmış Milli Eğitim İstatistikleri." 2011. http://sgb.meb.gov.tr/istatistik/arsiv.html (accessed March 2011).
Official Gazette. No: 27305. July 31, 2009.
Özdalga, Elizabeth. "Education in the Name of 'Order and Progress,': Reflections on the Recent Eight-Year Obligatory School Reform in Turkey." *The Muslim World* 89, no. 3–4 (1999): 414–438.
Pak, Sun Y. "Articulating the Boundary between Secularism and Islamism: The Imam-Hatip Schools of Turkey." *Anthropology and Education Quarterly* 35, no. 3 (2004b): 324–344.
———. "Cultural Policies and Vocational Religious Education: The Case of Turkey." *Comparative Education* 40, no. 3 (2004a): 321–341.
Seçginelgin, Hakan. "Democracy, Civil Society and Women's Public Personae: Turkish Women and Muslim Headscarves." In *Globality, Democracy and Civil Society*, edited by Terrell Carver and Jens Bartelson, 133–148. New York: Routledge, 2011.
Tanilli, Server. *Nasıl bir eğitim istiyoruz?* Istanbul: Cem Yayınevi, 1994.
Yuval-Davis, Nira. *Gender and Nation*. London: SAGE Publications, 1997.

14
Body Politics and Sexual Education under AKP Rule

Serdar M. Değirmencioğlu

This chapter examines how body politics are shaped under the Justice and Development Party (AKP) governments. Body politics encompasses practices and policies through which social forces regulate the human body, as well as the struggle over the degree of individual and social control of the body. Historically speaking, totalitarian and conservative regimes have been very interested in regulating the human body, particularly women's bodies. In recent years the AKP has been very eager to take command of young people's bodies both in and outside of school.

Surprisingly little attention has been paid to body politics. In his book examining the history of childhood in Turkey, Bekir Onur (2005) captures the overpowering role of the state and the stifling effect of religion on many realms of daily life, including the lives of children, but neglects how young bodies have been regulated. Body politics have only recently been addressed explicitly, either by feminist scholars or by those promoting Islam (e.g., Okumuş 2009). It is therefore necessary to rely on various sources, including personal accounts, and disciplines to gain insight into the way in which body politics were shaped before and have been shaped during the AKP regime.

This chapter first examines the body politics of the early republic and of the 1980s. It highlights the linkages between AKP politics and the military regime, and examines in particular the continuities between the Motherland Party (ANAP) and AKP policies. Next, the enigmatic nature of the AKP is examined to better situate the AKP on the conservative spectrum. The AKP is run in a top-down fashion; therefore, it is useful to examine the links between AKP policies and Recep Tayyip Erdoğan's personality and body politics. The chapter focuses on three areas in which AKP body politics are most evident: regulations about contact, sexuality, and public ceremonies.

The Republican Legacy

In the late Ottoman Empire, students had to follow a strict and all-encompassing moral code (Fortna 2002). There was very little distinction between public and private life, and very little room for a student to make decisions to offset social control of his body. The founders of the Republic of Turkey were intent on breaking with the Ottoman past and modernizing the country along Western lines. There was, however, an inherent contradiction in that the leading reformers were all military men and, in keeping with the military tradition, all believed in the sacredness and the power of the state.

The move to create an educational system in line with republican ideas was powerful but contained inherent contradictions, particularly those that had to do with the power of the state. In a nutshell, the body politics of the new regime was heavy-handed and authoritarian: The country was poor, and the people had poor health. The recurring wars of the late Ottoman period and the War of Liberation produced a large number of orphaned, sick, or frail children who needed state protection on the one hand and a good education on the other (Akbaş 2008).

The society as a whole needed to be disciplined in order to create a modern citizenry. Modern societies consisted of healthy and dutiful citizens—both men and women—and regulating the human body in many spheres of life could serve the desired goal of quick but orderly social progress (Akın 2004, Alemdaroğlu 2005).

Two primary goals, establishing national unity and modernizing the country, were often linked with the transformation of the human body in line with modern, rational, and scientific values (Alemdaroğlu 2005). The body politics of the new regime aimed to discipline society in order to create modern, healthy, and dutiful citizens by regulating the human body in many spheres of life, including clothing, aesthetics, health, reproduction, childcare, and housekeeping.

Eugenics emerged as a part of the state's hygienic and ethical regulation of the human body (Alemdaroğlu 2005): Abortion was abolished, a premarital examination of couples was mandated, and childcare institutions were established. Prevention of epidemics and alcoholism became a priority. These ideas were not entirely original: Eugenics was quite popular in the West. Under the nation-building frenzy, a collectivist and authoritarian discourse emerged, producing an ultranationalist ideology that bordered on racism (Maksudyan 2005).

In the early 1950s, the single-party regime and its heavy hand gave way to a new, somewhat liberal regime with a new government that aligned itself with conservative social forces. The new government was not against militaristic practices in schools, except those that did not fit with gender segregation. The new government pushed some of the reforms back, but the military coup in 1960 put an end to this, at least for a while.

With the progressive 1960 constitution, a more vibrant political climate emerged. However, two parties dominated politics until 1980: a left-of-center party that represented the heavy-handed and authoritarian republican tradition, and a right-of-center party that aligned with conservative forces—including religious movements—and served small and big capital. Both parties regarded education and schools as the breeding ground for acceptable and unacceptable social forces. More than ever, schools became the battleground between so-called "progressive" and "reactionary" forces.

The Legacy of the Military Coup

In 1980, Turkey was rocked twice. On January 24, the government of Turkey announced a set of liberal reforms. On September 12, a military coup followed. A reign of ruthless terror began. The military eliminated all political movements and any existing democratic practices and institutions (Doğan 2010). As the military furnished the path to a neoliberal economy, it solidified ideological control over all institutions, regulating scientific, cultural, and educational affairs.

An authoritarian framework, which increased the power of executive organs, was established with the 1982 constitution. In 1983, Turgut Özal, chief architect of the January 24 decisions, came to power with his ANAP. Özal served as prime minister for two consecutive terms and later as president (1989–1993). Since then, Turkey has been under the influence of neoliberal, neoconservative, and oppressive government policies (Bedirhanoğlu 2010).

The military government promoted a "Turkish-Islamic synthesis," a conservative doctrine that was produced to offset socialist influences in the 1970s. The official discourse had always promoted nationalism, but nationalism alone was not sufficient—nationalist movements in Turkey often drew on socialism in the past. Religion would be a much stronger antidote. In line with this doctrine, the 1982 constitution mandated religious education in schools.

Teacher-training institutions were always seen as a key mechanism to produce the ideologically ideal teacher. In the 1970s, these institutions became a major battleground between "progressive" and "reactionary" forces and were controlled by ultranationalists by the end of the decade. After the coup, these institutions were officially cleansed of the leftist elements. Soon these institutions were producing large numbers of teachers who were equipped with the "Turkish-Islamic synthesis."

By 1984, these new teachers were in classrooms. The military government introduced strict dress codes for teachers and students, and cleansed schools of leftist teachers. Özal's ANAP endorsed these policies. Özal proudly claimed that he had brought together four political traditions, but that the Ministry of National Education (MoNE) was reserved for his conservative associates.[1]

The Enigma

For many foreign observers, the social and political history of Turkey presents a story that is too complex to fathom. Many observers fail to capture the links between the 1980s and the AKP regime. The AKP appears to be very eager to dismantle old mechanisms, including the constitution put in place by the military government, and has earned a reputation of a prodemocracy party despite the fact that the AKP was an outcome of the political climate the military government produced.[2]

The enigma—or the apparent reformist character—of the AKP stems from the determination of its leaders to break away from the heavy-handed republican tradition. For many observers, reforms and election victories are nothing but a democratic success story. To more inquisitive observers, however, the AKP agenda reflects authoritarian and oppressive policies that serve a neoliberal and a neoconservative order (Bedirhanoğlu 2010). Under the AKP, the regime has become more and more like single-party rule. Party leaders allow little criticism or debate even within their own ranks.

With the AKP's economic policies, more wealth is produced, but it is distributed unequally, as reflected in the increase in poverty (Köse and Bahçe 2010). This appears to contradict the popular support for the AKP: With increasing poverty, popular support should decline. What appears to be the case, however, is that the AKP has effective tools to produce popular consent despite difficult living conditions for millions of people.

The new order AKP has built needs the state apparatus less. Public life is controlled through various channels: the local government, local conservative nongovernmental organizations, and an obedient media. The republican tradition employed the army as the ultimate force whenever it needed. The new order regards the police force as a safer mechanism: A force directly under the orders of the government can control public life more effectively. The ultimate force to sustain the neoconservative order is, of course, religion.

The Leader

In order to understand AKP politics, it is necessary to pay attention to the way in which the party functions. The AKP, just like Özal's ANAP, was engineered to function in a top-down fashion. Just like Özal, Erdoğan has ruled single-handedly. Not surprisingly, his personality and life history have made a strong impact on the party. One of these areas that has felt his influence is body politics.

In his recent book, Cemal Dindar (2010) examines the links between Erdoğan's tendencies and his upbringing, and reveals his notions about body politics. This is not an unwarranted exercise, because Erdoğan often presents himself as a model and uses his own experiences as an example in his speeches. To him, this is natural because his life reflects a good Muslim upbringing and success despite challenges.

For Erdoğan, family is the natural, god-given social arrangement, ruled by the father/husband. In fact, it is the only arrangement he recognizes. The wife (or the wives) and children obey the authoritarian and pious husband/father. For Erdoğan, his upbringing and his own family simply reflect the proper roles family members are supposed to play, exactly as portrayed in popular books about children under Islamic Law (e.g., Canan 2001).

This puts other social arrangements in jeopardy. Single women are considered women "without a husband"; hence, a moral liability. Single men are considered potential hazards: They are full of desires that may be hazardous if not brought under control (Çelik 2008). Erdoğan presents himself as an example: He was able to manage his youthful urges through early marriage (Dindar 2011). The society, thus, needs proper body politics, and the AKP should promote the family, sexual abstinence, and strict gender roles.

Body Politics in Public Areas

The emphasis on family in the AKP discourse is reflected in body politics across the country. Various developments reveal a consistent pattern, one that is often neglected. This is partly due to the heated debate about the veil in Turkey and elsewhere (see Scott 2007). An overemphasis comes at the expense of understanding the negative influence of religion-inspired regulations on various aspects of public life.

Local governments under AKP control have asserted considerable pressure on public areas, such as public parks. Policing in parks reveals important clues as to how public life is governed by the local AKP governments. A police presence in public parks has increased over the years, and there is an effort across the country to eliminate alcohol use and "indecent behavior" (e.g., hugging) in public areas.

In Ankara, the capital city, and elsewhere, parks are portrayed as a family domain and municipality or "security" staff police the parks accordingly. This means heavy pressure on single men—young men under 30—who are portrayed as potential hazards (Alkan Zeybek 2011). If a park is to be a family place, women should feel comfortable and safe—particularly safe from moral hazards. Only if single men are kept at a distance, women—young and/or old—can be at peace.

Moral sensibilities have made it very difficult for university students to find a rental apartment in many cities. Single women, in particular, face an offensive reasoning: They are considered a moral liability. A university student was told, just like many others, that she could not rent an apartment because the residents of the building were "good Muslims."

Body Politics at Large

Images, too, can be moral hazards. In 2003, a large, billboard-size swimsuit advertisement at the Istanbul airport, featuring a woman in a bikini, was removed by the airport authority, under directions from the ministry. The ministry argued that this image did not suit the tastes of pilgrims traveling to Mecca. A lawsuit followed: The airport authority lost the case and had to pay compensation to the swimsuit company.

The swimsuit controversy or other debates have not affected the AKP's resolve to bring public life in line with religion. Municipalities under AKP control have been repeatedly criticized for putting pressure on stores selling alcohol. This wave finally reached the Istanbul city center in 2011: Beyoğlu Municipality used force to cleanse the streets of alcohol in the city center. Streets full of cafés, bars, and restaurants turned silent almost overnight.

With subsequent election victories, the AKP leaders firmly believe they have consolidated power, and they have become bolder with their demands. Erdoğan has repeatedly demanded that women produce at least three children. In 2012, he declared that the AKP strives to build "faithful generations."

Ruling by Rulers

As noted earlier, body politics in schools started changing in the early 1980s. The military desired disciplined schools: strict dress codes, and a lot of nationalism and religion. There was little overt resistance among teachers because the military government considered resistance as subversion. Each and every act of subversion was classified and used against individuals or their family members.

Under the Özal governments, forms of gender segregation became more common. Previously, body politics had more to do with hairstyles and dress codes. Sexuality was managed by the hidden curriculum. With Vehbi Dinçerler as the minister of education, new teachers with distinctive markers (e.g., hair- and mustache styles, or suits popular in pro-Islam movements) held positions in classrooms across the country. Many teachers started to demand gender-segregated seating in the classroom.

Under the AKP, it became more common for school staff to enforce gender segregation. In less conservative cities, such as Antalya and Mersin, school principals are setting limits as to how close girls and boys can be to one another. In one high school, students were asked to follow a 45-cm-rule: Boys and girls were to keep this distance. In another school, the distance was set at one meter (Değirmencioğlu 2011a).

It was clear that the authorities were interested in policing students as if they were following an old phrase: *Ateş ile barut bir arada olmaz* (Fire and gunpowder do not mix). Contact between boys and girls must be controlled. Under the AKP, schools are ruled by a ruler.

Control in Private Schools

Private schools used to be reserved for the privileged in the 1970s. With neoliberalism and government support, private schools grew in number in the post-1980 period. Many parents who were afraid of the inadequacies of public schools chose private schools as the last resort in the past. However, the picture changed with Fettullah Gülen schools. Many of these schools operated outside of Turkey, particularly in countries that were formerly part of the Soviet Union. Leaders from various parties regarded Gülen schools as a tool for expanding Turkey's influence and actively supported them (Balcı 2003).

Gülen schools served as a springboard for the Gülen movement in Turkey. In less than 20 years, the Gülen movement built a network of schools, tutorial institutions, student dormitories and guesthouses, and several publishing companies, as well as a major daily newspaper, several radio and television channels, and a news agency. This expansion and the power it generated inspired other religious movements to start their own schools and student housing arrangements.

These developments resulted in a large number of private schools, governed in accordance with Gülen's teachings or another version of Islam. Leaving aside the problem that the Gülen movement presents for democracy, the fact is that religious private schools can control students to a greater extent. Various accounts indicate that body politics in religious private schools can amount to total control.

Many religious private schools present control as an advantage. The argument is often presented in terms of harmony: If school and home are in harmony, as if school is a natural extension of the home, the student will benefit. If public life is also under control, harmony will expand to the society.

The AKP has close and not always obvious ties with various religious groups, including the Gülen movement (Çınar 2010). As noted earlier, the AKP needs the state apparatus less than the previous regimes because it can rely on other forms of control, including religious movements, networks, and communities. Not surprisingly, harmony is the common element in the AKP discourse.

Sexuality and Sex Education

Turkey has always had a young population. The basic response in the field of education to young people's sexual development has always been avoidance. After 1980, in particular, sexuality did not fit well with the notion that children and youth needed protection: Youth, in particular, required protection from politics and bad habits.[3]

An official convention was held in 1988 to discuss youth issues and inform the government (Gençlik Hizmetleri Genel Müdürlüğü 1988). Many topics were discussed and common themes (e.g., values) were repeated. A few young people voiced a demand for sex education. These voices were not heeded: Sexual development and the influence of the media were neglected.[4]

Sexual education per se used to be available only in private schools. This is still true but only in some private schools: Sexuality in religious private schools is simply off-limits. In public schools, however, there were feeble attempts to introduce some form of sexual education in the 1990s. Topics such as pubertal development were introduced in a course on health in the eighth grade, but it was too little and too late.

Under the AKP, pubertal development was placed under the subject "Science and Technology" in the sixth grade, and more advanced topics, such as AIDS, were introduced in a course on health in the ninth grade. But the content steered clear of sexuality per se. Despite the fact that a hypersexualized media surrounds young people, the curriculum is kept free of real-life sexuality.

In a setting where sexuality is taboo and sexual development is not supported, confusion arises and a hypersexualized media can be more appealing. When tensions surrounding sexuality surface, the AKP and pro-Islam media outlets always offer the same response: more religion. If a sex scandal surfaces, the response is a cover-up.[5]

The Battle over Ceremonies

Celebrations marking a historical achievement (e.g., the founding of the republic) or a valued element of the society (e.g., children) were deemed important in the republican tradition. But thematic celebrations were nevertheless coupled with a historical turning point: Children's Day was celebrated on April 23—the day the first parliament was convened. Youth and Sports Day was celebrated on May 19—the day portrayed in official history as the beginning of the War of Liberation.

The military government added a third component to Youth and Sports Day—it was to be celebrated as the birthday of Mustafa Kemal. During the 1980s, Youth and Sports Day was turned into a massive event, performed in stadiums in Soviet-bloc style. For youth, big celebrations were bureaucratic exercises and deserved little or no enthusiasm.

The debate over the Commemoration of Atatürk, Youth, and Sports Day (also known as May 19 Ceremonies) began in 2003, when a group of university students demanded that the event be celebrated outside of stadiums. The AKP minister of education sided with the students, and this sparked a controversy. The controversy had little, if anything, to do with whether the youth had a right to determine whether and how the celebrations should take place. The demands were voiced again for a year or two, and then the protests subsided.

In 2012, however, the Ministry of National Education declared that the celebrations would be held outside of stadiums, except for Ankara. A careful analysis reveals, however, that the Ministry had neither any hard evidence against the celebrations, nor any interest in what youth really wanted. The decision was made on ideological grounds: Adolescent girls wearing tights and miniskirts in public, and performing side-by-side with boys could not be tolerated anymore by the AKP (Değirmencioğlu 2012).

Conclusion

It is clear that the AKP has emerged from the political vacuum created in the 1980s. Just like the military, the AKP solidified ideological control over all institutions regulating scientific, cultural and educational affairs. Just like the ANAP, the AKP has championed neoliberal, neoconservative, and oppressive government policies, but in a bolder and stronger fashion. For the AKP, "development" means a neoliberal order and "justice" is nothing more than the legitimization of a conservative agenda. It is no surprise, therefore, that this conservative agenda is now clearly reflected in the AKP's body politics.

Believing that their hegemony is firm, the AKP leaders have become bolder with their demands regarding proper body politics: control of sexuality and contact through gender segregation, sexual abstinence, strict gender roles, family, and patriarchy. The state apparatus is needed less because other forms of "civil control" (i.e., religious movements, networks, and communities) are at work. In private schools, for instance, students are under the total control of an ideology that is keen on regulating bodies.

The regulation of bodies according to religion has become more forceful under the AKP. The party is eager to police bodies in parks, on the streets, or in images, directly or with help from civil forces and a pro-Islam media. Single men are labeled as moral hazards, single women as moral liabilities. Official public events where girls' bodies were not covered or where girls and boys mixed freely could not be tolerated anymore: These events have been discontinued.

School life has clearly changed under the AKP. In many school, urinals were removed or broken because they meant improper manners. Forms of gender segregation were introduced and monitored. Previously unheard of practices (e.g., the one-meter rule) are being used to keep boys and girls apart. Abstinence and self-discipline, clearly enforced by various authorities, are integral elements of the AKP's body politics, and sex education in schools is considered off-limits.

Control in schools is a major goal, and under the AKP, body control is further consolidated through the introduction of police into the schools. Local governments in major cities have started showing an interest in scouts—a tradition that originally served as a means of control. The debate around school uniforms has already begun. It is expected that the AKP will use this debate to pave the way for allowing religious attire in schools.

Notes

1. Vehbi Dinçerler (1983–1985), İmren Aykut (1985–1987), and Hasan Celal Güzel (1987–1989).
2. Over the years, the AKP has benefited from a power vacuum and unfair election regulations—both a product of the 1980s. The fact that the AKP was founded in 2001 and in only 15 months received about 35 percent of the vote is a clear indication of a volatile political climate. In only three years, the AKP gained control over municipalities in most major cities, with about 42 percent of the vote. In the 2007 elections, the AKP increased its vote to about 47 percent. In 2011, only ten years after its birth, the AKP received almost 50 percent of the vote.
3. In the 1982 Constitution (Article 58 "Protection of Youth"), the state was given the role of raising youth in the light of science and the teachings of Atatürk (i.e., official ideology) and protecting youth from separatist ideologies, ignorance, alcohol and illicit substances, delinquency, gambling, and other bad habits.
4. Özal started the process that eventually led to the abolishment of the state monopoly over broadcasting. During what used to be the news hour in the evening, some private channels broadcasted sexually explicit films. Next the Internet and mobile phones started to penetrate the society. As control over the media decreased, forms of hypersexualized media emerged. Pornography became more accessible via the Internet. Men were very eager to consume hypersexualized media. These developments generated a lot of concern among conservatives, and body politics in schools became even more instrumental for steering young people away from moral hazards.
5. In 2010, two scandals surfaced in Siirt, historically a very religious area. Many officials, including school staff, were charged with molesting or raping four girls repeatedly. The second scandal involved eight adolescent boys sexually blackmailing a classmate: She had to offer two cousins, a two-year-old and a three-year old girl, to the boys. The two girls were raped and later killed. The response from the government and the Ministry of National Education, in particular, amounted to avoidance and denial, and did not reflect any intention to address underlying causes (Değirmencioğlu 2011b).

References

Akbaş, Emrah. "Construction of the Child Question in Early Republican Turkey and Social Services as an Art of Government." *Vulnerable Children and Youth Studies* 3, no. 1 (2008): 24–30.

Akın, Yiğit. *"Gürbüz ve Yavuz Evlatlar"*: *Erken Cumhuriyet'te Beden Terbiyesi ve Spor*. Istanbul: İletişim Yayınları, 2004.
Alemdaroğlu, Ayça. "Politics of the Body and Eugenic Discourse in Early Republican Turkey." *Body & Society* 11, no. 3 (2005): 61–76.
Alkan Zeybek, Hilal. "Bir Aile Mekanında Cinsiyet, Cinsellik ve Güvenlik." In *Neoliberalizm ve Mahremiyet: Türkiye'de Beden, Sağlık ve Cinsellik*, edited by Cenk Özbay, Ayşecan Terzioğlu, and Yeşim Yasin, 227–243. Istanbul: Metis, 2011.
Balcı, Bayram. "Fethullah Gülen's Missionary Schools in Central Asia and Their Role in the Spreading of Turkism and Islam." *Religion, State and Society* 31, no. 2 (2003): 151–177.
Bedirhanoğlu, Pınar. "Türkiye'de neoliberal otoriter devletin AKP'li yüzü." In *AKP Kitabı: Bir Dönüşümün Bilançosu* (2nd ed.), edited by İlhan Uzgel and Bülent Duru, 40–65. Ankara: Phoenix Yayınevi, 2010.
Canan, İbrahim. *Allah'ın Çocuklara Bahşettiği Haklar*. Istanbul: Timaş, 2001.
Çelik, Kezban. "'My state is my father': Youth Unemployment Experiences under the Weak State Welfare Provisions of Turkey." *Journal of Youth Studies* 11, no. 4 (2008): 429–444.
Çınar, Menderes. "AKP ve İslami hareketler: Defansif ve dağıtıcı iktidar kardeşliği." In *AKP Kitabı: Bir Dönüşümün Bilançosu* (2nd ed.), edited by İlhan Uzgel and Bülent Duru, 307–315. Ankara: Phoenix Yayınevi, 2010.
Değirmencioğlu, Serdar M. "Cinsel Gelişim ve Cinsel Haklar Işığında Cinsel İstismar." *8 Mart (Eğitim Sen Kadın Dergisi)* (2011b): 19–21.
———. "En İleri Namus." *Eğitim Sen Bülteni* 8–21 (2011a): 17–19.
———. "Törene güle güle, dayatmaya devam." *Evrensel*, February 5, 2012.
Dindar, Cemal. *Bi'at ve Öfke: Recep Tayyip Erdoğan'ın Psikobiyografisi*. Istanbul: Cadde Yayınları, 2011.
Doğan, Mustafa G. "When Neoliberalism Confronts the Moral Economy of Workers: The final Spring of Turkish Labor Unions." *European Journal of Turkish Studies* 11 (2010). http://ejts.revues.org/index4321.html (accessed September 2011).
Fortna, Benjamin. *Imperial Classroom: Islam, Education and the State in Late Ottoman Empire*. Oxford: Oxford University Press, 2002.
Gençlik Hizmetleri Genel Müdürlüğü. *I. Gençlik Şurası (24–28 Ekim 1988): Raporlar, Görüşmeler, Kararla*r. Ankara: T. C. Milli Eğitim Gençlik Spor Bakanlığı, 1988.
Köse, Ahmet Haşim, and Serdal Bahçe. "'Hayırsever' Devletin Yükselişi: AKP Yönetiminde Gelir Dağılımı ve Yoksulluk." In *AKP Kitabı: Bir Dönüşümün Bilançosu* (2nd ed.), edited by İlhan Uzgel and Bülent Duru, 492–509. Ankara: Phoenix Yayınevi, 2010.
Maksudyan, Nazan. "The Turkish Review of Anthropology and the Racist Face of Turkish Nationalism." *Cultural Dynamics* 17, no. 3 (2005): 291–322.
Okumuş, Ejder. "Bedene müdahalenin sosyolojisi." *Şarkiyat İlmi Araştırmalar Dergisi* 2 (2009): 1–15.
Onur, Bekir. *Türkiye'de Çocukluğun Tarihi*. Ankara: İmge, 2005.
Scott, Joan W. *Politics of the Veil*. Princeton: Princeton University Press, 2007.

15

Early Childhood Education in Turkey: A Critical Overview

Mehmet Toran

The fact that studies on Early Childhood Education (ECE) in Turkey have recently been put on the agenda together with changes in the field of education reveals the importance of ECE in general. The lack of critical and historical studies on ECE makes it especially difficult to obtain a general point of view, and causes us to neglect any review of the problem. Therefore, a review of the historical process is required to understand the structural and legal arrangements related to ECE. This article, in this context, will focus primarily on the historical process of ECE and then determine its current status.

The Last Decade of the Ottoman Empire: Laboratory of the Republic

Contemporary policies related to various spheres of life in Turkey date back to the final years of the Ottoman Empire. In particular, constitutional and legislative amendments implemented by the Party of Union and Progress (PUP) in 1908, which corresponds to the Second Constitutional Monarchy Period, constitute, in a sense, the basis of the republic that would be founded. The PUP determined the system of ideological, political, and economic thought of modern Turkey in a political sense (Deringil 2002). A bourgeois movement, PUP, which started the process of nationalization, is considered as a movement that supports the Western sense of political life (Gündüz 2008).

The movement also acted as a political laboratory of the Republic of Turkey to be established (Alış 2010). The Second Constitutional Monarchy Period is a movement of nationalization, and also a movement to restructure all segments of society. It possessed an economic point of view and aimed to create a new society for the bourgeoisie of the republic. The first tasks related to the implementation of the project were carried out in the field of education, and attempts were made to define a new type of citizen through a series of laws and regulations (Akyüz 1996, Akyüz 2001, İnal 1999). Not surprisingly, the PUP viewed children as the future of Turkish society, and thus expanded preschools across the country, equipping them to train future generations in civic awareness, which was on their agenda as a step in achieving their goal (Uyanık 2009).

Although the Ottoman elementary schools[1] were known to be the first ECE schools, according to the literature on the history of education in Turkey, the first ECE schools in the modern sense were opened by the PUP for Turkish children against the minority schools during the Second Constitutional Monarchy period (Öztürk 1998, Uyanık 2009). Even though these schools belonged to an association, they were fee-charging schools, and they aimed to raise Turkish children loyal to their national and moral values, and individuals who would be useful to their own homeland and nation. Teachers working at these schools had to be of Turkish origin so as to teach children their mother tongue, Turkish (Akyüz 1999a, İleri 2005). In addition, teachers of Turkish origin claimed that the education the children received from Jewish and Armenian teachers was not appropriate from the perspective of Turkish ethics and morality. Therefore, particular attention was paid to teacher training in the years that followed, and relevant legal regulations were instituted (Akyüz 1999b).

During the disintegration of the Ottoman Empire, after the Armenian revolt that occurred in Adana in 1908, a school named *Darüleytam-ı Osmani* (Orphanage of Ottoman) was opened especially for the assimilation of Armenian children whose families were forced to emigrate. The medium of instruction in this school, which was composed of Turkish and Armenian children, was Turkish, following a curriculum that aimed to instill Turkish social and cultural values into these children. Therefore, this school took its place in history as the first place where the assimilation policies of the newly established republic were carried out (Çelik 2007, Akyüz 1999a).

As a result of the effort to make ECE widespread, the *Ana Mektepleri Nizamnamesi* (Preschools Regulation) was prepared in

1915 regarding the operation of preschools (Deretarla Gül 2008, Gözütok 2003). The aims of preschools, and the duties and responsibilities of teachers who would be employed in these schools were determined in this regulation. The regulation aimed to support the growth and development of the children and raise them in accordance with Turkish traditions and Islamic values (Deretarla Gül 2008).

A transition from Ottomanism to Turkism was seen in the field of education during the Second Constitutional Monarchy Period, and this transition period played an important role in determining the ECE policies of the republic (Yetim 2008). The Preschools Regulation was also enforced during the republican period until 1952, and new nursery schools were restructured in accordance with this regulation (Yazar 2007). The Second Constitutional Monarchy Period, which was seen as a laboratory for the republic that would be established, provided a basis for the establishment of a new country with its new paradigm of ideology, and all tasks carried out, including those in the area of education, were done within this framework (Karataş 2003). In this respect, it is possible to see traces of this period in ECE.

The Structuring of ECE in Turkey (1923–1980)

Despite the new policies put in place in many fields when the republic was established in 1923, one can easily see that tasks carried out in the field of education date back to a few years before the establishment of the republic. In the thirteenth session of the Assembly, in 1920, education was put on the agenda, and the attitude of the republic toward education was defined. The aims of education that were particularly discussed and clarified in this session consisted of strengthening the national and religious values of Turkish children, helping children to gain an understanding of national history, teaching the Turkish language to children, promoting the richness of the Turkish language, and achieving these aims in education (Taş 2003). In his speech in 1921, Mustafa Kemal (Atatürk) highlighted the importance and the necessity of a national culture and defended the need to remove the division between education and culture (MoNE 2011). With this understanding, the republic aimed for a new type of citizen, and education was included within a central structure as defined by the *Tevhid-i Tedrisat Kanunu*[2] (Law on Unification of Education). The Ministry of National Education (MoNE) was established in 1923, and the Ministry undertook the responsibility of structuring programs and disseminating them, and forming budgets (Gözütok 2003).

Investment in ECE was mainly entrusted to the private sector and local administrations in the early years of the republic; however, the state made some attempts to open teacher education programs. To address the problem of a teacher shortage, it was proposed at the Congress of Inspectors of Education in 1925 that an institution for preschool teaching should be founded, but this proposal was not implemented (Öztürk 1998). A preschool teaching institution was opened in Ankara in 1927 (Öztürk 2001), yet this institution was closed when the resources allocated for preschools were transferred to primary education in the subsequent two years. A legal structure to support preschool teaching institutions could not be established until the 1960s (Oktay 1999). The high rate of the participation of women in the labor market in the 1960s, urbanization, internal immigration and changes in the family structure revealed the need for ECE. As a response to these changes, legal arrangements were made to educate more preschool teachers (Ural and Ramazan 2007).

Analysis of the pre-1980 development plans shows the main issues that the republic focused on. These plans focused on spreading preschool education, particularly in regions with low socioeconomic status, and the teaching of Turkish to children in those regions; expanding preschools to protect the children of single-parent families, and providing information to parents through handbooks. However, the Third Five-Year Development Plan, formed in 1973, states that the private sector would need to be supported by the MoNE and its relevant institutions in order for preschool education to be expanded due to the lack of public resources (DPT 1973, Çelik 2007). It was also emphasized in the same plan that education, in order to create manpower to fulfill the requirements of industrialization, should start at the earliest grades (DPT 1973). The Fourth Five-Year Development Plan, formed in 1978, also underlined the lack of resources for preschool education. The plan states that the expansion of preschool education would be promoted by both the public and private sectors. As discussed, after the 1960s, the MoNE supported the private sector in the effort to expand ECE, yet the Ministry also tried to preserve the central structure of ECE, that is, the fundamental values of the republic, through supervising the private sector. In other words, because public preschools' needs for budgets, equipment, and teachers were not met satisfactorily by the state, private preschools were supported (DPT 1979).

Preschool education was referred to in the *National Education Basic Law* (no. 1739), which was enacted in 1973 and which is still in force, for the first time in a comprehensive manner. According to this law, children younger than the compulsory school age were defined as "preschool children." The purpose, duties, and responsibilities of preschool education were defined by the law. With the survival of the state as its main objective, the law aimed to bring up citizens who are aware of patriotism, family values, national values, duties, and responsibilities for the Republic of Turkey, and to support the growth and development of children. The law also aimed to prepare children for primary education in compliance with the fundamental aims of national education; provide children, especially those whose families live in poverty, with preschool services; support children's physical, mental, and emotional development and help them acquire good habits; and enable them to speak Turkish correctly and properly (Official Gazette 1973). With law no. 1739, all levels of education were centralized and preschool education was defined comprehensively for the first time. It is clearly seen in the law that pluralist culture in education is ignored. Efforts are made to create a homogeneous society with Turkish and Islamic traditions from the early years of development of children. However, this situation poses an obstacle to democracy and pluralism, and to the quality, expansion, and different practices in preschool education (*Official Gazette* 1973).

The Breaking Point in Education: The Current Status of ECE (from 1980 till Now)

The 1980 military coup played a major role in the determination of policies, especially by providing a large area of movement for the conservative right and liberal tendency in which they set their own cadre in public offices, implementing liberal policies, and controlling government institutions. ECE was placed as the main issue on the agenda of the Tenth Ministry of the National Education Council in 1981. In the Council, it was decided that preschool classes would be opened for children in the age group of six years old. The basics of the program, including the objectives, duties, and responsibilities of preschool education institutions, were also determined in the Council. The ECE program outlined at the Tenth Ministry of the National Education Council listed the objectives of the ECE program as contributing to political integration in line with Kemalism, meeting the developmental needs of children, and helping middle-class children from regions with a low socioeconomic status to develop competence in academics and in Turkish. To put it differently, children who followed the ECE program were expected to develop basic skills, and to be proud of being a Turk, respect the flag, know and respect Atatürk, speak Turkish properly, know Turkish traditions and customs, exhibit moral behavior (MoNE 1981). In the Twelfth Council of the Ministry of National Education, it was determined that the implementation of guidance services in preschool education would be in line with the economic and social conditions of the state in order to achieve the national objectives as soon as possible (MoNE 1988). Preschool education was also discussed in the Fourteenth Council of the Ministry of National Education, and the "build-operate-transfer" model was adopted for the expansion of preschool education. ECE was left to the free market. In the Seventeenth Council of the Ministry of National Education, it appeared that there would be a tax break for entities in the private sector that offered ECE service. Thus, international nongovernmental organizations (NGOs), local associations, and foundations were encouraged to take responsibility, and they would be allowed to contribute to the expansion of preschool education (MoNE 1993, MoNE 2006a). In the Eighteenth Council of the Ministry of National Education, held in 2010, the open market was considered, and educational levels, including preschool education, were structured for a qualified work force. Further, it was decided that preschool children would be canalized into their prospective professions beginning with preschool education. Also, while it was emphasized that preschool children should be educated in values, the content of those values was not specified clearly (MoNE 2010).

The five-year development plans formed in the post-1980 period show a parallel with the decisions taken at the Councils of the Ministry of National Education. In the Fifth Five-Year Development Plan for the dissemination of ECE it was decided to benefit from actual situation on maximum level and to support private schools (DPT 1985). In the Sixth Five-Year Development Plan it was aimed to start to promote early childhood education and to increase the schooling rate (DPT 1990). In the seventh five-year development plan, the need for an increase in the quality of education starting from preschool was underlined in order to increase the quality of the workforce quality and to regulate preschool education in accordance with European Union (EU) norms (DPT 1996). In the Eighth Five-Year Development Plan, carried out in the early years of the government of the Justice and Development Party (AKP), the development of standards to eliminate the differences between institutions offering preschool education was the goal. It was determined that the development of written, and audio-visual programs would be encouraged as a way to make children at preschool institutions loyal to national, moral, and spiritual values; implementation of a holistic approach, and use of Turkish at preschool education effectively were decided (DPT 2001). In the Ninth Five-Year Development Plan, which corresponded to the AKP's second government era (2007–2011), the importance of the private sector in education was underlined again, and it was highlighted that education services offered by the private sector, from preschool education to higher education, were of high quality, and that support for the private sector in the field of education would continue (*Official Gazette* 2007).

Taking the Ministry of National Education Councils and the five-year development plans into account since 1980, it is noticeable that the structure of the status quo has been maintained in education in general, and in ECE in particular, whereas ECE was also entrusted to the private sector, and the private sector continued to be supported by the state. ECE was frequently discussed both in the Councils and in plans, and the aim was to spread this form of education. Moreover, the nationalist understanding as articulated by conservatism continued, and manpower was structured in such a manner that it would contribute to the market economy. This understanding came to the fore with the government of the AKP, and the process accelerated.

The studies about ECE were not limited with councils of Ministry of National Education and Development Plans. The studies were also done by institutions such as NGO's, government institutions, universities, and so on. With circular no. 2004–71, issued by the Directorate General of Preschool Education, the MoNE designated 2004–2005 as the "breakthrough in preschool education." In this circular, the following aims were adopted: using temporarily employed expert trainers as much as possible to meet the teacher shortage so as to expand preschool education, supporting all sectors that invest in preschool education, meeting the developmental needs of children, and helping them develop national and moral values in accordance with the law (no.1739) (MoNE 2004).

According to the law no. 2547 which was enacted in 1981 the responsibility to train teacher was given to universities. During the late 1990s with the support of the World Bank (WB), the Council of Higher Education (CoHE) structured the institutions that train teachers and established the National Committee For Training Teachers (CoHE 2007a). As a result of this structural amendment, teacher education was incorporated into the faculties of education, and departments of preschool teaching were opened within departments of primary school teaching starting in 1998. With this regulation, preschool teacher education departments were opened in many universities in a short time to meet the need for preschool teachers (CoHE 2007b). According to the data for 2010–2011, there are 98 preschool teaching departments within the universities (OSYM 2011). However, the total number of instructors in these departments is 260, of whom 130 have doctoral degrees (OSYM 2010). While the concern for meeting the basic needs of the market is included in the Bologna Process, inadequate numbers of faculty members lead to a lowering of the quality of teacher candidates. Although the CoHE claimed that the era was defined by the updating of undergraduate teacher education programs in accordance with international standards, considering that courses developed in parallel to the Bologna Process are aimed at growing the workforce as based on criteria predicted by the market (COHE 2011; Atay-Turhan et al. 2009), centralism thus still holds the authority to decide what the courses at the universities will be.

Starting in 1981, efforts to improve the quality of ECE programs were made within the framework of the law (no. 1739), and were redesigned in 1994, and while the program designed for children aged 0–36 months is still in operation, the program for children aged 3–4 years was revised in 2002 and finalized in 2006. The basic philosophy of the program is developmental, and it prioritizes individual differences and student-based learning and active participation. Nevertheless, the aim and principles of the program still follow the national approach (MoNE 2006b). However, with the recent amendment made in 2009, a framework conforming to international standards was set for the aims of the institutions in the regulation of preschools, staff, and organization. In practice, none of the standards was realized. The teacher shortage still continues, the objectives of the institutions are still in the nationalist line, and the lack of equipment for the effective operation of these institutions continues to create problems (MoNE 2009a).

A book on ECE published by the Turkish Industrialists' and Businessmen's Association (TUSIAD) in 2005 suggested that preschool education institutions should be opened in the industrialized cities to increase the labor-force participation of women, and also in the regions where ethnic groups, especially Kurdish people, live, in order to eliminate ethnic problems and encourage diversity in the cultural formation of children. TUSIAD also emphasized that the budget allocated to preschool education is inadequate and that the private sector should be supportive in this regard (TUSIAD 2005). Budget statistics of the MoNE show that the budget allocated to preschool education is at a very low level within the overall education budget. In addition, 40 percent of the budget allocated to preschool education is funded by the private sector, while 60 percent is funded by the state (MoNE 2009b). Statistics also highlight that annual spending per child in preschool education by the government is US$171 in Turkey. This amount is very low when compared to other Organization for Economic Cooperation and Development (OECD) countries (OECD 2009). The inadequacy of the budget allocated to preschool education had a negative impact on schooling, and school enrollment of children between three and five years was 27 percent in 2009–2010. The figure for children between four and five years remained at around 40 percent (MoNE 2009c).

In contrast to official statistics, research conducted by the Bogazici University Social Policy Forum (2009) determined the preschool enrollment rate in Turkey to be 16 percent. Having received academic and financial support from the WB and the United Nations Children's Fund (UNICEF), the government speeded up expansion and made preschool education compulsory for the five- to six-year-old children by issuing a circular in 2007 due to the fact that school enrollment rate was low in Turkey (MoNE 2007). A pilot study was conducted first in the selected provinces, and then new provinces were added later in 2011. Lack of statistical information about the recruitment of teachers, schooling rate and assisted services in pilot provinces, where preschool education is compulsory, makes it difficult to reach to scientific data on how the pilot study was implemented. As the preschool education with tuition fee was made mandatory with this implementation, the government imposed the costs of preschool education on families in a sense. However, as no legal arrangement has been made on this issue, the student's right to education is interrupted by the state when s/he cannot pay school fees for 15 days (Eurydice 2010, MoNE 2009a).

Conclusion

A review of the documents and implementations on ECE in Turkey illustrates that a structure based on centralized and national values has been built particularly by destroying differences. Although the expansion of ECE continues, these institutions are very far from meeting the needs of society. In particular, support to capital that is, entrusting the work on ECE to the private sector, reduces the quality of preschool education. The undergraduate program for ECE teachers ignores the best interests of children, and preschool education programs are far from meeting the needs of children and also lead to problems in practice.

The decisions of the governments in the development plans and in the Councils of Ministry of National Education were adopted especially in the interests of capital, and it was also decided that it would be necessary to train a future labor force starting at an early age. Studies focusing on the schooling rate and based on fully numerical data made the quantity in the ECE come to the forefront. However, the fact that the central government audits both public and private preschool education institutions and imposes the implementation of a central program obstructs the work being done on alternative approaches to curriculum development for ECE, as well as the qualities of democracy, pluralism, social sensitivity, awareness, and a culture of peace.

Notes

1. Ottoman Elementary Schools (890–1923) were founded for five- to six-year-old children to teach the Koran, math, and literacy, and these schools were not compulsory.
2. When the madrasas were abolished by the *Tevhid-i Tedrisat* (law of the Unification of Education) on March 3, 1924, all schools in the territory of the Republic of Turkey were attached to the MoNE, and the government aimed to achieve a national standard by bringing them together under one roof. However, the goal of this law was to have coeducation of boys and girls.

References

Akyüz, Yahya. "Anaokullarının Türkiye'deki Kuruluş ve Gelişim Tarihçesi." *Milli Eğitim Dergisi* 132 (1996): 11–17.

———. "Osmanlı Son Döneminde Kızların Eğitimi ve Öğretmen Faika Ünlüer'in Yetişmesi ve Meslek Hayatı." *Milli Eğitim Dergisi* 143 (1999b). http://yayim.meb.gov.tr/dergiler/143/1.htm (accessed May 2010).

———. "17. Yüzyıldan Günümüze Türk Eğitiminde Başlıca Düzenleme ve Geliştirme Çabaları (Genel Özellikler ve Doğrultular)." *Milli Eğitim Dergisi* 144 (1999a). http://yayim.meb.gov.tr/dergiler/144/akyuz.htm (accessed July 2011).

———. *Türk Eğitim Tarihi*. Istanbul: Alfa Yayınları, 2001.

Alış, Ahmet. "Üç Devrin Tanığı: Modern Kürt Siyasi Tarihinin İçinden Musa Anter'i Okumak." *Birikim Dergisi: Güncel Makaleler* (September 2010). http://www.birikimdergisi.com/birikim/makale.aspx?mid=661&makale (accessed June 2011).

Atay-Turhan, Tülay, et al. "The New Turkish Early Childhood Teacher Education Curriculum: A Brief Look." *Asia Pacific Education Review* 10, no. 3 (2009): 345–356.

Boğaziçi Üniversitesi Sosyal Politika Forumu. "Türkiye'de Çocuk Bakım Hizmetlerinin Yaygınlaştırılmasına Yönelik Bir Öneri: Mahalle Kreşleri." 2009. http://www.spf.boun.edu.tr/docs/MAHALLE%20KRESLERI%20-%20 ARASTIRMA%20RAPORU.pdf (accessed April 2010).

CoHE (Council of Higher Education). *Öğretmen Yetiştirme ve Eğitim Fakülteleri (1982–2007): Öğretmenin Üniversitede Yetiştirilmesinin Değerlendirilmesi*. Ankara: Yükseköğretim Kurulu Yayını, 2007a.

———. *Programlar ve Ders İçerikleri*. Ankara: Government Printing Office, 2011. http://www.yok.gov.tr/component/option,com_docman/task,cat_view /gid,134/Itemid,215/ (accessed October 2011).

———. *Türkiye'nin yükseköğretim stratejileri*. Ankara: Yükseköğretim Kurulu Yayını, 2007b.

Çelik, Meryem. "Türkiye'de Okul Öncesi Eğitimin Gelişimi." Master's thesis, Atatürk Üniversitesi Sosyal Bilimler Enstitüsü, Erzurum, Turkey, 2007.

Deretarla Gül, Ebru. "Meşrutiyet'ten Günümüze Okul Öncesi Eğitim." *Ç.Ü. Sosyal Bilimler Enstitüsü Dergisi* 17, no. 1 (2008): 269–278.

Deringil, Selim. *İktidarın Sembolleri ve İdeoloji*. Istanbul: Yapı Kredi Yayınları, 2002.

DPT (State Planning Organization). *Altıncı Beş Yıllık Kalkınma Planı: 1990–1994*. Ankara: Government Printing Office, 1990. http://ekutup.dpt.gov.tr /plan/plan6.pdf (accessed March 2011).

———. *Beşinci Beş Yıllık Kalkınma Planı: 1985–1989*. Ankara: Government Printing Office, 1985. http://ekutup.dpt.gov.tr/plan/plan5.pdf (accessed March 2011).

———. *Dördüncü Beş Yıllık Kalkınma Planı: 1979–1983*. Ankara: Government Printing Office, 1979. http://ekutup.dpt.gov.tr/plan/plan4.pdf (accessed March 2011).

———. *Uzun Vadeli Strateji ve Sekizinci Beş Yıllık Kalkınma Planı: 2001–2005*. Ankara: Government Printing Office, 2001. http://ekutup.dpt.gov.tr/plan /plan8.pdf (accessed March 2011).

———.*Üçüncü Beş Yıllık Kalkınma Planı: 1973–1977*. Ankara: Government Printing Office, 1973. http://ekutup.dpt.gov.tr/plan/plan3.pdf (accessed March 2011).

———. *Yedinci Beş Yıllık Kalkınma Planı: 1996–2000*. Ankara: Government Printing Office, 1996. http://ekutup.dpt.gov.tr/plan/plan7.pdf (accessed March 2011).

Eurydice. "Avrupa Eğitim ve Yetiştirme Sistemlerinin Yapısı: Türkiye 2009/10." 2010. European Commission Database. http://eacea.ec.europa.eu/education /eurydice/documents/eurybase/structures/041TRTR.pdf (accessed March 2011).

Gözütok, F. Dilek. "Türkiye'de Program Geliştirme Çalışmaları." *Milli Eğitim Dergisi* 160 (2003). http://yayim.meb.gov.tr/dergiler/160/gozutok.htm (accessed April 2010).
Gündüz, Mustafa. "Son Dönem Osmanlı Aydınlarının Yeni Birey ve Toplum Oluşturma Düşünceleri." *Erdem Dergisi* 51 (2008): 137–169.
İleri, İlay. "Batı Gözüyle, Meşrutiyet Döneminde Osmanlı Hükümetlerinin, Dil ve Eğitim Politikalarına Karşı Tepkiler." *Ankara Üniversitesi Osmanlı Tarihi Araştırma ve Uygulama Merkezi Dergisi* 18 (2005): 213–220.
İnal, Kemal. "Paternalist Politikanın İdeal Türk Çocuğu." *Ankara Üniversitesi Eğitim Bilimleri Fakültesi Dergisi* 32, no. 1 (1999): 195–212.
Karataş, Süleyman. "Osmanlı Eğitim Sisteminde Batılılaşma." *Sosyal Bilimler Dergisi* 5, no. 1 (2003): 231–242.
MoNE (Ministry of National Education). *2009–2010 Eğitim Öğretim Yılında Okulöncesi Eğitimde (Resmi+Özel) Okul, Şube, Derslik, Öğretmen ve Öğrenci Sayıları*. Ankara: Government Printing Office, 2009c. http://ooegm.meb.gov.tr/istatistik/Okul_oncesI_sayilarI_genel.pdf. (accessed August 2011).
———. *Milli Eğitim İstatistikleri: Örgün Eğitim 2008–2009*. Ankara: Milli Eğitim Bakanlığı Yayınları, 2009b.
———. *Okul Öncesi Eğitim Kurumları Yönetmeliği RG:29/08/2009–27334*. Ankara: Government Printing Office, 2009a. http://mevzuat.meb.gov.tr/html/25486_.html (accessed August 2011).
———. *Okul Öncesi Eğitimi, Genelge No:2007/89*. Ankara: Government Printing Office, 2007.
———. *Okul Öncesi Eğitimin Yaygınlaştırılması, Genelge No:2004/71*. Ankara: Government Printing Office, 2004.
———. *Ondördüncü Milli Eğitim Şurası*. Ankara: Milli Eğitim Basımevi, 1993.
———. *Onikinci Milli Eğitim Şurası*. Ankara: Milli Eğitim Basımevi, 1988.
———. *Onsekizinci Milli Eğitim Şurası*. Ankara: Government Printing Office, 2010. http://www.meb.gov.tr/duyurular/duyurular2010/ttkb/18Sura_kararlarI_tamami.pdf (accessed August 2011).
———. *Onuncu Milli Eğitim Şurası*. Ankara: Milli Eğitim Basımevi, 1981.
———. *Onyedinci Milli Eğitim Şurası*. Ankara: Milli Eğitim Basımevi, 2006a.
———. *36–72 Aylık Çocuklar İçin Okul Öncesi Eğitim Programı*. Ankara: Milli Eğitim Yayınları, 2006b.
———. *Tevhid-i Tedrisat Kanunu ve Medreselerin Kaldırılması*. Ankara: Government Printing Office, 2011. http://www.meb.gov.tr/belirligunler/10kasim/inkilaplari/egitim/tevhidI_tedrisat.htm (accessed August 2011).
OECD (Organization for Economic Cooperation and Development). "Education at a Glance 2009: OECD Indicators." 2009. http://www.oecd.org/dataoecd/41/25/43636332.pdf (accessed October 2009).
Official Gazette. *1739 sayılı Milli Eğitim Temel Kanunu, 24.06.1973/14574* Ankara: Government Printing Office, 1973. http://mevzuat.meb.gov.tr/html/88.html (accessed October 2011).
———. *Dokuzuncu Beş Yıllık Kalkınma Planı: 2007–2013*. Ankara: Government Printing Office, 2006. http://ekutup.dpt.gov.tr/plan/plan9.pdf (accessed March 2011).

Oktay, Ayla. *Yaşamın Sihirli Yılları: Okul Öncesi Dönem*. Istanbul: Epsilon Yayıncılık, 1999.
OSYM (Student Selection and Placement Center). *2010–2011 Öğretim Yılı Lisans Eğitimi Veren Yükseköğretim Programlarında Görevli Öğretim Elamanlarının Öğretim Alanlarına Göre Dağılımı*. Ankara: Government Printing Office, 2010. http://www.osym.gov.tr/dosya/1-58228/h/29lisansogretimalan.pdf (accessed October 2011).
———. *2011-ÖSYS Yükseköğretim Programları ve Kontenjanları Kılavuzu*. Ankara: Government Printing Office, 2011. http://www.osym.gov.tr/belge /1-12584/2011-osys-yuksekogretim-programlari-ve-kontenjanlari-ki-.html (accessed October 2011).
Öztürk, Cemil. *Türkiye'de Dünden Bugüne Öğretmen Yetiştiren Kurumlar*. Istanbul: Marmara Üniversitesi Yayınları, 1998.
———. "21.yüzyılın Eşiğinde Türkiye'de Öğretmen Yetiştirme" In *21. yüzyılda Eğitim ve Türk Eğitim Sistemi*, edited by Orhan Oğuz et al., 223–280. Istanbul: Serdar Eğitim Araştırma Yayıncılık, 2001.
Taş, N. Fahri. "Türk Milli Eğitiminin Yenileşmesi ve Öncelikleri." *Milli Eğitim Dergisi* 159 (2003). http://yayim.meb.gov.tr/dergiler/159/tas.htm (accessed March 2011).
TUSIAD (Turkish Industrialists' and Businessmen's Association). *Doğru başlangıç: Türkiye'de okul öncesi eğitim*. Istanbul: TUSIAD Yayınları, 2005.
Ural, Ozana, and Oya Ramazan. "Türkiye'de Okul Öncesi Eğitimin Dünü ve Bugünü." In *Türkiye'de Okul Öncesi Eğitim ve İlköğretim Sistemi: Temel Sorunlar ve Çözüm Önerileri*, edited by Servet Özdemir, Hasan Bacanlı, and Murat Sözer, 11–61. Ankara: Türk Eğitim Derneği Yayınları, 2007.
Uyanık, Ercan. "II.Meşrutiyet Dönemi'inde Toplumsal Mühendislik Aracı Olarak Eğitim: İttihat ve Terakki Cemiyeti'nin Eğitim Politikaları (1908–1918)." *Amme İdaresi Dergisi* 42, no. 2 (2009): 67–88.
Yazar, Ayşenur. "1914–2006 Okul Öncesi Eğitim Programlarında Yaratıcılığın İncelenmesi." 2007. Master's thesis, Atatürk Üniversitesi Sosyal Bilimler Enstitüsü, Erzurum, 2007.
Yetim, Fahri. "II. Meşrutiyet Döneminde Türkçülüğe Geçişte Kapsayıcı Formül: 'Millet-i Hâkime' Düşüncesi ve Etkileri." *SDÜ Fen Edebiyat Fakültesi Sosyal Bilimler Dergisi* 18 (2008): 65–80.

16

Fights over Human Rights: A Strange Story of Citizenship and Democracy Education

Tuğba Asrak-Hasdemir

In Turkey, some important steps have been taken to incorporate the notion and the teaching of human rights and freedom into the educational system. With the wave raised by the United Nations declaration of the Decade for Human Rights Education for the 1995–2004 period and also the curriculum studies conducted by the United Nations Educational, Scientific and Cultural Organization (UNESCO) in this context, the efforts to teach human rights, especially in the primary schools, gained momentum at the end of the 1990s in Turkey. Therefore, a national committee was formed and a national action plan was prepared to teach human rights issues across the country. The curriculum has since been modified. The course on citizenship and human rights became part of the educational system in 1998 as a required course in primary schools. Since 1999, another course titled Democracy and Human Rights Education has been taught in high schools as an elective course. However, this situation changed in 2005. Although the nature and importance of human rights and democracy has been frequently emphasized by the leaders and the cadre of the Justice and Development Party (AKP), the Ministry of National Education (MoNE) has removed the Citizenship and Human Rights Education course from the primary school curriculum and determined that the subjects and themes related to human rights and freedoms would be taught in other courses. This chapter proposes that the pragmatic ideology of the AKP has had certain effects on the changes related to human rights education. The lack of consistency in educational policies and the lack of uniformity among the official plans and programs have shaped, in particular, the story of the courses on human rights and citizenship during the 2000s.

The 2005–2010 period was an interregnum for the course on human rights education during the rule of the AKP. At the end of the first decade of the 2000s, the MoNE declared that the curriculum would be modified in the context of a project prepared in collaboration with the Council of Europe, called the Democratic Citizenship and Human Rights Education Project. To this end, a course entitled Citizenship and Democracy Education was included in the curriculum of primary education as an elective for the 2010–2011 academic year, and another course "Democracy and Human Rights" was made a part of the high school curriculum.

This chapter will discuss the short history of the courses on human rights, focusing on the AKP era, that is, 2002 to present. Recalling the changes in the curriculum, briefly described above, this history will be analyzed in two parts: 1998–2005 and 2010–2011, following the interregnum for human rights education in primary schools in Turkey. And then, the concluding part will deal with the products of the aforesaid evaluation and offers suggestions.

Human Rights Education and a Story from Turkey

There are two main forms of human rights education in schools: human rights can be taught as an independent course, or human rights can be discussed within different courses. In Turkey, these two forms of human rights education have been especially put into practice in the primary schools.

Since the establishment of the republic in 1923, citizenship education has become a part of the curriculum. With the division of the course Social Sciences into three parts, "Citizenship Education" was included in the secondary education program from the beginning of the 1985–1986 academic year. Until 1995, some changes were made in the content of the course. In this year, the course title was changed to Citizenship and Human Rights Education by the decision of the Ministry of National Education-Board of Education (MoNE-BoE 1995a), its content was restructured, and topics directly related to human rights were included (MoNE-BoE 1995b).

In 1997, the length of compulsory education became eight years by the combination of the five-year primary and three-year secondary education.[1] After this change, the course Citizenship and Human Rights Education came to be taught in primary schools. In 1998, a new curriculum for the course was accepted (MoNE-BoE 1998). Until 2005, the course was taught as a required course in the seventh and eighth grades in the primary schools in accordance with the aforementioned decision of the MoNE-BoE.

Another institutional development on human rights education was the establishment of a National Committee at the end of the 1990s. In relation to the Action Plan of the UN Decade for Human Rights, the High Coordination Board for Human Rights established the National Committee on the Decade for Human Rights Education (NCDHRE). In the first meeting, held on September 3, 1998, the National Committee underlined the problems of and priorities concerning human rights in Turkey. Human rights education is among the priorities. One of the objectives in this regard was to revise the curriculum of human rights courses in primary schools as well as high schools, and to take the necessary measures to provide instructors with the necessary skills to teach human rights in accordance with the objectives of the courses (NCDHRE 1999, 15). Depending upon the results of the inquiry directed by the National Committee, some proposals were put forward, including human rights education in primary schools, high schools, and also universities. In relation to a "required course" on human rights, the Committee stated its decision: "Our committee deems it necessary that the Ministry of National Education, in collaboration with our Committee, revise this programme once again" (NCDHRE 1999, 16–17).

From the 1998–1999 academic year to 2005, the Citizenship and Human Rights Education course has been part of the curriculum as a required course. Yet this situation changed in the early 2000s. The AKP came in power after the 2002 general election. Although the leaders and the cadre of the AKP have frequently emphasized the nature and importance of human rights and democracy on different occasions, the Citizenship and Human Rights Education course has been removed from the primary school curriculum. It was preferred that human rights issues be integrated into the other courses rather than taught as a separate subject. As Abraham Magendzo stated about the practices of Latin American countries, "Incorporating human rights into the school curriculum is fraught with difficulties and tensions.... A major tension producing question is about the place of human rights in the curriculum: whether they are to become a separate subject-matter or to be addressed in all subjects" (1994, n.d.).

Human right issues lost ground in the curriculum between 2005 and 2010. Now, I can briefly talk about the place and content of the Citizenship and Human Rights Education course in relation to certain criticisms between 1998 and 2005.

Human Rights Education: Some Criticisms and a Strange Solution

The National Committee, the Turkish Academy of Sciences, and the History Foundation of Turkey have collaborated to revise "major textbooks used in primary and secondary education in Turkey from the point of view of human rights issues" (Tarba-Ceylan and Irzık 2004, 1). In the project titled Promoting Human Rights in Primary and Secondary Schools Textbooks, the curriculum and the textbooks of the major courses were reviewed and evaluated in accordance with the criteria for qualitative analysis, determined in/for this study. At the end of an extensive review, valuable evaluations were made and shared with officials, academicians, and teachers. The study was also opened up to public through conferences, with the results of the study published in different books between 2003 and 2009. In this part, I will focus on the main points of the evaluations of the textbook for the course Citizenship and Human Rights Education.

Referring to passages in different textbooks, including human rights textbooks, Semih Gemalmaz asserts that restrictions on freedoms as well as expectations of duty and obedience to authority are prioritized over human rights and freedoms. The legitimization of war and the use of nuclear weapon, disregard of the problem of the death penalty, and an approach that instills prejudices against certain social groups are the main points of criticism that Gemalmaz directs at the textbook for the human rights course (2004, 9–39). Similar to Gemalmaz, Çayır states that a duty-oriented outlook is dominant over a rights-oriented one in textbooks, and argues that human rights education should adopt different teaching methods instead of traditional ones: "According to educators, however, successful human rights education cannot limit itself to the cognitive domain. An effective human rights education should also promote inquiry and action" (2003, 399).

Kenan Çayır (2004) also evaluated human rights education textbooks by taking into account the relationship between democracy and human rights. Besides the vague definition of the term "democracy" in certain textbooks for the course Citizenship and Human

Rights Education, he points out that "democracy" and "participation" are reduced to "electoral politics" (Çayır 2004, 96). Insisting on the strong relationship between democracy and human rights, he states that "democracy is a style of life or government which provides the framework for the realization and the practice of human rights. Human rights, however, is an 'ontological' end (not a means to any other end)" (Çayır 2004, 94). In addition to these problems, the glorification of the state or disregard of the relation between the state and its citizens as the basis of this foundation renders the situation more problematic (Çayır 2004, 98–99). Fatma Gök (2004) also underlines the overemphasis on the limitations of rights and freedoms, and also on duties and responsibilities in the textbooks. In short, human rights education has become a lack of the necessary understanding of human rights issues.

In one of the most referenced studies on human rights education, Mesut Gülmez (2001) points out that the approach to teaching the basic terms of human rights is not well ordered. For instance, the term "right" is separated from "freedoms," and explained in different units of the seventh grade textbook. Only the term "universality" is specified as a quality of human rights in the framework of the understanding of natural rights, but other qualities like "inviolability" or "interdependency" are not mentioned (Gülmez 2001), 298).

In addition to the criticisms at the national level, some deficiencies in human rights education, especially in primary and secondary education, have been noted at the international level. The Council of Europe, for instance, reported its criticisms and advice regarding the efforts to raise awareness on human rights, democracy, and citizenship in 2002. The Council asked Turkish authorities to take the necessary actions to establish democratic citizenship and human rights education. The Council insisted on the importance of education in the primary and secondary schools to promote human rights and raise awareness of human rights and democratic citizenship. The related courses were criticized as being teacher-centered, and it was recommended that the course materials and curricula of the existing courses should be revised to ensure participative consciousness of citizenship and human rights (Köylü 2002).

In an interview dated March 2004, Ionna Kuçuradi[2] shared her important advice regarding human rights education in Turkey:

> At present human rights education is conceived as teaching human rights instruments and, sometimes, as intercultural education or civic

education. But in my view, the aim of human rights education should be first and foremost to awaken people about the sincere will to protect human rights.... The second aim of human rights education is to provide people with knowledge of the concepts of human rights, that is, what a human right practically demands and why it demands it. And a third aim is to train people in evaluation, so that they become able to decide, in concrete situations, how to act in order to protect the human rights of those to whom their actions are directed or to avoid damaging others' rights out of ignorance. (2004, n.d.)

The criticisms directed at human rights education that are noted above were also shared and discussed by the officials and authorities of the MoNE. It was expected that some/all of the criticisms would be taken into consideration in the revision of the teaching curriculum of the primary schools that was made in 2005 as a part of regular process of the elaboration of curriculum every five years. However, on the contrary, this revision was a sign of a kind of "end" for the Citizenship and Human Rights Education course, since it was removed from the curriculum and lost the status of being "a separate subject matter." As Abraham Magendzo (1994) reminds us, this is one of the major tensions in the incorporation of human rights into the curriculum: whether to teach the subject as a separate course or whether to address the subject in other courses. It was decided that human rights issues were dealt with in the content of other related courses, and specifically incorporated into the curriculum of the social sciences course. The media literacy course is another course in which human rights issues can be taught. Yet the curriculum and textbook of the course are not suitable for this purpose (Asrak-Hasdemir 2009, 333–334). In the curriculum of media literacy, it is stated that this course is planned as student-based. There is no student textbook to provide active participation of students in the course by letting them prepare their course materials such as collecting news in printed and/or visual forms, and sometimes creating their media products et cetera. Teacher's handbook with its didactic nature, on the other hand, is not in conformity with this curriculum. Also, there are other problems encountered in the process, like who educates and how. Indeed, this course could provide important opportunities for students to learn and practice a wide range of human rights, from the child's rights to freedom of thought and expression, to the right to Internet access.

It is important to note that the year 2005 was, on the one hand, a sort of "end" or the beginning of an "interregnum" for a separate course on human rights; on the other hand, it was The European

Year of Citizenship through Education (Council of Europe 2004). In Turkey, with the approval of the MoNE, a national committee was set up to organize the activities related to the Year of Citizenship. The committee planned to carry out different activities, but could achieve only small portion of them under the headings of Presentation of the Year and Education of Educators. In relation to human rights education, 20 social sciences teachers attended a seminar sponsored by the British Council on Human Rights, Democracy and Citizenship Education in July 2005. Yasemin Karaman-Kepenekçi, the national coordinator, declared that a limited number of the activities was carried out due to budget problems (Karaman-Kepenekçi 2009, 430–431). Of these limited activities, a very small portion of social sciences teachers (20) could have participated in the training. If we set aside the total number of social sciences teachers within the whole system and take into account only the numbers for 2005, the number of social sciences teachers appointed or recruited part-time in this year was 1,091 (MoNE 2011).

The results of different activities undertaken[3] in terms of educational policies between 2007 and 2009 were listed in *Turkey's Activity Report* to the Council of Europe Standing Conference of Ministers of Education (2010). In relation to the issue being discussed here, it is reported that educators from different disciplines, especially philosophy teachers, participated in the training seminars. Within the system of the United Nations, national initiatives undertaken by Turkish authorities in the first phase of the World Program for Human Rights Education were summarized under the heading for projects called Human Rights and Democracy (Office of the UN High Commissioner for Human Rights, 2005–2009). In these projects, there were no curricular activities and studies for a separate course on democratic citizenship and human rights education. Also the majority of the activities were not comprehensive since they were directed at certain groups of students or were realized as pilot projects rather than being nationwide projects.

In the White Paper Final Draft (2007) that reported the evaluations of the curriculum changes within the European Union Support to Basic Education Project 2002–2007, human rights and citizenship were considered as interdisciplinary skills rather than as common core skills in the new curriculum base, as in the report titled *Structures of Education and Training Systems in Europe-Turkey* (Turkish Eurydice Unit 2009–2010,19). Although some characteristics peculiar to democratic citizenship and some issues related to human rights education have found a place in some important official documents like the Ninth National Plan (2007–2013) and the Special Commission Report on Education that were prepared for the Plan, we cannot talk about comprehensive, well-established short, middle, and long-term policies on human rights education. This situation conforms with the "pragmatic" outlook of the AKP. To put it differently, as Ziya Öniş says, "The AKP is a broad-based political movement with a pragmatic ideology" (2006, 132).

In the Ninth National Plan, *Program of 2011*, it is stated that persons in the age of the information society, who adopt national and moral values, will be equipped with different skills and values, including democratic values and critical minds, and will contribute to contemporary civilization (DPT 2010, 206). In the Special Commission Report on Education within the Plan, in the vision of education for the future, the model for individuals created through the educational process is described as "individuals loyal to the Republic and to *democratic values*, and who practice these values in their lives; who have free minds and who are *good citizens and respectful to human beings and human rights*" (DPT 2009, 58) (emphasis added). It is also stated that the "internalization of the education of democracy and the consciousness of development within the curriculum and educational processes will serve the purpose of stability and sustainable development" (DPT 2009, 77). Despite the fact that important official documents gave importance to democratic values and human rights, citizenship and human rights education would wait until 2010 to be a separate course.

From the Status of an Interdisciplinary Branch to a Separate Course: A Cinderella Story of Human Rights Education in Turkey?

Human rights education came on the scene again with the project called Democratic Citizenship and Human Rights Education. As part of this project, supported by the Council of Europe and prepared in collaboration with the MoNE, the Citizenship and Democracy Education course was included in the curriculum of primary schools as a separate course at the end of 2009. An informational meeting and workshop were held on November 2009 in Ankara in which officials of the Council and the MoNE-BoE, academicians, teachers, and representatives of several NGOs participated (MoNE 2009, 1–19). The total period of the Project was 36 months, and its budget was

9.1 million Euro. A high-ranking official of the MoNE-BoE stated that the impetus for this project had come from experts in the body of the MoNE-BoE. However, projects financed with foreign credits have become an important part of the policies and practices of national education since the 1980s. As a common tendency, neoliberal policies with a strong emphasis on the "free market" have influenced national education policy (Adıgüzel 2010, 38–42). Such project-based education can be treated as an example of the financing of education from other resources instead of public ones, which is due to the withdrawal of the state from public services, including education. However, public sources are important for consistent policies and those that can provide outreach. In the follow-up reports of the Educational Reform Initiatives (ERG)[4] on education, the main conditions of education are elaborated and certain policies are suggested by which public authorities can improve the conditions. This improvement will positively affect the quality of education, which guarantees the enjoyment of human rights (ERG 2010, ERG 2011). This improvement contributes to enjoyment of basic rights by children including the right of the child to education specified in the Convention on the Rights of the Child.

The main goals of the Project can be summarized as follows: to revise the program and curriculum of primary and secondary education by focusing on human rights; to prepare suitable materials for students, teachers, and school administrators as well as parents; to create a democratic school culture, and to include the participation of non-governmental organizations (NGOs) in the process (MoNE Project Coordination Center, 2011). As part of the project, the Citizenship and Democracy Education course would be added as a separate course to the curriculum of the primary schools. The MoNE-BoE decided that this course would be taught in the eighth grade as an elective course for the 2010–2011 academic year. It will be a "required" course in the 2011–2012 academic year (MoNE-BoE 2010a). In the curriculum of the Citizenship and Democracy Education course, there are four themes: all human beings are valuable, the culture of democracy, our rights and freedoms, and our duties and responsibilities. It is stated that the program is children-based rather than teacher-centered and that its activities are designed in accordance with this understanding (MoNE-BoE 2010b). Thanks to the Commission that prepared the program, certain criticisms of the prior programs on human rights education were taken into consideration.

In the information meeting and workshop of the Democratic Citizenship and Human Rights Education project in 2009, the participation of the NGOs in the process was one of the issues stressed by the authorities of the MoNE (MoNE 2009, 6–8). At the beginning, different actors in society, such as academicians and representatives of NGOs, took a role in shaping the program and curriculum of the course. The report by the ERG that was made public on June 26, 2011, states that a participative outlook in the preparation process and preferences for student-centered education and practices are positive aspects of the Project. However, this positive aspect could not be long-lived: some of the actors were restricted from the evaluation and measurement process of the pilot application of the course. This is another point that indicates the gap between the promises and the reality of the Project. The textbook was prepared and presented to the commission in April 2011 without waiting for the assessments of the contributors, such as teachers, to be collected. According to the ERG, this situation damaged the participative nature of the process (2011, 22). To some extent, it is related to the position of the AKP toward democratic culture and human rights. As Erdem Türközü states, the AKP is in an ambivalent position in terms of human rights. The heterogeneous nature of the party and the pragmatic nature of its relation with the human rights issue are the main causes of this position (2010, 233). He also added that the party seems to treat human rights as if it is an activity of public relations. That is, although the main actors of the party insisted on the role of the NGOs as a part of democracy and human rights, the AKP still considers NGOs as bodies of confirmation: "We do it and you confirm that we do it well" (Türközü 2010, 237).

Some Remarks and Conclusions

Interdependency is one of the main attributes of human rights. Also, promoting human rights and raising awareness of human rights are closely dependent upon the conditions of education. In that respect, the AKP's educational policies and practices strongly affect human rights education as well as the practice of education in conformity with the main principles of human rights. As we have seen in the different chapters of this book, the market-oriented policies of the AKP and in some respects, the lack of consistency in educational policies shaped the story of human rights education. These attitudes provide a certain explanation for the discontinuities and dilemmas in human rights education in Turkey during the 2000s.

Practicing human rights is an inseparable part of human rights education. In the report titled *Eğitimde Haklarımız Var!* (We have rights in education!), the conditions of education are seen under five headings and certain suggestions are made for strengthening the legal instruments in Turkey. Child-based education is one of the headings, and the importance of the participative nature of the educational environment and processes is stressed for the practice of child's rights in education to the full capacity (ERG et al., 2009). Such participation is especially important for the Citizenship and Democracy Education course. In addition to education on rights and responsibilities, a course on citizenship and human rights should also enable students to practice their rights and responsibilities in the community of the school, including the classroom. A well-known *Crick Report* insisted on education for "active citizenship" with a republican perspective, and in that respect, citizenship education aims at increasing "knowledge, skills and values" that are pertinent to "participative democracy" (Lockyer 2008, 22–23).

In conclusion, human rights education, including citizenship, has different dimensions and is closely related to the general preferences and conditions of education. The AKP's political ideology and preferences cannot provide a suitable environment for consistent educational policies, including citizenship and human rights. In its private history, the curriculum and the curriculum of the course were constructed because of the effects of national or international waves of relevant activities rather than being established based on comprehensive studies that ask, "Why and how we educate on human rights and citizenship." In the story of Cinderella, we do not know whether she and the prince "live happily ever after." To have a "happy ending" for the human rights course in the case of Turkey, it should not be forgotten that citizenship and human rights education are a complex whole with ties with democratic and civic culture within the school environment as well as within the country.

For an affirmative conclusion: We have important experiences, both positive and negative, to establish a course that fosters civic virtues and gives weight to the "public" and to "participation." We should do it, and we can do it!

Notes

1. The decision on the eight-year mandatory education was taken during the coalition government (Democratic Left Party and Motherland Party) that was in authority between June 30, 1997 and January 11, 1999. The Minister of Education was Hikmet Uluğbay from the Democratic Left Party. This

decision and its application strongly contributed to the schooling of children aged 11–13 in general, especially of girls.
2. Elected chair of the High Advisory Council for Human Rights in Turkey in 1994. Under her leadership, the Council introduced the teaching of human rights in primary and secondary education. She was also chair of the Turkish National Committee of the United Nations Decade for Human Rights Education.
3. The commitments related to democratic citizenship and human rights education were decided in the twentieth Session of the Council of Europe Standing Conference of Ministers of Education.
4. The ERG was one of the actors taking a role in the preparation of the curriculum at the beginning of the project.

References

Adıgüzel, Ergül. "Eğitimde Yapısal Dönüşüm, Fonlanmış Eğitim Projeleri ve Bıraktığı İzler." *Eleştirel Pedagoji* 2 (2010): 37–53.
Asrak-Hasdemir, Tuğba. "Medya Okuryazarlığı ve İnsan Hakları: Türkiye Örneği." In *Ders Kitaplarında İnsan Hakları II*, edited by Gürel Tüzün, 313–336. Istanbul: Tarih Vakfı Yayınları, 2009.
Çayır, Kenan. "Consciousness of Human Rights and Democracy in Textbooks." In *Human Rights Issues in Textbooks: The Turkish Case*, edited by Deniz Tarba-Ceylan and Gürol Irzık, 91–107. Istanbul: The History Foundation of Turkey, 2004.
———. "Human Rights Education Scenarios." *Educational Sciences: Theory & Practice* (2003): 398–400. http://search.ebscohost.comlogin.aspxdirect=true&db=a9h&AN=9187632&site=ehost-live.pdf (accessed October 2011).
Council of Europe. "Launching Conference of the European Year of Citizenship through Education." December 13–14, 2004. Sofia, Bulgaria. http://www.coe.int/T/E/Com/Files/Events/2004–12-EYCE/communique-final.asp (accessed June 2011).
Council of Europe Standing Conference of Ministers of Education. "Turkey's Activity Report." June 4–5, 2010. Ljubljana, Slovenia. http://www.coe.int/t/dg4/education/standingconf/Rapports%20des%20Etats/MED-23–37%20turkey.pdf (accessed June 2011).
DPT (State Planning Organization). "Dokuzuncu Kalkınma Planı Eğitim: Okul Öncesi, İlk ve Ortaöğretim" 2009. http://www.dpt.gov.tr/DocObjects/View/4822/oik-egitim-i.pdf (accessed June 2011).
———. "DokuzuncuKalkınmaPlanı2011YılıProgramı." 2010. http://www.kalkinma.gov.tr/DocObjects/View/10044/PROGRAM_2011_BakanlarKK-26112010.pdf. (accessed November 2011).
ERG (Educational Reform Initiatives). "Eğitim İzleme Raporu 2009." 2010. http://erg.sabanciuniv.edu/sites/erg.sabanciuniv.edu/files/izlemeraporu2009_0.pdf (accessed June 2011).
———. "Eğitim İzleme Raporu 2010 Basın Paketi." 2011. http://erg.sabanciuniv.edusiteserg.sabanciuniv.edufilesEIR2010_BasinToplantisI_BasinPaketi.pdf (accessed June 2011).

ERG et al. "Eğitimde Haklarımız Var!" 2009. http://erg.sabanciuniv.edu/sites/erg.sabanciuniv.edu/files/bildirge_savunu_dosyasi.pdf (accessed June 2011).
Gemalmaz, Semih. "Evaluation of Data concerning Human Rights Criteria Obtained from a Survey of Textbooks." In *Human Rights Issues in Textbooks: The Turkish Case,* edited by Deniz Tarba-Ceylan and Gürol Irzık, 9–48. Istanbul: The History Foundation of Turkey, 2004.
Gök, Fatma. "Citizenship and Human Rights Education Textbooks." In *Human Rights Issues in Textbooks: The Turkish Case,* edited by Deniz Tarba-Ceylan and Gürol Irzık, 108–122. Istanbul: The History Foundation of Turkey, 2004.
Gülmez, Mesut. *İnsan Hakları ve Demokrasi Eğitimi.* 2nd ed. Ankara: TODAİE, 2001.
Karaman-Kepenekçi, Yasemin. "Türkiye'de Demokratik Yurttaşlık Eğitimi Konusunda Yapılan Çalışmalara bir Örnek: Avrupa Konseyi '2005-Avrupa Eğitim Yoluyla Yurttaşlık Yılı' Projesi." In *Uluslararası Avrupa Birliği, Vatandaşlık ve Vatandaşlık Eğitimi Sempozyumu Bildiri Kitabı,* 426–432, 2009. http://eupecit.orgindex.htm (accessed July 2011).
Köylü, Hilal. "Avrupalı Çocuk Yetiştirin." *Radikal,* March 18, 2002. http://www.radikal.com.tr/haber.php?haberno=32226&tarih=18/03/2002 (accessed June 2011).
Kuçuradi, Ionna. "Interview with Ioanna Kuçuradi, Turkish philosopher." March 31, 2004. http://www.unesco.org/new/en/media-services/single-view/news/interview_with_ioanna_kucuradI_turkish_philosopher/ (accessed June 2011).
Lockyer, Andrew. "Education for Citizenship: Children as Citizens and Political Literacy." In *Children and Citizenship,* edited by Antonella Inverzinni and Jane Williams, 20–31. London: Sage, 2008.
Magendzo, Abraham. "Tensions and Dilemmas about Education in Human Rights in Democracy." *Journal of Moral Education* 23, no. 3 (1994): 251–259. http://web.ebscohost.com.proxy1.lib.uwo.ca:2048/ehost/detail?vid=3&hid=119&sid=1a2e03bb-71b3-4042-a438-2ec6a07fa6f3%40sessionmgr14&bdata=JnNpdGU9ZWhvc3QtbGl2ZQ%3d%3d#db=a9h&AN=9411091717 (accessed June 2011).
MoNE (Ministry of National Education). *Demokratik Vatandaşlık ve İnsan Hakları Eğitimi Projesi Bilgilendirme Toplantısı ve Çalıştayı.* Ankara: MoNE, November 11–12, 2009.
———. "2005 Yılı Sayısal Verileri." 2011. http://personel.meb.gov.tr/sayisal_veriler.asp?ID=207 (accessed July 2011).
MoNE-BoE (Ministry of National Education-Board of Education). "Decision No: 56." March 6, 1995a. http://ttkb.meb.gov.tr/kurul.aspx?ilk=1&aranan=&tarihi=1995 - &kararno=56&sayfa=1 (accessed June 2011).
———. "Decision No: 75." July 20, 2010a. http://ttkb.meb.gov.tr/kurul.aspx?ilk=1&aranan=&tarihi=2010 - &kararno=75&sayfa=1 (accessed May 2011).
———. "Decision No: 82." June 25, 1998. http://ttkb.meb.gov.tr/kurul.aspx?ilk=1&aranan=&tarihi=1998 - &kararno=82&sayfa=1. (accessed June 2011).
———. "Decision No: 289." January 8, 1995b. http://ttkb.meb.gov.tr/kurul.aspx?ilk=1&aranan=&tarihi=1995 - &kararno=289&sayfa=1. (accessed June 2011).
———. *İlköğretim Vatandaşlık ve Demokrasi Eğitimi Dersi (8. Sınıf) Öğretim Programı.* 2010b. http://ttkb.meb.gov.tr (accessed June 2011).

MoNE Project Coordination Center. "Demokratik Vatandaşlık ve İnsan Hakları Eğitimi." 2011. http://projeler.meb.gov.tr/pkmtr/index.php?option=com_content&view=article&id=126%3Ademokratik-vatandalk-ve-nsan-haklar-eitimi-projesi&catid=70%3Adevam-eden-projeler&Itemid=83&lang=tr (accessed May 2011).
NCDHRE (National Committee on the Decade for Human Rights Education). *Human Rights Education Programme of Turkey 1998–2007*. Ankara: NCDHRE Publications 2 1999.
Office of the UN High Commissioner for Human Rights. "Summary of National Initiatives." 2005–2009. http://www2.ohchr.org/english/issues/education/training/Summary-national-initiatives2005–2009.htm (accessed June 2011).
Öniş, Ziya. "Globalisation and Party Transformation: Turkey's Justice and Development Party in Perspective." In *Globalising Democracy*, edited by Peter Burnell, 122–140. London: Routledge, 2006.
Tarba-Ceylan, Deniz, and Gürol Irzık. "Introduction." In *Human Rights Issues in Textbooks: Turkish Case*, edited by Deniz Tarba-Ceylan and Gürol Irzık, 1–8. Istanbul: The History Foundation of Turkey, 2004.
Turkish Eurydice Unit. "Structures of Education and Training Systems in Europe-Turkey." 2009–2010. http://eacea.ec.europa.eueducationeurydicedocumentseurybasestructures041_TR_EN.pdf (accessed May 2011).
Türközü, Erdem. "AKP ve İnsan Hakları." In *AKP Kitabı Bir Dönüşümün Bilançosu*, edited by İlhan Uzgel and Bülent Duru, 225–263. 2nd ed. Ankara: Phoenix, 2010.
White Paper Final Draft. 2007. http://tedp.meb.gov.tr/doc/Pubs/07.01.29%20White%20Paper%20Final%20Draft%20January%202007.pdf (accessed June 2011).

17

The System of Teacher Training during AKP Rule

İ. Rıfat Okçabol

The Turkish education system and teacher-training system was inherited from the Ottomans. The first Ottoman teacher-training school was opened in 1848, and there were 20 such schools for primary education and one for secondary education when the Republic of Turkey was established in 1923 (Okçabol 2005a, Okçabol 2005b). The numbers and types of teacher-training schools expanded after 1923. These schools were run by the Ministry of National Education (MoNE) until 1982. Some universities began to set up a school of education to provide teaching certificate programs based on 7 to 8 teaching-methods courses, following the establishment of the Faculty of Educational Sciences at Ankara University in 1965 (Küçükahmet 1976, Okçabol 2005b). These certificate programs were generally for undergraduate students in the schools of arts and sciences.

The *Basic Law on National Education Act* of 1973 (no. 1739) is probably the most important law in Turkish education and for the teacher-training system. Article 43 of this law indicates that teaching is a special profession, and that teachers should be trained in programs in higher education institutions, of which the curricula consist of courses in general cultural subjects, the specialized subject matter a person will teach, and pedagogy. The *Law of Higher Education Act* of 1981 (no. 2547) is another important law in Turkish education that details various aspects of higher education and establishes the Council of Higher Education (CoHE).[1] The CoHE has regulated, managed, operated, and inspected the inputs, teaching-learning process, and outputs of the higher education system since 1982.

This chapter examines the changes made in the teacher-training system since the early 1980s, mainly focusing on the AKP era. This chapter asserts that the system was modified as an educational tool by the AKP to train an Islamist cadre in the schools.

A General Overview

<u>Teacher Training after 1982:</u> In the changes described above, departments of education and teacher-training schools that train secondary school teachers were converted into schools of education; those that train primary school teachers were converted into two-year higher schools of education at universities. Teacher-training schools that train vocational and technical school teachers were then converted into schools of vocational and technical education.

<u>Basic Characteristics of Teacher Training:</u> Schools of education were established on a departmental basis by the CoHE. A department of educational sciences is the core department, and it exists in each school of education to provide undergraduate studies in various programs related to this department[2] and teaching-methods courses for students in other departments. Other departments vary from one school of education to another and train teachers in the related programs.

<u>Staffing:</u> The CoHE has been the main force in defining who is chosen as a university president as well as a dean, and has been selecting relatively conservative people for these positions since its establishment. The Atatürk Higher Council of Culture, Language, and History[3] accepted on June 20, 1986, a report[4] that was in line with Turkish-Islamic understanding of the essence of the educational and cultural life of Turkey. The administrative staffs at schools of education look like those at a madrasa.

<u>Curricula:</u> Curricula for the new programs were also set by the CoHE. Curricula are based on courses that provide teaching skills, general cultural courses, and subject-matter courses. Courses on teaching methods are more or less fixed for each program and include the following courses: introduction to education, sociology of education, psychology of education, educational technologies, guidance and counseling, measurement and evaluation, educational administration, educational principles and methods, special teaching methods, and special teaching practices. Some schools offer the history

of education, the philosophy of education, and program-planning courses in addition to certificate courses. Schools of education that were converted from an educational institute have continued their tradition of offering subject matter courses for their students in their schools/departments. Students in other schools of education take subject-matter courses in the schools of arts and sciences.

<u>Student Selection:</u> Formerly, students who desired to go to a university took two different university entrance exams, called the Student Selection Exam and the Student Replacement Exam.[5] Those who received predetermined scores from the first exam were eligible to apply to take the second exam, with a list of their choice of programs. For each program, applicants were put in a descending order based upon their scores on the second exam. Based on the quota for a program, the top applicants are admitted into that program. Some programs requiring special talent conduct their own special exam instead of the second exam. The MoNE established the General Directorate for Teacher Training and Education and teaching high schools[6] were attached to this directorate. A scholarship was provided for the graduates of teaching high schools when they entered a teacher-training program that they had ranked between their first to tenth choices in 1989, because the Ministry desired that "teacher high schools should be the main student sources for faculties of education."

The World Bank-CoHE Project

A major transformation in the system of teacher training took place as a result of the project titled Preservice Teacher Training that started in 1994 and ended with a new teacher-training model in 1997 (Okçabol 2005b). This project was initiated, financed (as a loan), and carried on under the expertise of the World Bank (WB), with the cooperation of the MoNE and the CoHE. This new model (referred to as the WB-CoHE model in this chapter), which was based on suggestions of the Carnegie Forum on Education and the Economy, had been used to address the educational needs of the United States (Carnegie Forum 1986, 55–57). Five main characteristics of the new system are summarized below:

Reorganizing the Faculties of Education

According to this WB-CoHE model, the Departments of Art and the Departments of Music were united as the Departments of Fine Art.

Departments of Computer Technologies and Education were established. Teacher training at the four-year schools of higher education became primary education departments[7] of the schools of education, and programs in preschool education, the classroom teacher, Turkish, math, science, and social sciences were attached to these departments. Teacher candidates began to take their subject matter courses in the related departments of faculties of arts and sciences.

The length of teacher-training programs has been differentiated. Programs to train primary school teachers, and teachers of Turkish, foreign language, music, art, physical education, and computer in secondary schools continue to be four years long, but the length of the programs was expanded to five years for remaining subjects like math and physics for secondary schools. This new five-year program is called the "joint undergraduate and master degree program" and identified as (3.5 + 1.5) numerically. The number 3.5 means that teacher candidates take subject-matter courses from the related faculties of arts and sciences for the first 3.5 years and then take teaching-methods courses in the remaining 1.5 years in the school of education.

Existing teaching-certificate programs were eliminated, and three new certificate programs that were initiated for preschool, classroom, and English teachers were designed for university graduates only. A new master's degree program called the Teacher-Training Master's Degree and that did not require a thesis was also created for university graduates. Teacher-training master's degree programs (without a thesis) consist of only teaching-methods courses that are consistent with all teacher-training programs, as well as three additional courses.

The CoHE opened two programs to train teachers for preschool education and English in the School of Open Teaching.[8] The CoHE started a program to train teachers of religious culture and moral education in schools of theology, and permitted graduates of this program to teach Turkish or social knowledge at primary schools upon taking required courses taken in a school of theology.

New Curricula

New curricula were designed for each teacher-training program as part of the CoHE model (CoHE 1998a, CoHE 1998b). The numbers of theoretical courses like sociology of education, philosophy of education, and educational administration have been dropped from the curriculum in order to transform schools of education into institutions based on practical knowledge for students. Teacher candidates' academic experience has been emphasized during their preservice training, and practice in teaching-methods has been increased (CoHE 1998c).

Assessments of the WB-CoHE Model

The WB-CoHE model was criticized heavily. The points that drew the heaviest criticism were as follows:

- This new model did not cure the weaknesses of teacher-training programs. In terms of providing secular, scientific, and democratic understanding and love for the teaching profession, the new model was even weaker than the old one.
- The unity of the teacher-training system would be destroyed.
- The teacher-training responsibility of schools of education as mandated by law (no. 2809[9]) would be shared illegally by other faculties.
- In the process of the development of this model, valuable teacher-training experiences and suggestions of previous Supreme Councils, and other meetings and conferences as well as the specific conditions of Turkey, such as problems of religious fundamentalism, separatist movements, and economic conditions were ignored.
- The draft was prepared without consulting schools of education, without undertaking any research, and without paying attention to the conditions of faculties.
- The draft would lead to statute differentiation among teachers.
- The new master's program without a thesis was based upon only pedagogical formation courses, and the closing down of undergraduate study in guidance and counseling was unrealistic and contradictory to the law (no. 2547), since the law requires research for the master's degree, which is lacking in the new program (Okçabol 2005b, 161–165).

Changes in the Subsequent Years

Two university entrance exams were converted into a single exam in 1999, and extra points began to be awarded for those graduates of vocational and technical high schools who applied to higher education programs related to the area in which they graduated. In the early 2000s, two new exams were initiated for graduate studies. One of the exams was the Graduate Degree Education Exam for those applying to master's degree programs, and another exam was called the Language Exam for Public Employees (KPDS). The KPDS has been also used for those applying to doctoral programs. The candidates who receive the required minimum points on these exams become eligible to take additional exams conducted by the departments offering graduate study.

Teacher Training during the AKP's Administration

The AKP governments attempted to change the higher education law twice, but were not able to succeed because this draft legislation generated heavy opposition. Even those who were anti-CoHE did not support these proposed changes, because of their antidemocratic content. The AKP tried to change educational regulations and implement some decisions such as letting girls attend a university while wearing a *turban* (headscarf), eliminating extra points for vocational school graduates, selecting students who are going to be trained as academicians through interviews conducted by the MoNE, initiating a new certificate program conducted by the MoNE, and so forth. But most of these attempts were rejected by official authorities because of their antisecular and anticonstitutional nature.

These and similar issues and the AKP's attempt to reorganize the CoHE caused some conflicts between the CoHE and the AKP right after the AKP came to power. Conflicts with the CoHE continued until the former AKP leader, Prime Minister Abdullah Gül, won the presidency. He appointed Yusuf Ziya Özcan as the head of the CoHE. At the beginning of Gül's presidency and Özcan's leadership, nearly 21 members of the CoHE were selected from those who would be affiliated somehow with the AKP in a couple of months. That is, the AKP took full control over the CoHE. Therefore, in terms of what happened in the teacher-training system, the AKP's administration period could be separated into before and after the AKP's full control over the CoHE.

Before the AKP's Full Control over the CoHE

Various research findings indicate that teachers are not trained properly and programs are not designed to provide effective dimensional changes on candidate teachers (Kavak et al. 2007, 82–84; Okçabol et al. 2003). Moreover, research findings show that the competencies of schools of education became questionable in the light of the Public Employees Selection Exam (KPSS).[10] Then, the CoHE implemented the following changes in teacher-training programs in July 21, 2006:

- The percentages of courses in teaching skills and in general culture were increased. Many courses were identified as new teaching-methods courses.

- The responsibility for training religious culture and moral education teachers was transferred from the schools of theology to the schools of education. But the teacher candidates continued to take their subject-matter courses in schools of theology.
- Additional teacher-training programs were initiated, such as in the Japanese and Arabic languages, and for teaching students with special needs, such as the deaf, the blind, and the gifted.
- The program in guidance and counseling was renewed.
- Undergraduate programs in the educational sciences that had been closed were reopened in July 11, 2007, and restructured to offer only graduate studies in schools of education (Kavak et al. 2007, 68).

In February 2007, to select those who were applying to a graduate program or to be instructors at universities, the CoHE initiated a new exam by expanding the Master's Degree Education Exam into a new one called the Academic Staff and Graduate Degree Education Exam (ALES), and established a requirement of a minimum of 72 points requirement out of 100. Whoever received 70 points or higher on the ALES was eligible to take the written and oral exams conducted by the department to which they were applying. The CoHE began a new movement to change the status of schools of vocational and technical education that train vocational/technical teachers.

Assessments of the 2006 Changes

Kavak et al. indicate that these new changes that were implemented will train teachers to be intelligent, able to solve problems, and able to teach students how to learn instead of providing them with direct information (2007, 67). It seems that their claims do not have enough evidence, however, because the curricula expansion of 2 to 3 courses in 2006 could not possibly provide these kinds of major changes in teacher candidates. The WB-CoHE model as well as the changes implemented in 2006 are not sufficient to provide the teacher competencies[11] established by the MoNE (2008) either.

Kavak et al. (2007) think that many educators support the decision to train teachers of religious culture and moral education in schools of education. However, these researchers also believe that this change may create new problems and that these problems could be overcome by a special effort on the part of educators. It also seems that their expectation is unrealistic, because after such programs were transferred to schools of education, these schools began to employ mostly theologians for these programs during the AKP's administration. Therefore, the number of theologians has been increasing in the schools of education, where secular and scientific education must reside. Such a newly appointed theologian thinks that families are degenerating and that this degeneration began after reforms took place in the mid-nineteenth century. He criticizes people who travel abroad instead of obeying the religious rule to sacrifice in the month of Ramadan, as well as suggests that "reading the Koran appropriately" will save families (Okçabol 2010). Theologians who have similar ideas will most likely receive more employment.

After the AKP's Full Control over the CoHE

The following changes in the teacher-training system were instituted after the AKP took full control over the CoHE.

Reducing University Autonomy

The ALES score became a major defining factor in selecting instructors and graduate students after the CoHE's decision of July 2008. According to the CoHE, the ALES will have to be weighted as 55 percent, with the Grade Point Average (GPA) and the KPDS as 15 percent of an applicant's total score. That means, departments' own entrance exams (written and oral) will have the weight of only the remaining 15 percent in determining their selection of applicants.

Closing Schools of Vocational/Technical Education

All schools of vocational and technical education were converted into schools of technology, art and design, or trade and tourism after the decision of the government in November 2, 2009. As a result of this decision, nearly 73 years of experience in vocational and technical teacher training were erased and came to an end. Most likely, there will be no academic unit to carry out research in the field of vocational and technical education since the basic functions of these new schools are not teacher training. Those who would like to be teacher in a vocational/technical area will have to apply to teaching-certificate programs in these newly established schools. However, the establishment of these new schools has not yet been fully completed.

Muhammet Eltez, Hüseyin Ekiz, and Abdullah Sönmez (2008) state the following four reasons behind the plan to change the status of schools of vocational and technical education. First, the MoNE is able to employ only 5 percent of the graduates of these schools per year. Second, when these graduates are employed in nonteaching positions, they experience confusion about their responsibilities and the statutes. Third, industry needs engineers in technology fields, not vocational and technical teachers. Last, there are difficulties in identifying equivalencies and accreditation of these schools in the Bologna Process. As seen from these reasons outlined above, the closing down of these faculties has nothing to do with the betterment of education and teacher training.

Restarting the Certificate Programs

For unplanned reasons and actions by the MoNE and the CoHE, schools of education were established, and the expansion of the quotas for teacher-training programs was greater than the demand for teachers. Over 300,000 graduates of schools of education are looking for teaching jobs, while the MoNE needs some 130,000 new teachers. Even under these circumstances, the CoHE decided to restart teaching-certificate programs for all undergraduate students in August 27, 2009. Upon the implementation of this decision, some schools of education started such programs willingly and immediately, because students have to pay high tuition to enroll in such programs in general. Some faculties' councils decided that opening such programs is neither educationally logical nor ethical, as thousands of teachers are looking for teaching jobs, and certificate programs intend to double their numbers in a couple of years. The faculty councils therefore decided not to be involved in such programs at all. There were only two universities that respected their faculty's council's point of view and decided not to open such programs, but the rest opened such programs based on a vote in the university senate. Luckily, the Council of State decided to stop the implementation of this certificate program in October 20, 2010.

Marketing and Privatization of Teacher Training

Training teachers in the Second Teaching Programs,[12] allowing private universities to train teachers, and opening certificate programs are indicators of the marketing of teacher training. Graduates of teacher-training programs have to take the KPDS and score high enough to be employed as teachers in public schools. Many graduates attend expensive special preparatory courses before they take the

KPDS. Therefore, the more students pay, the easier it is for them to become teachers.

Piety of Teacher Training

In addition to providing theologians to staff the programs that train teachers of religious culture and moral education in schools of education, the CoHE stopped opening new schools of education at public universities, but in March 2009, it permitted piously affiliated foundation universities to open schools of education to train teachers.

Activating the Turkish National Committee on Teacher Training[13]

This committee has been activated with new members who are affiliated with the AKP. Therefore, this committee works mostly as a political unit rather than as a scientific one, and it approves whatever the CoHE decides.

Conclusion

A basic qualitative issue related to teacher training is the quality of students entering teacher-training programs. Quite a large percentage of incoming students, who favor the Ottoman rather than the republican regime, come from both public and private high schools that are controlled by reactionary people. Some high school students as well as students in the schools of education attend to class in private classrooms and live in private dormitories or private houses whose owners are reactionary pious people or organizations. These students receive special religious enculturation from what they call "their big brothers and sisters."

Another qualitative issue is the quality of the existing teacher-training system. The existing system is unable to make significant changes in teacher candidates. Candidates come to schools of education and leave four to five years later without experiencing any major changes in their worldview, scientific thought, understanding of the importance of their profession and the essence of education, and democratic attitudes. They do not gain the theoretical and philosophical background necessary to be considered as good teachers and educators. They graduate without acquiring the spirit of teaching, without questioning the attitudes and habits that they took on from their earlier education, and without understanding why they are becoming teachers. If they gain anything in the schools of education, it is only some teaching skills and knowledge about their subject matter.

The basic quantitative issue is the lack of academicians in schools of education. There were 33 students per academician in the schools of education, and only 3 students per academician in the schools of theology. There were 397 students per a full professor in education and only 14 per a full professor in theology (Okçabol 2007, 278).

There are several reasons for the insufficiencies of schools of education. First of all, the CoHE and schools of education are staffed by people who favored a Turkish-Islamic synthesis when those institutions were first established. On the other hand, the CoHE was structured in an inadequate way to be able to deal with educational issues effectively. Primarily, the CoHE does not have expertise in education because there is almost no "educator" who holds a degree in educational sciences among the members of the CoHE, especially since the AKP has taken full control. There is an Educational Committee in the CoHE, but its head was a theologian for a while and then an agriculturalist took over this position for the time being. Secondly, the CoHE has been generally working to please the governments, and thus their decisions are more political than educational. Moreover, the CoHE appoints deans according to their affiliation with the AKP's worldviews, and sometimes even appoints noneducators as deans of schools of education.

The changes of 1997 and 2006 in the teacher-training system were not aimed at reshaping or altering the Turkish-Islamic understanding either. Initiating the training of teachers for religious culture and moral education at theology schools, starting a teacher-training master's degree program that does not require a thesis and letting these students applying to doctoral programs, and closing undergraduate programs in educational sciences in 1997 weakened the scientific side but strengthened the Turkish-Islamic understanding of teacher training.

Since 1997, there has been more small-scale research about classroom teaching-learning than general educational issues. Schools of education have moved away from their concern about issues related to educational science and become alienated from the education system in general as well as from the teacher-training system. There have been major changes in the education system of Turkey, such as renewing the primary school education programs and restructuring secondary education under the guidance of international organizations, instituting new entrance exams at all levels of education, and so forth, but there has been no major research about these changes.

Teacher's unions serve as other indicators about what the graduates of schools of education do. There are three teacher's unions with more than one hundred thousand members. The two largest unions are pro-Turkish-Islamic to varying degrees, and most graduates of schools of education join these two unions. Therefore, some of the graduates are becoming a major force in pushing Turkey to become an Islamic country.

Notes

1. For the position and structure of CoHE, see Okçabol 2007.
2. The School of Education is structured in eight departments: Educational Sciences, Educational Sciences, Social Sciences Education, Turkish Language and Literature Education, Foreign Language Education, Music Education, Art Education, and Physical Education and Sport. Each department has its own programs (see Kavak et al. 2007).
3. This Council was established in August 11, 1983, to investigate, introduce, disseminate, and publish articles about Kemalist thoughts, principles, and reforms.
4. According to this report, "Religion means state; nation is religious community; national culture is Islamic culture; nationality is the Muslim world; nationalism is Pan-Islamism; the Turkish nation is 99 percent Muslim Turks; secularism is religious enmity; and science is the knowledge in the Koran" (cited in Güvenç et al. 1991, 49). When this report was accepted, the head of the CoHE was among the members of the council.
5. These exams are conducted by the Student Selection and Replacement Center that is attached to the CoHE.
6. High schools whose curricula include two education courses to prepare students for the teaching profession are called "teacher high schools."
7. Meanwhile, compulsory education was expanded from five years to eight in August 1997, and five years of elementary school and three years of junior high school were combined together as primary school.
8. This faculty provides distance learning where students do not have to attend regularly.
9. This law has been effective since March 30, 1983.
10. Graduates of teacher-training schools used to be employed immediately after their graduation. A Teacher Training and Replacement exam was initiated to employ teachers in 1985. Implementation of this exam was stopped in 1991, but reinitiated for not only teachers but also for all public employees and renamed as the KPSS in 2002.
11. Teacher competencies include the following domains: personal and professional values-professional development, recognition of student, teaching-learning

process, tracing growth-learning-measurement, school-family-society relations, and knowledge of programs and contents.
12. The Second Teaching programs were initiated in 1992. These are evening programs for those who were not able to get enough points on the university exam to attend regular programs that are conducted in the daytime. Tuition for these programs is much higher than the daily regular programs, and staffs working in these programs receive double payments for each hour they teach over their weekly load.
13. This committee was established by the CoHE in 1997, but has never been active since then. The duty of this committee is to provide guidance services on teacher-training matters to the CoHE, develop related curricula and update it, cooperate with the MoNE, and coordinate activities and interactions between the CoHE, the MoNE, universities, and schools of education (CoHE 1998a, 26).

References

Carnegie Forum. *A Nation Prepared: Teachers for The 21st Century. The Report of the Task Force on Teaching as a Profession.* New York: Carnegie Forum on Education and the Economy, 1986.
CoHE (Council of Higher Education). *Eğitim Fakülteleri Öğretmen Yetiştirme Lisans Programları.* Ankara, 1998b.
———. *'Eğitim Fakülteleri Öğretmen Yetiştirme Programlarının Yeniden Düzenlenmesi.* Ankara, 1998a.
———. *Fakülte-Okul İşbirliği.* Ankara, 1998c.
Eltez, Muhammet, Hüseyin Ekiz, and Abdullah Sönmez. "Teknik Eğitim Fakültelerinin Yeniden Yapılanması." 2008. http://www.obitet.gazi.edu.tr/tek_fak.htm (accessed August 2010).
Güvenç, Bozkurt et al. *Türk İslam Sentezi.* Istanbul: Sarma Yayınevi, 1991.
Kavak, Yüksel, Ayhan Aydın, and Sadegül Akbaba-Altun. *Öğretmen Yetiştirme ve Eğitim Fakülteleri (1982–2007).* Ankara: YÖK Yayını, 2007.
Küçükahmet, Leyla. *Öğretmen Yetiştiren Kurum Öğretmenlerinin Tutumları.* Ankara: Ankara Üniversitesi Yayınları, 1976.
MoNE (Ministry of National Education). "Öğretmenlik Mesleği Genel Yeterlikleri." 2008. http://otmg.meb.gov.tr/YetGenel.html (accessed December 2010).
Okçabol, Rıfat. "Bir 'İlmi' Toplantı!" May 7, 2010. www.haber.sol.ogr.tr.
———. *Türkiye Eğitim Sistemi,* Ankara: Ütopya Yayınevi, 2005a.
———. *Öğretmen Yetiştirme Sistemimiz.* Ankara: Ütopya Yayınevi, 2005b.
———. *Yükseköğretim Sistemimiz.* Ankara: Ütopya Yayınevi, 2007.
Okçabol, Rıfat et al. *Öğretmen Yetiştirme Araştırması.* Ankara: Eğitim-Sen Yayını, 2003.

18

Transformation of the Teaching Profession in Turkey

Esin Ertürk

Over the last 20 years, national education systems all over the world have undergone many reforms due to the growing influence of neoliberal globalization. These reforms usually resulted in the adoption of market rationality to the content of education as well as to the employment regime and the managerial and financial aspects of education. The neoliberal approach to education as an area of private investment not only legitimized the commodification of educational services and teachers' labor, but it also paved the way for the intensification of market principles in every sphere of public education, including the management of schools, which is called the "new managerialism." New managerialism is the reflection of a corporate culture in public institutions, and mainly aims to transform the idea of public services into the effective, efficient, and economic management of human capital resources by introducing private sector management techniques to the public sector (Beckmann and Cooper 2004). In terms of teachers, one of the most important outcomes of the reforms in education is the destruction of the professional identity of teachers and the corrosion of the culture and character of teaching (O'Brien and Down 2002, 113).

Until the 1980s welfare states regulated their relationship with teachers according to the idea of professionalism. As public sector teachers did not produce commodities for profit in the marketplace and instead produced use value, skills, and knowledge that placed future workers in a position to sell their labor, they were not directly controlled by market mechanisms. In return for the security of tenure, status, adequate income, and state support for professional closure, the relationship between the welfare state and teachers was based on an implicit and embedded contract, symbolized in the notion of goodwill. And due to their relative autonomy from the market as professional service class, teachers were able to exercise great control over their work and classrooms. Today, with the intensification of neoliberal reforms in education, teachers' work has been restructured and their limited, but existing professional autonomy has been challenged. First, teachers' labor has been commodified, deregulated, flexibilized, and as a result, they have been directly and indirectly caught up in the selling of products and services for profit. Second, their control over their work and classroom practices has been weakened through the mechanisms of performance appraisal, teaching councils, and new professional career categories. Teachers have started to be monitored more closely and placed in a position where they are accountable to their peers and superiors for the work they do in schools (Robertson 2000, 157–161).

In parallel with the marketization of education at the global level, market-friendly policies in Turkish education began in the 1980s and continued into the 1990s, making parents more responsible for educational expenditures and encouraging the privatization of education (Ercan 1999). Later, market-friendly reforms in the educational system gained momentum when the Justice and Development Party (AKP) came to power in 2002. The government has made reforms in many areas related to education. One of these reforms is the curriculum reform that redefines the aim and content of education in accordance with the needs of a global competitive market economy (İnal 2011). The other one is the introduction of Total Quality Management (TQM) and the Performance Appraisal and Career Exam for teachers, which create differences in status among teachers and a competitive culture in schools. Furthermore, within the framework of TQM, School Development Teams, which are responsible for creating educational projects and finding financial resources for these projects, were established. Furthermore, Parent-Teacher Association were given the status of firms in order to be able to finance some of the school expenditures with the support of families and local community. Thus, contrary to the constitution, which provides for compulsory elementary education for all citizens, and which is to be free in the public schools, the existing informal practice of collecting money from the parents and local community has gained a formal and institutional status.

However, the most crucial reform related to the teaching profession during the rule of AKP is the radical changes in the employment status of newly appointed teachers. In the last six years, teachers' employment status and working conditions have changed due to the general usage of precarious labor that has resulted from the dramatic rise in the number of contracted and temporary teachers in schools to create wage flexibility and reduce the financial burden for education in the government budget.

In this chapter, based on interviews conducted in 2009 with five elementary school teachers of different employment status, the transformation of the teaching profession under the rule of the AKP, will be discussed. In this framework, the chapter is composed of four parts. First, I will review the degradation of teachers' labor and the differences in working conditions among teachers with diverse employment status. This will be followed by a discussion of the effects of TQM applications on teachers' work. The next part is devoted to current teachers' experiences and feelings about being a teacher under such changing conditions. Finally teachers' common reactions to the reforms and the government's political response will be discussed.

Creating Flexible Teachers

Teachers are the largest group in the public service sector, constituting 40 percent of public employees (about 650,000) (*Radikal* August 22, 2011). In the public sector, they are mainly employed in regular status, subject to the *Law on Civil Servants*, code 657, 4/A clause, and have job security. However, except for article 4/A, two other irregular employment types have been described in the law passed in 1975, as contracted in the 4/B clause and as temporary labor in the 4/C clause, and it recommended that they be used when the teacher shortage cannot be filled with existing employees, mainly in extraordinary situations such as during the maternity leave and military service of regular teachers (MoNE 1965). Although the Council of Education agreed to the employment of contracted teachers as routine practice in 1988, it was not applied widely until the 2000s. First, in 2005, the AKP government introduced the assignment of thousands of contracted teachers with one-year job contracts. Five years later, in 2010, the number of contracted teachers reached to sixty-eight thousand. Furthermore, during these years, number of temporary teachers subject to the 4/C clause also increased dramatically. The number of temporary teachers reached seventy-eight thousand in 2011, while it was fifty-five thousand in 2008 (MoNE 2011, MoNE 2008).

One of the most important differences between regular, contracted, and temporary teachers is the temporary teachers' lack of job security. Contracted teachers are assigned for one year by the Ministry of National Education (MoNE). Until 2007, they could be discharged at the end of the year by the decision of local educational authorities without any justification. Besides the lack of job security, contracted teachers did not have the right to unionize. Fortunately, in 2007 they gained this right by the decision of the State Council upon the litigation of the teacher unions. As for temporary teachers, who are different from regular and contracted teachers, they are recruited by a district's directorate of education and they do not have even a one-year job contract. They always face a risk of losing their job during the semester. If a regular teacher is appointed to his/her school, or the principal of the school terminates the contract, the temporary teacher will lose his/her job the next day. Although contracted teachers do have one-year contracts, their position in their daily relations with the school management is just as fragile as that of temporary teachers. As one of the contracted teachers points out in an interview, they are obliged to face drudgery beyond their specified responsibilities for fear that the directors' negative attitude might affect their employment in the same school for the following year. Moreover, their vulnerable position forces them to become members of unions that are supported by the school management or the government so that they can receive individual advantages, as one contracted teacher wrote in the Internet forum for teachers (*Sozlesmeliogretmenler* May 11, 2008).

Selection criteria for employment also differ according to the status of teachers. For the recruitment of temporary teachers, there are no objective criteria. Therefore, this means that the political pressures and personal biases of the local authorities and school directors are crucial in the selection process. Regular and contracted teachers are appointed according to the scores they receive on the central exam, which is called Personal Selection Examination. This exam began to be used in 1999 to bring objective criteria into the selection and placement of civil servants. However, since 2009, it has come up as an issue many times due to allegations about leaked questions and cheating scandals that have left both the reliability of the exam and the organizing institution under suspicion. Today, the exam, with its minimum scores required for assigning an individual as a regular or contracted teacher, is used by the MoNE as the legitimate excuse for employing teachers with different status. Contracted and temporary teachers who receive scores lower than the minimum required to be hired as regular teachers usually blame themselves for their failure.

There is no huge gap between the salaries of contracted teachers and regular teachers. Regardless of the number of years of service, contracted teachers' salary is defined by the Council of Ministers, and it is almost the same amount as the salary of newly employed regular teachers. However, contracted teachers lack some rights that regular teachers have. First, they are outside the tenure system that provides a slight increase in salary as the years of service increase. Second, they do not have the right to be a director and they are outside the new career system. Third, they do not receive family and children benefits. Last, they do not have the right to change their workplace except in certain extraordinary situations, such as to facilitate the unity of family members and to deal with health problems (*Habergo* January 19, 2011). When it comes to temporary teachers, they do not have a fixed wage because it is determined according to the number of hours they teach. When they get sick and/or during the public holidays, the payment for the missing hours is cut from their wages. Furthermore, they are not paid for weekends. A one-hour course fee is equal to a regular teacher's overtime pay. At best, temporary teachers' wages are nearly one-third of the salary of regular and contracted teachers who do the same work. Moreover, contracted teachers are paid by the provincial administrations' budget or by the parent-teacher associations, whereas regular and contracted teachers are paid from the government's central budget. These teachers do not have any social and economic rights. If they take sick leave for ten days, then they lose their job and have to wait until the next semester for reappointment (*Memurlar* October 29, 2011). Just for the total hours they teach in a month (for instance, the insurance payment for temporary teachers' 120 hours of teaching in a month is counted as 15 work days with eight-hour days a month), temporary teachers do not have the right to retire. It is estimated that they must work until the age of 120 to be eligible for retirement. In terms of receiving free health services, they also have some difficulties because of their missing monthly insurance payments.

Teachers' experiences regarding the reforms are varied in terms of their status. Actually, temporary teachers are the most vulnerable group. They are always in an ambiguous position and always face the threat of unemployment. Yet, it is necessary to underline that both contracted and temporary teachers see their position as transient, as is pointed out in the words of these teachers:

There is always unforeseen risk. Suppose that, if a regular teacher is assigned, you lose your job. The director may say: "Don't come to school tomorrow." This is very common. Sometimes you may not have time to say hello to your children. I have seen some teachers in this position. They even cry because they have to leave the school, their students.... When you are temporary, you think, "I do not really belong to this school." So, I don't think that precarious teachers could concentrate on their job. You just think of the day to day. But to be teacher is not like producing refrigerators in a factory. You work with the children; there should be love and trust between teachers and students. It requires time and continuity. You have to be close to the children. But in this situation, I would not dare to have close relations with the children and parents. They also know that I am not permanent. I say myself, "You don't know if you will be here or not." I do something for children but...(M. Ç., temporary-status elementary school teacher, 42, Istanbul)

I don't know if they will renew my contract because I am critical of some practices of the director. So sometimes I feel that it is meaningless to continue to work here. I thought about quitting the job, but I do not want to leave the children in the middle of the term. But, I think I would quit next term.... There are discriminatory practices toward the contracted and temporary teachers. We are even humiliated. (F. A., contracted-status English teacher, 26, Muş)

Employing contracted teachers is not suitable. You are contracted, you come to class, what can you do? If you are temporary, what can you give to students? It's not your classroom. But if I'm permanent in the classroom, if I am the teacher of the classroom, I work effectively. Contracted teachers always feel anxious. They think about their own position. What can I do next year? Which school can I work for? If you do not get on well with the director, or if the director does not accept you, you cannot work there. If we are going to educate free minds, then the state should quit employing contracted teachers. (N. E., regular-status elementary school teacher, 48, Istanbul)

Creating a Hierarchy among Teachers

In addition to the employment of teachers with different status—regular, contracted, and temporary, the MoNE has also created a hierarchical status among regular teachers to establish wage flexibility through the application of TQM. TQM started to be applied in 2000 in the pilot schools, and was generalized to all schools in 2005. For teachers, one of the most important aspects of TQM is the measurement of their performance. However, a performance appraisal that produces a decisive impact on teachers' wages cannot become a routine practice in the Turkish educational system. This is because the performance-based wage system is not compatible with the current *Law on Civil Servants*. Actually, the government tried to make more radical changes in the law in 2004 and proposed an amendment to the *Law on Civil Servants* in order to normalize the deregulation of the status of civil servants. However, it encountered a strong reaction by the trade unions, and the draft law was suspended. The government also proposed a public reform draft bill that decentralized the public administration, as well as the finance and administration of education in the same year and changed the employment regime in the public sector. However, this reform attempt could not be realized either because the president vetoed it. Fear of the growing administrative and political power of the Kurdish regions' elected municipalities that are governed by the Peace and Democracy Party was decisive in the decision to abandon administrative reform. For this reason, the deregulation or flexibilization of the teaching profession can only be realized to the extent that the existing *Law on Civil Servants* and the central public administration system permit.

To overcome these limitations to a degree, the MoNE introduced the Career Exam in 2005 with a revision in the *National Education Law*. The Career Exam is part of the TQM applications and aims to create wage differences and competition among teachers. Based mainly on the scores of teachers (50 percent) on the exam and other criteria, such as education level, service years, administrators' and school principals' opinion, teachers were given the titles of head teacher and professional teacher and received wages that reflected their new status (MoNE 2006). However, this exam could be done only once in 2005 because the implementation of the law was suspended by the Council of State upon the protests and claim of the teacher's unions. Then, the Supreme Court omitted the decision of the Council of State and simply suggested some revisions. Today, the outcome of the test is valid, and head teachers and professional teachers still receive some extra payment. Furthermore, a new exam for teachers that will be administered every three years was announced by the MoNE in September 2011.

Teachers mostly criticize the Career Exam, and there is a strong element of mistrust on the part of teachers toward performance appraisal. These feelings are evident in the following comments of three teachers interviewed:

> I think they want to drive wedge between teachers and create conflict.... In our school, performance evaluation was implemented four

years ago, and we evaluated each other. We gave good grades to each other. Because all of us work and try our best. (A.G., regular-status elementary school teacher, 50, Istanbul)

I think it is very bad because, it leads to discriminatory practices. They cannot measure a teacher's success through the written exam. To be a good teacher is to be experienced. (A.E., regular-status elementary school teacher, 52, Istanbul)

Career exams measure the cognitive capacity of teachers, but to be a good teacher does not mean having high cognitive capacity. Some of the teachers became a professional teacher. However, I know some better teachers who did not take the exam and are very good at their job. They did not take the exam because they were protesting against it. Teachers who took the exam or others say that the exam is not important and is not able to measure the teachers' success, but I think that competition among teachers is created implicitly. Competition is a concept of the market. It is not suitable for education. We can do well in education not through competition but through sharing and solidarity. For instance, to help my students improve, I set up groups in which there are students with different abilities, and I encourage solidarity, sharing their knowledge. I think this is also suitable for teachers. (M. Ç., temporary-status elementary school teacher, 42, Istanbul)

To Be a Teacher

As discussed in the previous parts, especially since 2005, teachers' working conditions have been restructured and the economic status of some teachers has deteriorated very seriously. However, the problem is not just economic. A spiritual crisis related to being a teacher also accompanies the economic problems. To be a teacher used to be thought of as a form of public work. However, the marketization of education, the deregulation of teaching profession, and a shift in educational philosophy from the public good to individual responsibility for delivering outcomes have led to the corrosion of the culture and character of teaching. The negative effects of the current policies on teachers' own perceptions about their work are evident in the statements of the teachers who were interviewed:

I think teachers are model for students. And if I give something to my students, I feel very happy. I feel responsibility for my students, because they are the future of society. But today, we are paid poorly. The education system has nearly collapsed, and our value system also has collapsed. Money has changed everything. While some teachers still try to do their best, some teachers and schools see the students as an income resource. (N. E, regular-status elementary school teacher, 48, Istanbul)

I want to work as a teacher, but everything is ambiguous for me. My wage is very low, and will not be possible to retire if I work under such conditions. I love teaching, but I am a "second class" teacher. (M. Ç, temporary-status elementary school teacher 42, Istanbul)

Teachers receive little respect. I feel myself to be a figurehead rather than an educator. The state sacrifices 95 percent of the population. The market economy constructed its own schools, and rich families' children receive a good education, but others do not. (A.E, permanent-status elementary school teacher, 52, Istanbul)

My father and my mother were teachers, and I am also a teacher. When I started to work, I felt that I could do this job happily until the end of my life, but I am not sure now. Having job security was also an important reason for me to choose this job, but I am contracted. I want to be a good teacher and I want my students to educated as free individuals, but I see that it might not be possible under the MoNE. But I like to be with students and feel their love. (F.A., contracted-status English teacher in an elementary school, 26, Muş)

My students are successful because their families do their best to educate them. But I feel depressed here. When I work in Anatolia, in less developed and smaller regions, I really feel myself to be a teacher. But in Istanbul, especially in the schools of rich districts, teachers are not happy, because parents evaluate teachers in terms of their clothes and lifestyle. They have the right to intervene in everything, because they are rich and support the school. Principals are always in favor of the parents. They try to control everything... When I am in my own neighborhood, I feel that I am respected, that I am a teacher. (A.G. permanent-status elementary school teacher, 50, Istanbul)

Conclusion

Teachers constitute 40 percent of the public employees in Turkey, and 65 percent of the annual education budget is spent on teachers' salaries. Therefore, for the government, the easiest way to reduce the financial burden of education is to deregulate teachers' status through the generalization of precarious labor in schools. However, as teachers are the largest unionized group in the public sector, it would be hard to change the employment status of teachers already employed. That is why the MoNE attempted to change the employment status of newly employed teachers who are not unionized and are waiting for recruitment. However, there is still widespread discontent about the deteriorating working conditions and about the prevalence of precarious labor in education. On the other hand, the support of teacher's unions contributes to the power of precarious teachers. For instance, the Precarious Teachers Commission has been established within the left-wing trade union called the Union of Education and Science Laborers, and they have come to the public agenda with demands for temporary-status teachers, such as the privilege to use travel discount cards, like other teachers have (*Sendika* May 15, 2005). Moreover, precarious and unemployed teachers also established a support organization in 2009 called the Platform of Unassigned Teachers. The Platform has organized many protests and provided widespread support from some media groups and opinion leaders, and succeeded in keeping the attention of the public focused on the problems of precarious teachers. It has also created pressure on the government to solve the problem of teacher shortages as well. In this regard, teachers are powerful social actors and have the potential to affect the public, which makes them an important group that the political powers must satisfy. Precisely for this reason, the MoNE announced a plan to transfer contracted teachers to regular status before the 2011 general election, and approximately seventy thousand contracted teachers were given the right to move to regular status right after the election (*Haber7* March 9, 2010).

First, this move by the government can be explained as a populist action before the election, made in an effort to suck away the opposition energy of the masses. The termination of an agreement with the International Monetary Fund (IMF) that imposes restrictions on the number of civil servants in the public sector has also provided the government with an opportunity to appoint more teachers with regular status. Second, the opposition parties' support for precarious teachers and their promise to end the employment of contracted teachers in their election campaigns was also an effective factor in moving the government to take action. Third, the government's stepping back from employing contracted teachers might be related to its policy in the Kurdish-speaking region where educational services are transient and irregular because of the teacher shortage. In recent years, the government has shown a special interest in providing educational services in the region, and it appointed twenty-two thousand of the newly assigned thirty thousand regular teachers to that area in 2011 (MoNE 2011). In this way, the AKP expects to strengthen its political power against its rival Kurdish actor, namely the Peace and Democracy Party, which is the other powerful political party in the Eastern Region, and which is demanding the Kurdish mother tongue be taught in schools. Therefore, government policy to ensure the satisfaction of teachers can be evaluated in accordance with its political goals and its search for alliances with teachers in the region.

Consequently, it could be argued that the neoliberal orientation of the government will aim for even more deregulation and flexibilization of jobs in public services in the near future. However, some recovery of working conditions is also possible as a result of the organized struggle of teachers or because of the short-term political interests of the government. Furthermore, putting an end to the recruitment of contract teachers will not prevent the usage of precarious labor in education, since the 47,000 regular teachers assigned in 2011 do not cover the actual number of teachers needed (i.e., 146,184) (*Memuruz* April 2, 2011). As a result, the growing number of temporary teachers are waiting to close the gap under worse work conditions.

References

Beckmann, Andrea, and Charlie Cooper. "'Globalization,' The New Managerialism and Education: Rethinking the Purpose of Education in Britain." *Journal for Critical Education Policy Studies* 2, no. 2 (2004). http://www.jceps.com/index.php?pageID=article&articleID=31 (accessed May 2009).

Ercan, Fuat. "1980'lerde Eğitim Sisteminin Yeniden Yapılanması: Küreselleşme ve Neoliberal Eğitim Politikaları." In *75 Yılda Eğitim*, edited by Fatma Gök, 23–39. Istanbul: Türkiye Ekonomik ve Toplumsal Tarih Vakfı Yayınları, 1999

Haber7. "Sözleşmeli Öğretmenler Kadroya Alınacak." March 9, 2010. http://www.haber7.com/haber/20100309/Sozlesmeli-ogretmenler-kadroya-alinacak.php (accessed September 2011).

Habergo. "Sözleşmeli Öğretmen ile Kardolu Öğretmen Arasındaki Farklar Nelerdir?" January 19, 2011. http://www.habergo.com/haber/20751/sozlesmeliogretmenilekadroluogretmenarasindakifarklarnelerdir-.html (accessed February 2011).

İnal, Kemal. "AKP, Bildungsreform und Anpassung an den globalen Wandel." In *Bildung und gesellschaftlicher Wandel in der Türkei-Historiche und aktuelle Aspekte*, edited by Arnd-Michael Nohl and Barbara Pusch, 45–78. Würzburg: Verlag Würzburg in Kommission, 2011.

Memurlar. "Kadrosuz Usta Öğretici Görevlendirmesiyle ilgili Sıkça Sorulan Sorular ve Cevapları." October 29, 2011. http://www.memurlar.biz/haber/kadrosuz-usta-ogreticiler-dikkat-9392.html (accessed November 2011).

Memurum. "Milli Eğitim Bakanlığının Kaç Öğretmene İhtiyacı Var?" April 2, 2011. http://www.memurum.biz/2011/04/milli-egitim-bakanliginin-kac-ogretmene-ihtiyaci-var.html (accessed November 2011).

MoNE (Ministry of National Education). "Devlet Memurları Kanunu." 1965. http://mevzuat.meb.gov.tr/html/dmk.html. (accessed June 2009).

———. "Öğretmenlik Kariyer Basamaklarında Yükselme Yönetmeliği." 2006. http://www.turkegitimsen.org.tr/mevzuat_goster.php?mevzuat_id=242. (accessed June 2009).

———. "Sayısal Veriler-2011 Yılı Sayısal Verileri." 2011. http://personel.meb.gov.tr/sayisal_veriler.asp?ID=207 (accessed September 2011).

———. "Sayısal Veriler-2008 Yılı Sayısal Verileri." 2008. http://personel.meb.gov.tr/sayisal_veriler.asp?ID=207 (accessed September 2011).

O ' Brien Pat, and Barry Down. "What Are Teachers Saying about New Managerialism?" *Journal of Educational Enquiry* 3, no. 1 (2002): 111–133. http://www.ojs.unisa.edu.au/index.php/EDEQ/article/viewFile/553/423 (accessed May 2009).

Robertson, Susan. *A Class Act: Changing Teachers Work, the State and Globalization*. New York: Falmer Press, 2000.

Sendika. "Sözleşmeli Ücretli Öğretmenlerden Paso Hakkı Kampanyası." May 15, 2005. http://www.sendika.org/yazi.php?yazI_no=2515 (accessed June 2009).

Sozlesmeliogretmenler. http://www.sozlesmeliogretmenler.com/showthread.php/3876-sendika-%C3%BCyesi-olanlar-ve-olmayanlar. May 11, 2008 (accessed June 2009).

19

Transformation of Adult Education in Turkey: From Public Education to Life-Long Learning

Ahmet Yıldız

In the last 30 years, global neoliberal policies and practices have radically influenced all educational processes. In line with the demands of the Organization for Economic Cooperation and Development (OECD) and the World Bank (WB), education has been reevaluated at a time of capital accumulation crisis and turned into a commodity (Mayo 2011, Rikowski 2002). The neoliberal movement asserts that the public role in directing education results in the irrational use of resources and the failure to adequately meet consumer expectations (Ercan 2006). In line with this perspective in an era of global economic competition, education has turned into a tool of economic policy rather than a right for citizens (İnal 2009, Mayo 2011, Sayılan and Yıldız 2009, Uysal 2009). The concept of "public education" has become obsolete in Turkey and given way to the concepts of "adult education" or "lifelong learning." Public education now refers to something in the past that is remembered with nostalgia, and is considered to be an archaic concept that bears no relationship to our day. Together with such transformations triggered by global neoliberal policies, education for adults has started to be defined in line with market demands and become more individualistic. This chapter focuses on the recent dramatic transformation in adult-education practices in Turkey, particularly since the Justice and Development Party (AKP) came to power in 2002.

Neoliberalism, the AKP, and Adult Education

The neoliberal policies that dominated Turkey after 1980 led to a radical change in adult-education practices and approaches, following the discourse and practices of the AKP, which came to power in 2002. The recent transformation in adult education closely mirrors the political stance represented by the AKP. This stance claims that the state should have a limited role, and that education should be considered as a gradual process of social change, family, and traditional values rather than being radical. In other words, the AKP is trying to reconcile the protection of traditional values, including religion, with the process of globalization (Uzgel 2009).

The stance developed by the AKP is also evident in adult-education practices. Indeed, this era has been marked by strong initiatives aiming to make education more religious and more aligned with the needs of the market. Accordingly, the adult-education approaches and practices that have gained ground since the AKP's rise to power can be divided into four themes: (1) approaches and practices that reduce adult education to workforce training, and in which the role of the civil society is particularly important; (2) adult-literacy endeavors; (3) educational services offered by the local authorities ruled by the AKP; and (4) religious courses.

Reduction of Adult Education to Workforce Training and the Increased Role of NGOs

An overview of basic official documents that have recently guided education in Turkey, as well as other reports and documents, reveals a neoliberal perspective that views education in relation to the demands of the economy and markets. For instance, law no. 3797, dated 1992, which outlines the organizational structure of the Ministry of National Education (MoNE), was amended in 2011 with a decree issued by the government, and the main mission of the Ministry was described as "designing, implementing and updating instructional programs that can equip students with the knowledge and skills necessitated by a globally competitive economic system; and managing instructional services for students and teachers within this framework" (MoNE 2011). The roots of these policies that require education to be guided by employment policies is traced back to the 1990s. During this process, the education-related discourses of the OECD, the WB, the

European Union (EU), and national capital frequently stated that education could not meet the demands of the market, and thus the state needed to take certain measures to transform it into a field that trained qualified workforce. Legal arrangements on the education-employment relationship developed in line with these views (law no. 4702 and law no. 5544, dated 2006) assert the following:

- Cooperation should be established between education-employment, and curricula and policies should be created to satisfy the workforce market.
- Education-employment policies should be integrated so as to train a workforce that possesses the various necessary qualities.
- Employers should be incorporated into the formulating of educational policies as a "social stakeholder."
- Education-employment policies should be made to meet both local and international market demands with the help of local boards and by identifying the demands of the local market (Uzunyayla 2007).

These policies, which aim to integrate education and employment, have been conceived in relation to "lifelong learning" (Bağcı 2007). Indeed, in the 2000 Lisbon Meeting of the European Council organized by the EU, which is a significant determiner of recent educational policies in Turkey, "lifelong learning" was mentioned as one of the main elements of the strategy adopted by the Union for continuous economic growth and social harmony. It was suggested that lifelong learning strategies should be implemented in order to meet the skills needed in the workforce market of member states, and that the quality of their educational and vocational training systems should be improved. The establishment of the European Employment Strategy (EES) by the EU with the aim of offering member states a broad, effective, and efficient platform to develop preventive and active policies to combat unemployment and transform work markets, and to achieve cooperation among the employment policies of member states has particularly helped open a new window on adult-education practices in Turkey. The Turkish Work Institution (İŞKUR) is responsible for implementing the EES and aligning informal education activities with the policies of work markets in the country. Thus, the İŞKUR has recently fulfilled an important task, and an increasing number of skill development programs have been implemented by the İŞKUR.

These practices emphasize the need to increase the quality of vocational training and reduce unemployment by offering vocational training to the public. Thus, they define unemployment through personal skills (Yaşot 2009). Further, lifelong learning has increased the demand for certification and professional documentation. What is important now is to acquire and continuously enhance personal skills through schooling, work, or other means (Uzunyayla 2007). This shows that adult education is bound by employment markets and reduced to workforce training. According to Ahmet Duman (2005), this trend, which is known by the term "new vocationalism," devalues lifelong education.

The discourse on the need for a qualified workforce so as to cope with global competition and changes also contributes to the justification for this transformation. The concept of employability has particularly stood out, drawn the boundaries of the concept of lifelong learning, and come to be mentioned only with market arguments, which draw on neoliberal economics, such as efficiency, quality, flexibility, and competition.

The WB is another organization that has recently helped shape educational policies. Particularly after the year 2000, educational projects funded by the WB have revolved around "equal opportunity" and the democratization of education (Orhan 2007), and nongovernmental organizations (NGOs) have been encouraged to take an active role in these endeavors. Educational projects funded by the WB have been initiated in Turkey in order to alleviate the negative economic and social effects of the privatization of public institutions. Indeed, the reduction in public spending dictated by neoliberal economic programs that are in effect in developing countries leads to the collapse of public health and education systems. In return, the WB loans money to health and education projects as a part of schemes to combat poverty (Çulha-Zabçı 2003). Thus, as stated by George Monbiot (2001), "First they [the World Bank] break your legs, then, by way of compensation, they offer you a pedicure" (cited in Çulha-Zabçı 2009, 101).

NGOs play a central role in these projects. Today, almost all institutions proclaim more cooperation with NGOs in their strategic plans and action-plan documents. The global rise of the civil society and their international collaborations, European Commission training programs, and funding allocated to NGOs in the process of integration with the EU have increased the volume of adult education activities in NGOs (Okçabol 2009). However, it should be noted that the NGOs that run adult-education programs have focused their efforts on micro problems and audiences (Alpaydın 2005). Further, the close cooperation between NGOs and public and international institutions has discredited their claims of being "close to the people" (Sinha 2005).

Adult-Literacy Practices

Currently, there are five million illiterate citizens living in Turkey, comprising approximately 10 percent of the adult population. The issue of adult literacy is thus one of the biggest educational challenges that the country faces. Similar to previous governments, the AKP initiated a campaign to combat this problem (the literacy campaign entitled "Mother and Daughter at School") (2008). As is evident from the title, the campaign was aimed at women. Indeed, females constitute 84 percent of the illiterate population, thus the problem is intertwined with the issue of gender.

The courses that have been launched with this campaign are being managed by Public Education Centers (PEC), which have always existed in Turkey at a national level with the aim of basic adult education. However, a study examining these literacy courses (Yıldız 2011) found that approximately 85 percent of their participants were not at an expected reading level. This suggested that some literacy courses fail to equip adult participants with adequate literacy skills and are dramatically far from meeting expectations. The reason behind this should be sought in the literacy practices in Turkey, including the "Mother and Daughter at School" campaign, which have always defined literacy as only a "skill." In this approach, literacy is reduced to a technical issue that bears no relation to certain life experiences (Nohl and Sayılan 2004, Sayılan 2009, Yıldız 2011, Yıldız 2008, Yıldız 2006), and the problem of literacy is perceived merely as a "statistical issue" that is fought against by a quantitative increase in the rate of literacy. This approach limits literacy training to a mechanical-skills acquisition process, and mostly fails to focus on the sociocultural context of literacy. However, as critical educationalists emphasize (see Freire 1995, Giroux and McLaren 1992), literacy training is not limited to learning how to read or write, but is also closely related to how and where reading and writing will be used, the socioeconomic status of the individual, gender, educational background and the position of the individual within the society in relation to her/his ethnic background. In sum, the literacy approach in Turkey assumes that problems can be solved in the classroom, devoid of a social context, and does not concern itself with the empowering of students by enabling them to actively participate in public/social life.

This traditional perspective has been even more strengthened by the AKP. It has not been possible in the AKP era to improve literacy, especially as a skill that facilitates the participation of women in public life and that enables them to cope with the vicissitudes of modern life. On the contrary, by suggesting at every opportunity that "women should have at least three children," Prime Minister Erdoğan reflects a conservative ideology that limits the place of women to the home and reduces their role solely to child care, which enhances women's literacy problem. This approach has thus failed to contribute to the development and implementation of effective literacy policies. It has resulted in the creation of a group of women who seem to be literate on paper—but not in practice—and are "desperate housewives" when viewed through the lens of social/individual empowerment.

The AKP's neoliberal and conservative ideology is also evident in adult-literacy curricula. The main tendency in this field is to standardize adult-literacy curricula and activities by considering quality criteria, and to treat literacy and basic arithmetic skills on a performance scale. At the same time, many of the values in the ideological universe of neoliberalism (entrepreneurship, career planning, communication skills, leadership) are considered life skills and included in literacy-training curricula (Sayılan 2009). Indeed, "developing citizens with entrepreneurship skills" was one of the main goals declared in the revised Adult Literacy Education Curriculum and Materials in 2005 (MoNE 2005).

Adult-Education Activities by Local Authorities

The ideological power of the "new right" at the end of the 1970s and the addition of market-based policies to that after the 1980s led to important transformations in the traditional management structure of local authorities. Appearing first in the United States and the United Kingdom, these transformations manifested themselves as privatization, entrepreneurship in municipalities, privatization of public services, and voluntary participation in local public services (Ben–Ellia 1996, Sezen 2008). With rapid urbanization and the booming need for infrastructure, work, education-health, housing, and sociocultural facilities, the responsibilities and tasks of local authorities have expanded greatly. In Turkey too, a significant increase developed in the tasks and functions of local authorities starting from the mid-1990s, particularly in social-policy fields such as social aid, social services, education, health, and housing (Erder and İncioğlu 2008, Ersöz 2007, Sezen 2008).

The emergence of comprehensive educational activities by Metropolitan Municipalities also started with the March 1994 local elections after the victory of the Welfare Party (RP), which won the highest number of votes in Ankara and Istanbul, the two largest cities in Turkey, and the educational activities offered by local authorities took on new aspects with the continuing "Islamic municipality tradition" (Doğan 2007), or in other scholars' words the "social municipality tradition" (Erder and İncioğlu 2008). This type of municipality management became more distinct with the gradual transformation of the methods developed during the search of the Islamist RP for more followers. Thus, the seeds of this tradition were sown in the RP era, but it was only declared as official party policy by the AKP after the 2004 elections (Erder and İncioğlu 2008).

Indeed, the local authorities that offer the most comprehensive educational activities in Turkey both belong to the AKP: Istanbul Metropolitan (IBB) and Ankara Metropolitan Municipalities (ABB). The IBB has institutionalized its adult-education activities and established large organizations to operate in this field. The largest of these organizations, the Istanbul Artistic and Vocational Education Courses (ISMEK) was established in 1996. The ISMEK has so far served over one million individuals. The courses include many areas, from vocational technical courses to sports. Similarly, the ABB offers adult-education activities through the Municipality Technical Education Courses (BELTEK) and the Municipality Handcrafts and Vocation Courses (BELMEK) for women.

The aims and tendencies of the AKP are evident in these endeavors. The following points are worth noting:

- These educational activities are not offered as a public service in municipality-owned buildings and by municipality staff, but through "bids" without "personnel employment." Thus, not only does funding go to companies that are close to the party, but educational activities are treated with a market mentality.
- Vocational technical education courses relate mostly to lower social-class vocations or skills required by these vocations, such as gardening and skin care. Even though the impact of these courses on the employment of the aforementioned social groups remains limited, they play an important role in communicating with and getting the support of particularly the unemployed and the poor who work in the informal sector.

Indeed, these courses give the poor hopes of "new work opportunities" at a time when the effects of the neoliberal destruction on the poor are perhaps at their worst.
- It is worth noting that the courses include Turkish Islamic arts, such as porcelain painting, paper marbling, and calligraphy, as well as languages, such as Arabic and Ottoman. These are typically valued by conservatives, and it is obvious that such courses provide Islamic socialization.
- ISMEK and BELMEK have both been structured to prioritize women. The majority of course participants at ISMEK were housewives (84 percent) (Ersöz 2007). However, this chapter asserts that these programs do not empower women or amend existing social injustice and inequalities. Indeed, the programs attended most frequently by women are those that reproduce the traditional worldview and gender roles that define the place of the woman as the home, and her main role as caring for children and other family members.

Koran courses

One of the most influential institutions in the field of religious education in Turkey is the Department of Religious Affairs (DIB). The DIB runs a major part of its religious education activities through Koran courses. Koran courses are defined as 32-week-long courses that offer basic religious education and help participants to read Koran accurately and appropriately, and memorize enough of it to practice their faith. However, these courses use state resources to teach the religious beliefs of only a certain portion of the population, not of everyone. In a way, the teaching conducted in these courses aims to Islamicize the entire population. Thus, Koran courses have always been a heated topic of debate in Turkey.

Traditionally, Koran courses bring to mind summer religious teaching activities for children. Koran courses for adults are a very recent occurrence. During the transition to eight-year compulsory basic education following the military intervention of February 28, 1997, which is known as a "post-modern coup," the interest in Koran courses for children waned so much that the courses ran the risk of closure. Indeed, a total of 1,989 Koran courses were closed down due to the lack of enough enrolled students between 1997 and 2001 (Klavuz 2002). It was during this period that adult Koran courses appeared.

Table 19.1 Koran courses and number of enrolled students

School Year	Number of Operating Koran Courses	Number of Enrolled Students
2000–2001	3,368	90,353
2001–2002	3,364	1,04,109
2002–2003	3,852	1,18,335
2003–2004	4,322	1,34,406
2004–2005	4,447	1,55,285
2005–2006	4,951	1,84,356
2006–2007	6,033	2,30,297
2007–2008	7,036	2,49,973
2008–2009	7,677	2,68,738
2009–2010	8,696	2,97,247

During the AKP era, Koran courses for both adults and children, and the number of their participants increased sharply. According to data from DIB and as shown in Table 19.1[1], the increase from 2001 to 2010 was threefold.

It should be noted that these are official numbers and are mostly misleading, because there have always been "pirate" courses not included in official statistical records.

It is worth noting that similar to literacy courses, Koran courses are mostly attended by women (90 percent). More interestingly, even though Koran courses last longer, they have a larger number of attendees than literacy courses. The Islamization policy seen in Turkey recently may explain why women with similar socioeconomic life conditions should prefer Koran courses. A patriarchal cultural climate devalues literacy skills that are tools of empowerment for women; what is more valued but less "dangerous" is religious knowledge. Influenced by the socialization processes within this cultural climate, women may tend to participate in religious activities and training. This climate prevents women from existing in public life and is unfortunately supported by recent public policies.

Discussion and Conclusion

It is true that the traditional line of adult education, which emphasizes public responsibility, was broken in the AKP era, and the content of adult education was reduced merely to the fields of private economy and religion. Indeed, most adult education today dwells on the economy and/or religion rather than education, and adult-education activities seem to be not the activities of the Ministry of National Education, but of the Ministry of Economy or the ministry in charge of religious affairs. The AKP's goal of bringing together traditional values, including religion, with globalization may seem paradoxical at first glance. However, the AKP has managed to construct these as mutually benefiting processes, rather than conflicting ones. In this regard, the AKP differs from the Islamic political parties and movements of the past that always approached "Western values" with suspicion and resisted them. Owing to this distinguishing trait of the AKP, it is possible to define it as a "neo-Islamic" party.

The neo-Islamic stance of the AKP in accord with global capitalism renders the provision of public adult education difficult. The dominant adult-education approach in Turkey is shaped by the needs of markets as influenced by global trends, and does not include egalitarian practices that demonstrate a sense of public responsibility, target the lack of education revealed by the demographic nature of the country, or extol the complementary/compensating function of adult education. Accordingly, adult education is largely evaluated in the context of market ideology, and is mostly defined as increasing the sensitivity of the workforce to the developing economy and developing employment skills for individuals. Furthermore, there is emphasis on putting adult-education activities on the market and supporting the private sector.

However, to have a high quality of life, every individual should have access to adult-education activities for lifelong learning, regardless of their education and income levels. The global market economy, nevertheless, is always keen to reduce social public expenses and increase competition and privatization (Ayhan 2005, Miser 2002). By following this model, adult-education practices, which have always had less access to public funds than formal education, have been stripped of their social content and reduced to personal development or workforce training (Sayılan 2001). Parallel to this transformation, the term "public" gave way to individual/adult, and "education" to learning. While the concepts of public and education refer to state responsibility and the public sphere, adult and learning emphasize the individual responsibility of the learner who is considered a client. In other words, the shift from the public to the individual and from education to learning has meant a shift from public right to charity and from public service to commodity.

It should be noted that the commercialization of adult education causes serious problems, particularly in developing countries such as

Turkey owing to the size of the population that is deprived fully or partially of institutional education and the right to basic education. Indeed, the gap between traditional literacy and the recent digital literacy has become bigger. As an end result, the economic, social, and cultural inequalities between the masses with little access to basic education and the qualified/educated masses that operate in international competitive markets have deepened on a global basis (Lam 2006; Hull, Zacher, and Hibbert 2009). In addition, the persistence of the educational trend that puts an emphasis on the role of individuals, the private sector, and NGOs in adult education, rather than that of the public, may result in public responsibility being transferred in full to the civil society or the private sector. The risk is obvious. Indeed, educational projects to be run jointly by private institutions, NGOs, and the Ministry of National Education have been offered as a prescription to solve the problems of education.

The majority of adult-education practices in Turkey may be evaluated, other than the market ideology, in the context of the Islamic socialization goal of the AKP. The acceleration in the activities of Koran courses organized by the Department of Religious Affairs in the AKP era is evidence of this.

One of the most important aspects of the practices outside the work orce market is that these activities appeal mostly to women. Indeed, women dominate the adult-education activities organized by municipalities, public education centers and the Department of Religious Affairs. However, far from providing employment for women or empowering them in public-social life, most of these courses reproduce traditional gender roles and target Islamic socialization, in line with the AKP's ideological position.

In conclusion, be it market-driven or for religious reasons, the recent increase in the adult-education practices offered by İŞKUR, PEC, DIB, and local authorities, and the extent of these activities may only be compared to the first years of the republic. Both eras saw the most widespread and effective adult-education practices in the country. The difference is the reformist-statist-secular goals of the early republican era as opposed to the market-religious goals of the recent era.

Note

1. Compiled and calculated from various statistical data at the website of DIB. http://www.diyanet.gov.tr/turkish/dinegitimi/Default.aspx (accessed March 2011).

References

Alpaydın, Yusuf. "Türkiye'de STK'ların Yetişkin Eğitimine Katkısı." *Sivil Toplum* 3 (2005): 81–90.
Ayhan, Serap. "Dünden bugüne yaşam boyu öğrenme." In *Yaşamboyu Öğrenme*, edited by Fevziye Sayılan and Ahmet Yıldız, 2–15. Ankara: PegemA Yayıncılık, 2005.
Bağcı, Erhan. "Avrupa Birliği Ülkelerinde Yaşam Boyu Eğitim Politikaları Almanya, Danimarka Ve Türkiye Üzerine Karşılaştırmalı Bir Çalışma." Master's thesis, Ankara University, Ankara, Turkey, 2007.
Çulha-Zabçı, Filiz. *Dünya Bankası: Yanılsamalar ve Gerçekler*. Istanbul: Yordam Yayınları, 2009.
———. "Sosyal Riski Azaltma Projesi: Yoksulluğu azaltmak mı, zengini yoksuldan korumak mı?" *Ankara Üniversitesi Siyasal Bilgiler Fakültesi Dergisi* 58, no. 2 (2003): 215–241.
DIB (The Presidency of Religious Affairs of the Republic of Turkey). Egitim Hizmetleri Genel Mudurlugu, 2011. http://www.diyanet.gov.tr/turkish/dinegitimi/Default.aspx.
Doğan, Ali Ekber. *Eğreti Kamusallık: Kayseri Örneğinde İslamcı Belediyecilik*. Istanbul: İletişim Yayınları, 2007.
Duman, Ahmet. "Türkiye'de Yaşamboyu Öğrenme SiyasalarıOluştu(a)mamanın Dayanılmaz Hafifliği." In *Yaşamboyu Öğrenme*, edited by Fevziye Sayılan and Ahmet Yıldız, 31–45. Ankara: PegemA Yayıncılık, 2005.
Ercan, Fuat. "Neoliberal Eğitim Politikasının Anatomisi İçin Bir Çerçeve" 2011. http://www.fuatercan.wordpress.com. (accessed March 2011).
Erder, Sema, and Nihal İncioğlu. *Türkiye'de Yerel Politikanın Yükselişi*. Istanbul: Bilgi Üniversitesi Yayınları, 2008.
Ersöz, Yunus. "Yerel Yönetimlerin Yetişkin Eğitimi Alanındaki Etkinlikleri." In *ISMEK Öğrenen Toplum İçin Yetişkin Eğitimi Sempozyumu*, edited by Muhammet Altıntaş, 44–67. Istanbul: ISMEK Yayınları, 2007.
Freire, Paulo. *Ezilenlerin pedagojisi*. Translated by Dilek Hattatoğlu and Erol Özbek. Istanbul: Ayrıntı Yayınları, 1995.
Giroux, Henry, and Peter McLaren. "Writing from Margins: Geographies of Identity, Pedagogy, and Power." *Journal of Education*, 174, no. 1 (1992): 7–30.
Hull, Glynda, Jessica Zacher, and Liesel Hibbert. "Youth, Risk and Equity in a Global World." *Review of Research in Education* 33 (2009): 117–159.
İnal, Kemal. "AKP'nin Neo-Liberal ve Muhafazakar Eğitim Anlayışı." *Eleştirel Pedagoji* 1 (2009): 37–50.
İŞKUR (Turkish Work Institution). "Yılı Faaliyet Raporu." 2010. http://statik.iskur.gov.tr/tr/rapor_bulten/2010%20Yılı%20Faaliyet%20Raporu.pdf (accessed April 2011).
Lam, Wan S. E. "Culture and Learning in the Context of Globalization: Research Directions." *Review of Research in Education* 30 (2006): 213–237.
Mayo, Peter. *Gramsci, Freire ve Yetişkin Eğitimi*. Translated by Ahmet Duman. Ankara: Ütopya Yayınları, 2011.
Miser, Rifat. "Küreselleşen" Dünyada Yetişkin Eğitimi." *Ankara Üniversitesi Eğitim Bilimleri Fakültesi Dergisi* 35 (2002): 55–60.

MoNE (Ministry of National Education). *Yetişkinler Okuma Yazma Öğretimi ve Temel Eğitimi Programı.* Ankara: MoNE Yayınları, 2005.

MoNE (Ministry of National Education). Millî Eğitim Bakanlığının Teşkilat ve Görevleri Hakkında Kanun Hükmünde Kararname. 14.09.2011 tarihli Resmi Gazete, 2011.http://mevzuat.meb.gov.tr/html/28054_652.html (accessed April 2012).

Nohl, Arnold M., and Fevziye Sayılan. "Türkiye'de yetişkinler için okuma yazma eğitimi. Temel eğitime destek projesi teknik raporu." 2004. Milli Eğitim Bakanlığı/Avrupa Komisyonu. http://www.meb.gov.tr/duyurular/duyurular/proj/tedpbilgilendirme.pdf (accessed March 2011).

Okçabol, Rıfat. "AKP'nin Eğitim Karnesi." *Eleştirel Pedegoji* 1 (2009): 26–32.

Orhan, Seçil. "Türkiye'de Eğitim Sisteminin Yeniden Yapılandırılması Ve Sivil Toplum Kuruluşlarıyla İlişkisi." Master's thesis, Marmara University, Istanbul, Turkey, 2007.

Rikowski, Glenn. "Education and Globalisation." House of Lord Select Committee on Economic Affairs Inquiry into the Global Economy, January 22, 2002, pages 1–9. http://www.ieps.org.uk.cwc.net/rikowski2002d.pdf (accessed January 2006).

Sayılan, Fevziye. "Paradigma Değişirken: Küreselleşme ve Yaşam Boyu Eğitim." In *Cevat Geray'a Armağan,* edited by Muhterem Orhan: 609–624. Ankara: Mülkiyeliler Birliği Yayını, 2001.

———. "Yetişkin Okuma Yazma Öğretimi ve Temel Eğitim Programı ve Ders Kitapları: Eleştirel Söylem Analizi." *Eğitim Bilim Toplum* 26 (2009): 39–68.

Sayılan, Fevziye, and Ahmet Yıldız. "Historical and Political Context of Adult Literacy in Turkey." *The International Journal of Lifelong Education* 28, no. 6 (2009): 735–749.

Sinha, Subir. "Neoliberalism and Civil Society: Project and Possibilities." In *Neoliberalism: A Critical Reader,* edited by Alfredo Saad-Filho and Deborah Johnston, 163–169. London: Pluto Press, 2005.

Uysal, Meral. "Adult Education in Developed Countries." *International Journal of Educational Policies* 3, no. 2 (2009): 17–23.

Uzgel, İlhan. "AKP: Neoliberal Dönüşümün Yeni Aktörü." In *AKP Kitabı: Bir Dönüşümün Bilançosu,* edited by İlhan Uzgel and Bülent Duru, 11–39. Ankara: Phoenix Yayınları, 2009.

Uzunyayla, Ferda. "Avrupa Birliği'ne Giriş Sürecinde Eğitim ve İstihdam Politikaları." Master's thesis, Marmara University, Istanbul, Turkey, 2007.

Yaşot, Berrin. "Türkiye'de Birikim Sürecinin Değişen Yapısının İstihdam ve Eğitimdeki Yansımaları." Master's thesis, Marmara University, Istanbul, Turkey, 2009.

Yıldız, Ahmet. 2011. "Okuma-Yazma Kurslarında Okuma-Yazma Öğreniliyor mu?" *Kuram ve Uygulamada Eğitim Bilimleri Dergisi,* 11: 403–421.

———. "Türkiye'de yetişkin okuryazarlığı: Yetişkin okuma-yazma eğitimine eleştirel bir yaklaşım." PhD diss., Ankara Üniversity, Turkey, Ankara, 2006.

———. "Yeni Okuma-Yazma Kampanyasının Düşündürdükleri." *ABECE Dergisi* 264 (2008): 4–11.

Contributors

Ergül Adıgüzel is currently working as a guide teacher at a vocational secondary education institution. His interests are education quality management, strategic planning, and process management applications, such as the effects of education on the components of areas. He is also an activist in *Eğitim-Sen* (Education and Science Workers' Union).

Güliz Akkaymak is a doctoral canditate in the Department of Sociology at the University of Western Ontario, London, Canada. Her research interests include social inequality, sociology of work, sociology of education, and migration studies.

Gülay Aslan is an assistant professor in the Faculty of Education at Gaziosmanpaşa University, Tokat, Turkey. She is interested in equality and discrimination in education, neoliberal education policies, and critical pedagogy.

Tuğba Asrak-Hasdemir is an associate professor in the Department of Public Relations, the Faculty of Communication, Gazi University, Ankara, Turkey. Her research interests include human rights, child's rights and communication; political communication and propaganda; public sphere, public relations and transnational civil society; information society, e-government and critical analysis; right to know; and media literacy. Her book is titled *Kamusal İletişimde Bilgi Edinme Hakkı* (Right to know in public communication) (2007).

Ömür Birler is an instructor doctor in the Department of Political Science at Middle East Technical University, Ankara, Turkey. Her works focus on political theory and philosophy of science. She has edited books on Turkish politics. Her books are *Turkey: Neo-Liberalism, Democracy and Nation-State* (2009) and *Winds of Politics and Economics in Turkey* (2011).

Ergin Bulut is a doctoral candidate in the Institute of Communications Research at the University of Illinois at Urbana-Champaign, Illinois, United States. His research interests broadly include critical theory, political economy, technology, labor, and education. He has published on labor in digital capitalism, cultural studies, child labor in Turkey, and labor in the creative economy. His ongoing dissertation work is on the labor process in the video-game industry. He has translated the works of Michael Apple and Aijaz Ahmad into Turkish. He recently coedited a volume titled *Cognitive Capitalism, Digital Labor and Education* (2011).

Mustafa Kemal Coşkun is an assistant professor in the Department of Sociology, Ankara University, Turkey. His book *Demokrasi Teorileri ve Toplumsal Hareketler* (Democracy theories and social movements) was published in 2007. Most recently he edited *Yapı, Pratik, Özne* (Structure, practice, subject) (2009).

Serdar M. Değirmencioğlu is a professor in the Department of Psychology at Cumhuriyet University, Sivas, Turkey. His work and activism focuses on children's rights and welfare, youth policy, participation, civic engagement, community psychology, and critical pedagogy. He is the editor of a book titled *Some Still More Equal Than Others: Equal Opportunities for All*, published by the Council of Europe in 2011.

Esin Ertürk is doctoral student in the Atatürk Institute History for Modern Turkey, at Boğaziçi University, Istanbul, Turkey. Her research interests are education history of early republican Turkey, women's history, labor history, critical sociology, and politics of education.

Duygun Göktürk is a doctoral student pursuing her PhD in the Cultural Foundations of Education at Purdue University, Indiana, United States. Her research interests are sociology of education, education policies, and sociology of religion with a special focus on feminist agenda and the new forms of hegemony.

Gökçe Güvercin is a doctoral candidate and a research assistant in the Department of Educational Sciences at Boğaziçi University, Istanbul, Turkey. Her doctoral dissertation is about the professional identity development processes of public school teachers through learning experiences. Her research interests are teacher professional development, informal learning, life history, and biographical research.

Kemal İnal is an associate professor in the Faculty of Communication at Gazi University, Ankara, Turkey. His studies are mainly on childhood, child labor, the Kurdish language, media literacy, textbooks, and curriculum in Turkey. He is the editor of the Turkish critical journal of education, *Eleştirel Pedagoji* (Critical pedagogy), and the author and translator of many Turkish, English, and French books and articles.

Hülya Koşar-Altınyelken is a lecturer and researcher at the Child Development and Education Department of the University of Amsterdam, the Netherlands. Her research engages with issues such as gender, migration, educational policy transfer, educational reforms, pedagogy, and teachers. She has published in journals such as *Journal of Education Policy, Comparative Education,* and *International Journal of Educational Development.*

Contributors 261

Nejla Kurul is a professor in the Faculty of Educational Sciences, Department of Educational Administration and Politics at Ankara University, Ankara, Turkey. She holds a PhD in Educational Administration and Planning from Ankara University, Turkey. Her works include critical books and articles on educational policies, the finance of education, and educational administration and universities in Turkey.

Erdal Küçüker is an assistant professor of Educational Sciences at the University of Gaziosmanpaşa, Tokat, Turkey. His field of study is educational economics and planning. He is presently doing research on the negative effects of neoliberal education policies on public schools.

İ. Rıfat Okçabol is a retired professor and currently a part-time instructor of Education at Boğaziçi University, İstanbul, Turkey. His books include *Türkiye Eğitim Sistemi* (Turkish education system), *Öğretmen Yetiştirme Sistemimiz* (Teacher-training system in Turkey), *Yükseköğretim Sistemimiz* (Higher education in Turkey), and his textbooks include *Halk Eğitimi* (Adult education) and *Eğitim Bilimlerine Giriş* (Introduction to the sciences of education).

Nevzat Evrim Önal is an assistant professor at Beykoz Vocational School of Logistics, İstanbul, Turkey. He is the author of *The 150-Year Story of Anatolian Agriculture* and the editor of *The Bologna Process in Question*, both of which have been published in Turkish. He has also written a number of articles on agricultural development and higher education issues in Turkey.

Ali Murat Özdemir is an associate professor in the Department of International Relations at Hacettepe University, Ankara, Turkey. He has published widely on the sociology of law and political economy in general and on the political economy of the Turkish legal system in particular, both in English and Turkish.

Gamze Yücesan-Özdemir completed her doctorate in Labour Economics at the University of Sussex in 1998 and became an associate professor in social policy in 2004. Since 2010, she has been a professor of economics in the Faculty of Communications at Ankara University, Ankara, Turkey. She has published books and articles widely on social policy and political economy both in English and Turkish.

Ünal Özmen is an executive editor of a journal, *Eleştirel Pedagoji* (Critical pedagogy) and a columnist for a newspaper, *BirGün*. Since his retirement in 2006, he has held different positions. He has worked as an elementary school teacher, as the president of the Counseling Commission of the Ministry of National Education, and as parliamentary adviser.

Onur Seçkin is a doctoral candidate and a research assistant in the Department of Educational Sciences at Boğaziçi University, Istanbul, Turkey. His master's thesis was on adult learning in social movements, and his ongoing doctoral dissertation is about lifelong-learning policy-making processes in Turkey. His research interests are social movements and learning, informal learning, sociology of education, and educational politics and policy.

Burcu Şentürk is a doctoral candidate in the Department of Politics, University of York, United Kingdom. Her book *İki Tarafta Evlat Acısı* (Agony of Losing a Child on Both Sides) was published by İletişim Yayınları in 2012.

Mehmet Toran is an assistant professor of early childhood education studies at Girne American University, Girne, TRNC. He holds a PhD in early childhood education approaches from Gazi University. He has a background as a preschool teacher. His research deals mainly with early childhood education curricula, early childhood education approaches, early childhood education policy, poverty and childhood, and critical pedagogy.

Hasan Ünder is a professor in the Department of Philosophy of Education at Ankara University, Ankara, Turkey. He is the author of *Çevre Felsefesi: Etik ve Metafizik Görüşler* (Environmental philosophy: ethical and metaphysical views) (1996). He is the editor of *Skolastik Eğitim ve Türkiye'de Skolastik Tarz* (Scholastic education and scholastic way of thinking in Turkey) (2002). He also has published articles on the early republican era in Turkey, philosophy of education, and environmental philosophy.

Ayhan Ural is an assistant professor in the Department of Educational Sciences, Education Administration and Supervision at Gazi University, Ankara, Turkey. He has publications on primary education, the quality of primary schooling, critical pedagogy, and the right to education.

Ahmet Yıldız is currently an assistant professor in the Adult Education and Lifelong Learning Department at Ankara University Faculty of Education, Ankara, Turkey. He is interested in issues of adult basic education, literacy, and critical education.

Index

Academic Staff and Graduate
Degree Education Exam
(ALES), 225, 226
adult education, 129, 245–55
Atatürk, 33, 38–9, 41, 193, 196
see also Mustafa Kemal, 187

behaviorism, 18, 23, 37, 38
behaviorist model, 61
Board of Education and Discipline
(TTKB), 48, 50, 52, 56
body politics, 179–89
Bologna Process, 125, 130–1, 134,
136, 198, 227

central exams, 92, 152
see also centralized exams, 155, 157
central university exam, 140, 141,
221, 223
see also university entrance exam,
158, 221
see also university exam, 167
commercialization
of adult-education, 254
of collective goods, 85
of education, 85–7, 89–90, 159
in the educational system, 97–8
commercializing education, 86
commodification
of collective goods, 85
of education, 27, 87–8, 93, 95
of educational services, 89, 233
of the educational system, 15, 104

of higher education, 146–8
in public services, 5
of public services, 4
of scientific research, 143
commodifying education, 86
commoditization of education, 159
competitive education, 92, 154–6,
160–1
compulsory education, 167, 206, 252
compulsory religious courses, 118
compulsory religious education, 19
conservative democracy, 165
conservative democrat, 19, 84
conservative democratic, 168, 174
conservative-Islamist ideology, 170
constructivism, 18, 23, 34–7, 39–44,
48, 60
constructivist educational models, 61
see also constructivist approach, 102
constructivist learning theory, 35
content of education, 19, 233–4
see also educational content, 102
contracted teachers, 235–8, 242
contractual teachers, 93
Council of Higher Education
(CoHE), 130–1, 133, 134, 135,
140–1, 145, 154, 197, 219–20,
221–2, 224–9
curricula, 17, 23, 34, 36, 38, 47–51, 55,
56, 141, 219, 220, 222, 225, 247
adult-literacy curricula, 250
literacy-training curricula, 250
standardized curricula, 130

curriculum, 19, 22–3, 36, 37, 50, 55, 59–62, 65–8, 71, 102–3, 144, 170, 187, 192, 205–8, 210–14, 215, 222
  hidden curriculum, 185
  laboratory schools, 21, 100
  reform, 23, 34, 43, 60, 234

distance education, 129–30
distance education programs, 133
distance learning, 132
distance learning courses, 133
distance learning programs, 129

early childhood education (ECE), 191–200
  see also preschool education, 194–195, 222
Eğitim-Bir-Sen, 110, 111, 115–19
  see also Union of Unity of Educators, 110
Eğitim-İş, 111
  see also Union of Education and Science Profession Public Employees, 111
Eğitim-Sen, 110, 111, 242
  see also Union of Education and Science Laborers, 110
electronic (text)books, 53–6
  see also tablet PCs, 53–6
  see also Electronic Book Project, 53
equal opportunity, 154, 159, 161, 248
European Union (EU), 23, 48, 49, 61–2, 72, 96, 114, 125, 159, 247
  funds, 54
  norms, 196
  supported projects, 86, 100

gender roles, 183, 188
gender segregation, 181, 185, 188
globalization, 18, 23, 26, 48, 61, 86, 111, 117, 165, 246, 254
governance, 99–100, 104, 117
governance of education, 90–1
  see also education governance, 90–1

Gülen movement, 171, 186
Gülen schools, 185–6

headscarf, 167, 173, 174, 175, 224
headscarf issue, 118, 168, 171–2
high schools, 99, 205, 207
higher education, 88, 125–35, 140–1, 154, 155, 197, 219, 222
  see also tertiary education, 125–35
higher education institutions, 131, 144, 219
higher education programs, 104, 223
higher education system, 139, 140, 142, 146, 220
human capital, 20, 24, 88
human rights education, 205–16
  see also human rights textbooks, 208

Imam-Hatip schools, 19, 38, 42, 43, 71, 165–72
  see also religious schools, 169
individualism, 11, 63, 65, 67, 156
International Monetary Fund (IMF), 5, 10, 12, 18, 83, 85, 90, 95, 242
  designed programs, 10
  oriented economic policies, 9
  policies, 10
Islamic clothing, 13
Islamic-conservative, 3
  see also Islamic conservatism, 11
Islamic discourse, 165
Islamic ideology, 47, 125
Islamist movement, 33
  see also Islamic movements, 47, 175

January 24 decisions, 7, 95, 109, 181
  see also stabilization program, 6
  see also January 24 adjustments, 83

Koran courses, 19, 167, 252–3, 255
Koran education, 43
Kurdish problem, 17

Language Exam for Public
  Employees (KPDS), 223, 226,
  227–8
lifelong learning, 68, 73, 78, 100,
  129, 245, 247–8, 254

Market Islam, 47
marketization of
  education, 18, 25, 85, 86–7,
    89–90, 234, 240
  the educational systems, 15, 48
  research, 129
military coup of 1960, 181
  see also 1960 coup, 111
military coup of 1980, 6–7, 47, 84,
    111, 130, 139, 140, 181–2, 195
  see also September 12 military
    coup, 89
Ministry of National Education
  (MoNE), 19, 23, 26, 27, 48,
    50–4, 61, 62, 86, 87, 89, 90,
    93, 95, 100–2, 117, 151, 159,
    167, 182, 187, 193, 194,
    205–6, 210, 211, 212, 219,
    221, 224, 225, 226, 227,
    236, 238–9, 241–2, 246,
    254, 255
Moderate Islam, 47

National Outlook, 17, 166, 168,
  171
Necmettin Erbakan, 17, 167, 171
neoconservative order, 181–3
neoconservative policies, 181, 188
neoliberal capitalism, 6, 128
neoliberal discourse, 23, 26,
  60–4, 67
neoliberal globalization, 223
neoliberal ideology, 18, 20, 23, 27,
  47, 64, 84, 85, 104, 128, 250
neoliberal imperialism, 126
neoliberal legal reform process, 5
neoliberal policies, 9, 47, 48, 85, 90,
  95–101, 104, 109–10, 119, 127,
  141, 181, 188, 213, 245–6

neoliberal reforms, 60, 234
neoliberal theory, 11
new right, 8–9, 250
1982 constitution, 6, 43, 181–2
1960 constitution, 181

Organization for Economic
  Cooperation and Development
  (OECD), 245, 246
  countries, 22, 27, 159, 199
Özal governments, 7, 185

parent-teacher associations (PTAs),
  86, 99, 234, 237
performance appraisal, 234,
  238–9
performance evaluation, 21, 65,
  109, 134–5, 142–3, 147, 239
Performance Management System
  (PYS), 101–2
performance systems, 18, 21
PIRLS, 61
PISA, 37, 61
positivism, 37–44
postmodern coup, 111, 167, 252
precarious teachers, 238, 241–2
preparatory courses, 11, 227
primary education, 22, 61, 194–5,
  208, 209, 219
  see also elementary education,
    156, 234
primary schools, 19, 67, 118, 152,
  205, 206, 207, 222
private colleges, 11
private education, 86, 133
private education institutions, 88
  see also private teaching
    institutions, 92, 151
private higher education, 131, 141,
  142
private higher education
  institutions, 131, 140–1, 142
private publishing houses, 50
private schools, 25–7, 152, 155,
  159, 185–6, 188, 196

Index

private tutoring courses, 24–5, 151
  see also dershane, 24, 151–61
  see also private tutoring, 66, 68, 152, 155, 156, 158
  see also private teaching/tutoring institutions, 88, 92
  see also private tutoring centers, 66
  see also private tutoring sector, 157
  see also private tutoring systems, 159
  see also tutorial institutions, 186
  see also tutoring institutions, 24–5, 27, 88
private universities, 27, 127, 131–5, 139–48, 227, 228
  see also foundation universities (FUs), 139–48, 228
privatization, 63, 127, 133, 135, 250, 254
  of education, 64, 86–8, 234
  of the educational systems, 15, 97
  of higher education, 127, 133, 141
  of public services, 159, 250
  of the universities, 148
public education, 12, 18–21, 24–7, 86, 87, 89–90, 154, 155–6, 160, 233, 245
Public Employees Selection Exam (KPSS), 224
public schools, 11, 20, 25–6, 27, 86, 89, 151–4, 155, 160, 185, 186, 227, 234
public universities, 127, 131, 133–4, 139, 141–5
  see also state universities, 139, 141, 143

Recep Tayyip Erdoğan, 17, 41, 44, 47, 180, 250
  see also Erdoğan, 183, 185
  see also Prime Minister Erdoğan, 27, 53, 55, 172, 174, 250
religious courses, 118, 246
religious education, 13, 19, 43, 118, 168, 175, 182, 252

religious private schools, 186–7
rote learning, 21, 23, 35, 37, 65

secondary education, 22, 154, 155, 208, 209, 219, 229–30
secondary schools, 19, 66–7, 101, 118, 129, 152, 209
sex education, 186, 188
social policies, 3, 5, 11–14, 47, 84–5, 93
social regime, 11, 12–15
social regulations, 9
student-centered education, 48, 214
student-centered educational models, 61
student-centered pedagogy, 18, 21, 59
Student Selection and Placement Center (OSYM), 131

teacher-training institutions, 182
teacher-training programs, 103, 221, 222–5, 227, 228
teacher-training schools, 219, 220–1
teacher-training systems, 219–20, 223, 224, 225, 226, 228–9
teacher's unions, 109–11, 118, 230, 239, 242
teaching certificate programs, 219, 222–7
temporary (status) teachers, 235–8, 242, 243
textbooks, 17, 23, 47, 48, 49–56, 60, 62–8, 90, 208–9, 210, 214
TIMMS, 37, 61
total quality management (TQM), 21, 77, 101, 234, 235, 238
trade unions, 92, 110–17, 239
tuition (fees), 126–7, 131, 133, 141, 146, 147, 199, 227
Turgut Özal, 181–2, 183
Turkish Higher Education, 125–37, 139–49
Turkish Industrialist' and Businessmen's Association (TUSIAD), 61–2, 72, 134, 198

Turkish-Islamic synthesis, 181–2, 229
Türk-Eğitim-Sen, 110, 111
  see also Education, Teaching and Science Professions Public Employee Union of Turkey, 110

vocational education, 72, 80, 100, 101, 103, 226
vocational high schools, 74, 80
vocational training, 71, 145, 247
vocational (training) schools, 27, 71, 140, 145, 147, 166, 168, 169
  see also schools of vocational and technical education, 225, 226
  see also vocational and technical education institutions, 98

World Bank (WB), 12–13, 18, 83, 85, 86, 90, 95–8, 99, 104, 126–8, 133, 134–6, 197, 199, 221, 245, 246, 248
  funds, 54
  supported projects, 86, 100

GPSR Compliance

The European Union's (EU) General Product Safety Regulation (GPSR) is a set of rules that requires consumer products to be safe and our obligations to ensure this.

If you have any concerns about our products, you can contact us on

ProductSafety@springernature.com

In case Publisher is established outside the EU, the EU authorized representative is:

Springer Nature Customer Service Center GmbH
Europaplatz 3
69115 Heidelberg, Germany

www.ingramcontent.com/pod-product-compliance
Lightning Source LLC
LaVergne TN
LVHW051914060526
838200LV00004B/142